I Have Something to Tell You

I HAVE

SOMETHING

NATALIE APPLETON

TO TELL

A MEMOIR

YOU

RAVENSCRAG PRESS

RAVENSCRAG PRESS
#3 2908 32 Street
Vernon, BC V1T 5M1
www.ravenscragpress.com

ISBN 978-1-7750044-0-0
ISBN 978-1-7750044-1-7

Produced by Page Two
www.pagetwostrategies.com
Cover design by Peter Cocking
Cover painting by Thai-British artist Kat Jones,
from her collection "Monsoon"
Interior design by Nayeli Jimenez
Printed and bound in Canada

For Noel, my love.
And our sons.

"We tell ourselves stories in order to live."

JOAN DIDION, *The White Album*

CONTENTS

PART III: MAGIC ROOSTERS

AUTHOR'S NOTE

I WROTE THIS story as it was happening. I wrote it much later. I wrote it in my dreams and when I couldn't sleep. I wrote it at once, and then for nearly a decade. Sometimes on and on for weeks. Some years, just a week.

This story lives on in my mind. And I wake to it. And as a former journalist, I wrote it with a great reverence for truth.

So, all these words are true. But they are my truth. And so this story is imperfect, in the way so many designs of humans are.

As a gesture of privacy for those whose paths I crossed and told of, and who had no idea they might one day feature in this story, nearly all names have been changed.

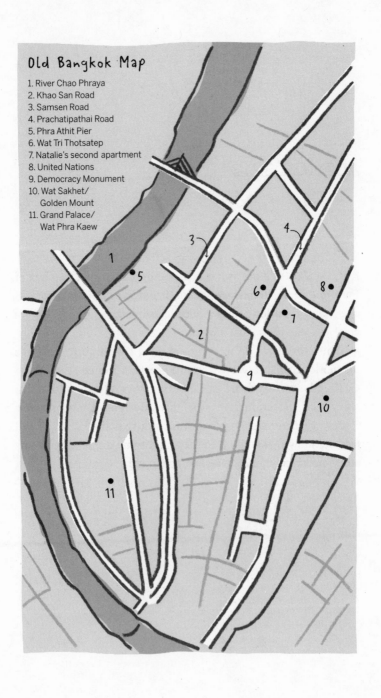

Old Bangkok Map

1. River Chao Phraya
2. Khao San Road
3. Samsen Road
4. Prachatipathai Road
5. Phra Athit Pier
6. Wat Tri Thotsatep
7. Natalie's second apartment
8. United Nations
9. Democracy Monument
10. Wat Sakhet/
    Golden Mount
11. Grand Palace/
    Wat Phra Kaew

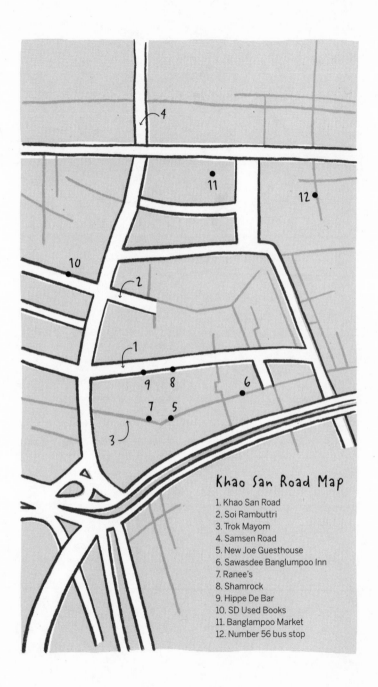

Khao San Road Map

1. Khao San Road
2. Soi Rambuttri
3. Trok Mayom
4. Samsen Road
5. New Joe Guesthouse
6. Sawasdee Banglumpoo Inn
7. Ranee's
8. Shamrock
9. Hippe De Bar
10. SD Used Books
11. Banglampoo Market
12. Number 56 bus stop

Above us, the moon inches up the sky
as if being lifted by string. Orange, pregnant with light
and hazy with waves of heat. He looks up, hopeful,
sweet. Innocent of all this.
My voice, it's a whisper. *I have*
something to tell you.

PROLOGUE
HOPE SINKS

ONG AND I are on our knees, crouching over the Phra Athit Pier. Strings of damp wood stamp my skin. Below, the River Chao Phraya slaps the pier. Planks shake with footsteps.

This is the night of the twelfth moon, and everyone in the kingdom is near a river to pay homage to Phra Mae Kongka, goddess of rivers. Thais call her festival *Loy Krathong*; the floats they release into her water, *krathong*.

Song blocks my *krathong* with her hand. "Wait," she says. "You must to make a wish."

"A wish?" I ask, taking my eyes off the fishy, muddy water and my beautiful *krathong*. It's like a little birthday cake, iced with banana leaves, yellow carnations and purple orchids, incense sticks and a single yellow candle. I don't want to let it go.

Song's cheeks, lit with the tiny flames, beat like butterfly wings. Her skin is tan, but barely. Her hair is bobbed, though most wear it long. Very, very long.

"Ahh, Nat-a-lieeee." Song's palm thumps her chest.

She nearly forgot to tell me about the last, most important part of *Loy Krathong*, the wish. In addition to apologizing for the pollution and thanking her for watering the rice, Thais offer the river goddess a *krathong* believing her waters will carry away their hopes and sorrows. Song nods. "Like good luck."

"Oh." Thousands of *krathong* candles light the water with the moon. Thousands of wishes bob in the wind. Even with the breeze, even in the dark, it's hot.

I lift my *krathong* onto my lap and think. Sorrows: I don't know anyone, save for Song and a toothy woman who cleans the ground-floor washroom. I'm a bad teacher. I killed an albino gecko. I left Stuart and our cat. And I just don't know if I can do this.

I wish...

The pier sways with passersby: uniformed children, teenage girls, elderly couples. I see flashes of school pins, of arms linked in arms, of missing teeth shed by smiles. Babies see me, my red hair and my forehead, white like the flesh of a plantain. They stare but not long because tonight their pudgy fingers and wide eyes are drawn to all the yellow wicks flickering on the water.

I think I could belong here. And I want others to think I know what I'm doing with this *krathong*. That Song and I are friends.

Our legs almost touch until she shifts off her heels and leans on her wrist.

I sigh.

"What are you wishing?"

Song is the size I was at age nine. I feel that young, a girl copying Song as we cross streets, eat without forks and return *wai*s from students. Really, she is almost as old as I am, twenty-four. Song, still dressed in kitten heels and a pink suit jacket, is a secretary at the *rajabhat* university where we work. Since

I left Canada ten weeks ago to teach English here, Song has become my unofficial translator and tour guide. She is the person I am closest to, and yet all I know about her is that she lives across the river in Thonburi with her family (parents, a sister, a brother, her brother's wife); that she leaves that house not long after dawn to journey into the city, to our office; that she leaves our office when it's dark to attend English classes (even though she is nearly fluent and a graduate of our program), or when it's still bright on a Saturday afternoon to work at her family's clothing stall at Chatuchuk Market.

I smile. Because I believe in wishes and because she is sweet. "If I tell you, it won't come true."

"Really?" she asks.

I shrug.

Song is much better at these kinds of cultural explanations. She tried to tell me about *Loy Krathong* on our way here, inside a swarming, rocking green bus from the fleet of "unloved buses," so nicknamed because of their age, erratic routes, doorless sides, fan-less roofs, hasty drivers, cheap fares and the dark, tarry smoke that huffs from their engines. Like Bangkok itself these buses, charring, dangerous by the West's design; these buses that one could never quite catch.

Normally, Song would never take me on a green bus, but she had to tonight because old Bangkok is choked with people on their way to the river to launch *krathongs*. "*Loy* means... It means..." Song's palm wormed in the air, to demonstrate, until the definition came to her. "To float!" And then she cupped her tiny hands. "*Krathong.*"

I trace the smooth green leaves, pinned to resemble the petals of a lotus. Hopes: That I'm not crazy. That the world really is whispering to me, with books and streets and people, to lead me along. That I'm figuring this out, this knowing when I'm going the right way. *I wish...*

The wax and smoke of other *krathong* candles saunter into my nose. That smell and the faces of those issuing it remind me of church. Of people lighting a candle, taking a breath and thinking, *God, help me. I'm sorry. Why? I need. Please, please. Make a wish already.*

A passenger boat chugs past, packed with people in suits. This is their life. They wake up sweating to a rooster's crow and step into stiff uniforms. They tiptoe around their half-naked infants and snoring mothers, and out a wooden door. They pay 15 *baht* for a spot on the boat. They shuffle off under the sun, *wai* their elders, offer Coca-Cola to the gods, and work until it's dark and wait for the boat back home.

I wait for the boat to cross the river, for the waters to become calm so my *krathong* will stay afloat, at least for a while.

I blink and make my wish: *I want to know why I'm here.* Just as quickly, I drop the *krathong* into the river. It bobs twice, then tips over. I gasp. My float's wet underside sails away into a stream of failed *krathongs*, lining the river like old boat ropes.

Song kneels back down. Her fingers warm my shoulder. "Natalie. Don't worry," she says. "Maybe next year will be better, *na.*"

PART I
WILD ROSE COUNTRY

December 2004–August 2005

SWIMMING
MAGGOTS

J UNIE AND I are sucking in our stomachs and studying the lineup on the stairs. He is wading through the peacoats and parkas. My whole world, until tonight, like the pop songs between us. Every verse familiar.

My mind flashes to Stuart, my boyfriend. Out somewhere with his friends, watching hockey. His eyes, so blue. The ring in the glove box of his Ford.

It's the night before Christmas Eve, and I'm at Gringo's with the kids who stayed and the kids who left. It's like a reunion: get drunk and brag about what you've been doing. And I was fine with that. Until I saw him.

My throat turns rusty. My palms sweat.

"Oh, 'Girls Just Wanna Have Fun'!"

Junie's cold, sticky hand yanks my wrist to the dance floor. So we slither, through all the other girls in sparkly shirts, fists knocking at the chorus. Chanting the words, pointing at each other's cheeks when Cindy sings, *Girls*.

Junie's arms ribbon around her hair. Her hair, as long and straw-yellow thick as the tail of a horse. Has the same musk too. She rides. Ran for Stampede queen with her blind Appaloosa and lost. Even though she was the prettiest. Even though she could ride, like hell she could ride.

"I love this song," she calls.

"I know," I say, drink jangling along my limbs, my lips. *I know.* Even though we're just twenty-three, our devils, they dance with us. Especially here.

My head draws a "W" at the *Oh-oh-oh* part. I pretend not to search, for him. Even when I find him. Dark hair, spiked like before. Brown eyes set close. A blue Ralph Lauren shirt with the sleeves rolled up. Mr. President.

Four years ago, Scott Wicks was the president of the Medicine Hat College Students' Association and I was the editor of the student newspaper, *Express This!* I didn't like him because he liked himself enough. He didn't like me because I didn't like him. I wrote editorials deflating him for his attachment to multisyllabic euphemisms, the least of which was "fiscally responsible." (At the time, where we come from, those were big words.) I didn't vote for him, and said so. Often.

Cindy's lyrics quaver, mute. The DJ's voice thumps and spits. Under the black lights, teeth and lint glow. The bar, about the size of a school gymnasium, is now packed. Like I knew I would, I'm shuffling toward him. He is talking to a few guys who mostly come up to his shoulders, one with fish eyes, one with salts of hair but mostly bald already.

And I just stand there, shy-like, nails scratching my bottle's label.

"Hey," says Scott.

"Hey."

"Jeez. It's been a while." He stops himself from looking me down and up. "What, uh, what have you been doing?"

"Graduated from J-school. Last year."

Back in college, before we both left to finish our degrees at university, there was tension between us. Even more than what might be expected from two people in these positions. If some of it was sexual, we ignored it at the time. But tonight, tonight he is suddenly that tension and that time, when we were two of a kind, about to take on the world.

"What?"

"Journalism school."

"Oh, right."

I went to the University of Regina. What I'd wanted was to become a foreign correspondent. Roam in the echo of bullets. Hole up in the shacks of son-less mothers and listen as they told. Win awards for stories that'd break your heart. Come back and give talks at the library.

"I got on at *The News*. I was really lucky. Most of the people I went to school with couldn't get a job. Or they did. In Butt-fuck, Saskatchewan."

My laugh, so awkward and rehearsed. I bite my straw, hold back that I left the *Medicine Hat News* months ago and am now a largely unemployed freelancer. That what I ended up writing about was corn-eating contests and community theater. That it turned out I liked it, being known. Calling familiar names for quotes. Feeling important at talks and meetings, with my ragged notepad and inky wrists. Big fish.

"You still with Stuart?"

"Yeah. We bought a house. A corner lot with a double garage."

Our black-and-white 1970s bi-level, just steps from the edge of my high school football field. When I was fourteen, a classmate, Grant Cuz, lived there. He wore Wranglers and chewed tobacco and had always been too big and goofy for his age. There was a sweetness to him, though. His family moved, to Grande Prairie or Fort Mac, one of those. And then a cube van hit his truck head-on.

There are three high schools in Medicine Hat. The one I went to. The one Scott went to. And the Catholic one Stuart went to. None of us knew each other then. Stuart didn't go to college so he doesn't know Scott, but he might know *of* him.

"Wow." Scott's forehead crumples. "Good for you. Good for you."

"And you?"

"Still with the party."

Scott, a gofer with the Liberals' last election. We ran into each other at a political columnist's book launch in Calgary two falls ago. I was a TV station intern capturing the fake smiles and frozen handshakes. He was handing them out. It had been the first time we'd run into each other since college. After the election, "the party" gave him a job as someone's assistant in Ottawa.

"I kept thinking you'd beat me there."

"What?"

"Natalie," he says, until we're in a gaze that storms up the truth, "I didn't think you'd be ... *here.*"

Here: This bar. The black cotton tube top I have on. My boyfriend who drives a backhoe and cheats at Scrabble. "Here," a bad word. Medicine Hat.

Thousands of moons ago, they say, in a battle with the Cree at the lip of the river, a Blackfoot medicine chief took an arrow in the heart. The wind took his headdress. The water took the chief. The Crees took their flag, the medicine man's hat, and the Blackfoot fled. Today, Medicine Hat is home to the world's tallest teepee but no First Nations people.

In a part of town near the river, old men get down on their knees with scissors to cut their green grass even. In other parts of town, men come home once a month in the big fat trucks they've bought with their big fat oil-patch paychecks. A lot of men are divorced. A lot of women are divorced. Remarriage brought my brother and me first to the freshly paved streets of Ross Glen, and later to a dusty rose bungalow in Crescent Heights, high above the train tracks and the tiny war-era houses of Riverside. I went to school with our blind paperboy, spent Saturdays at the mall, sitting around the fountain that divided its four aisles, and didn't see a traffic jam or a black person until I was nineteen. In Calgary.

"Scott, I love Medicine Hat."

A truth, and a lie. Hometowns, how they tug us. With memories of hide-and-seek in scorched coulees, and kissing in dusty trucks after dark. With streets and faces as familiar as a mother's breath. But it's not the place we leave or long for. It's how a town makes us feel. Like a child, loved. Like an old woman, rocking over boredom and regrets.

He pauses.

We take in the damp of the air, the snow and spilled drinks that streak the floor.

"Look," I say. "When I was in university, this documentary maker from Africa came to our class."

I've told this story so many times I nearly forget that it's not mine; it belongs to an older *News* colleague and fellow U of R alumnus. I've told this story so many times I nearly believe the ending.

"And he said you don't have to be in a big city to make a big difference, you know? I'm happy here."

Scott coughs, fists his chest. "Hey, that's good."

The story, what the man said, it's true. I just need to believe it myself. I need to see it's my ego that wants a bigger story in a bigger paper, not the world, not my writing. I need to be thankful I know that alive feeling that comes from being the conduit of strangers' stories.

He squeezes my arm. "It is."

I nod. "I need another drink."

Scott doesn't drink, so it's a phantom glass he raises to mine. "Well, good luck. OK?"

"Yeah. You too."

"And Merry Christmas."

"You too."

THE SCRATCHED-IN NAMES of other girls. Bitches, hearts. Why do they always do hearts? *Didn't expect to see me here.* Numbers and shoulds. The glint of amber glass, and puddles of beer or urine or both at my boots, a fluorescent light above. *Here.* Still as the door, save for my heart. Beating, beating. My fingers, vibrating. Finally, they turn the handle, creak open the door.

Me in the mirror. Me. *Natalie.* Seeing what is. Not freckles and scars and strands of red hair, but maggots swimming under the garbage bags at the back door. My browning, rippling article clippings. The Astroturf stoop where I smoke at night. The room, stealing a breath. My stomach, rocking, capsizing, sinking. Sinking.

I bustle out of the bathroom. Just a few steps out, Scott's eyes catch mine. Between us, swarms and totters of twenty-somethings. I search for Junie's hair, pick her out of the crowd, twirling, through the hazy blue of a strobe light. *She'll never know.*

Scott's eyes. My left hand. *The ring.* The rest of my life, like minnows at my shins.

My toes, they know I need to do something. So they start, for him. When our shoulders brush, my eyes, heavy with this charade, they target a table at the back.

"Natalie."

"Oh, hey." A smile. A blink, *slow, slow.*

So tall. Tall but sturdy. Maybe that's what it is, the skyscrapers and red ties ahead.

Scott looks at my hands, empty. "They run out of beer?"

"Lord, I hope not," I say. "Have you ever played Drink a Small Town Dry?"

It's a Saturday-night affair at university in Saskatchewan. So many one-bar towns; so little else to do but drink after them. Soon we're talking about something more important. The effects of mad cow disease on the economy. Noam Chomsky's theories, maybe. It doesn't matter.

Why do we ramble, when what we want to say, what we need to say—and do—is just there, six words or less?

The crowd bulges and someone's back presses me against Scott. My cheek at his neck, my breasts at his chest, slipping. The smell of men's shower soap. Like the kind of love I knew in high school. He catches me, a hand on each shoulder. Looks down, like he could kiss my forehead.

I say it: "You want to get a drink?"

Scott eyes the beer tubs, the main bar, the half-dozen lines ten people deep.

"Somewhere else," I say. "Where we can talk."

"Oh. Y—" His tongue lassos the word. Stills it. Then lets it off. "Yeah. Yeah, OK."

A few minutes apart, stepping *up, up, up* until we are out the doors and on the street. It's dark and snowing and we have no coats.

SINCE IT IS nearly one o'clock in the morning and since we are doing something we are not supposed to do and since he is only here for the holidays, we direct the cab to his mother's house. For a drink.

On the way, he says, "My mom, she has one of your old columns on the fridge."

It was about me and Junie driving my old Volkswagen convertible in the summer, and could there be anything better than being sixteen? The cab stops at one of the chicken coops, a type of row house with faded-green wood siding. And here I'd imagined a three-car garage, heated. His mom, I learn, was a divorcée. Like mine. A single mom. And then a married single mom. Like mine. These mothers, how they suffered.

His hands, still warm, hook my calves, unzip my boots. Sliding the wispy paper of that column from under a magnet tile to my fingers. Waving me to follow. We *tiptoe, tiptoe, tiptoe* down the stairs to a basement that's bare except for a dusty sofa. He doesn't have anything. So he leaves me there and walks to a convenience store seven blocks away in his dress shoes in the snow and returns, teeth tearing the plastic.

THE DOLL
HOUSE

I HAVE TO GO.

My insides are sore and knotted with knowing this, with trying to tell me for so long.

That's what I have to do. I have to go, soon.

Blue, winter light leaks through the blinds. Stuart, my boyfriend, is on the other side of the bed, snoring. My heel scratches the back of his leg, hairy and still.

I can't marry him.

Sorry kneads my stomach. Lying on my side, hands curled around each other like twist ties, I cry, eyes closed.

It's not him. Or last night. It's here. I'm not supposed to be here.

Scott's words, "I thought you'd be somewhere," replay and rewind in my mind. Not his fingers, not his lips. "But I'm happy," I said. "I'm happy."

It was barely light out when I got back. Too early to be awake, to face all of this. And so I went to my side of the bed, and lay down.

Hours—or is it just minutes later?—I buckle out of bed and wrap myself in The Cowboy, a blanket nicknamed for the bronc-riding man stitched on the front. It's a heavy, plush blanket, the kind you can buy at mall kiosks and the fair that feature wolves and Disney characters. Stuart doesn't move when I lift it off the bed. Two days before we'd had sex on The Cowboy, laid out on the carpet in front of the fireplace. My toes toasted and the TV, muted, flickered. Out of the corner of my eye I'd spotted a jewelry store Christmas flier under the coffee table and thought about the styles of rings I'd pointed out. Stuart was above, away. When it was over, we hugged, kneeling on the blanket with our underwear in our hands. I think he'd never felt so loved in his life.

Now, The Cowboy around my shoulders, feet half in Stuart's work boots, phone and cigarette in hand, I step outside. Across the street, a snowman beams. The lights on a Christmas tree blink. Every inch of me, awake. Alone.

Erin. I'll call Erin. We met as babies, possibly in utero. Our fathers ran heavy equipment together during the day and drank whiskey together at night. While they were off, our mothers ran birthday parties, fixed red Jell-O, birthed sons. We kids rode our trikes too far, swore at our mothers like our fathers did, and demanded shinier dolls and bigger bikes at Kmart. After my dad left, we all stopped seeing each other. Erin and I found each other again at thirteen when junior high brought us back under the same roof. Even though now we live in different cities from time to time because of school and practicums (she is studying to become a teacher), we know we can always call each other and ask for the truth.

The line rings and rings, and when I wipe my nose with The Cowboy, she answers.

"Natalie?"

"Yeah." I sniffle, strike a match from the book I keep in a cracked plant pot that's never had anything else inside it.

"What's wrong?"

"I don't know." My eyes follow the smoke as it poofs and fades above the white lawn. I loved him too. I did. But there have always been nags of questions: Is he the one? Is this it?

"Why are you crying?"

My lungs push up a breath. "Last night..."

I wait, remember his face, all dark and young in the cab. His footsteps on the stairs, how quickly sleep took me. His neck, dewy with sweat and snow when he returned. All of it, already buried, like a mitten after a blizzard. Hidden now, but sure to surface in the spring, soiled and thready.

"What about last night?"

"What do you think about me, in Medicine Hat? With Stuart? Honest."

She pauses, then reels off her answer. "Honestly, I didn't think you'd be here."

She's thought about this before.

A howl tips out of my mouth. I've found myself out.

"You just always seemed like someone who was going to go somewhere and be somebody, you know? In high school, I don't know, I just pictured you... somewhere else."

Somebody. Somewhere. I'd dreamed about those words all my life. When Erin and I were four we played on an old train carriage in a park by the river. I always wanted to be the conductor, pulling down on the whistle string. I didn't want to be one of the women with the babies in the back. I wanted to be Somebody, go Somewhere. I didn't care who or where. An aptitude test I took in eleventh grade showed I could form sentences and ask questions, and suggested journalism, so I thought, that's my ticket: I'll be a journalist, maybe a real writer. Then I got a reporting job in my hometown and wound up with a man who likes it here. What Stuart wants is to sit in his backhoe cab, scraping and shifting dirt from the earth's belly. To stand at the front door in muddy work boots at five o'clock and

feel little boys and girls clinging to his legs screaming, "Daddy!"
To have a wife who'll hug him, serve him a casserole. Save for
stays in two other towns—one in Saskatchewan, one in Texas,
where he moved both times to play hockey but returned early,
homesick—when I met Stuart, he'd only had one address, his
parents'.

"Natalie. What's *wrong*?"

I want to be a mom someday, but I don't want to wish I'd
waited or done it with a different man.

"Nothing's wrong. That's the problem." I'm yelling now.
Choking on the snot in my throat.

Stuart Tenney and I were introduced when I was twenty and
he was twenty-three, two and a half years ago, at the Corona
Tavern. It's in the Flats, not far from the two-story red-brick
house where he'd lived all his life. He was embarrassed about
being from the Flats, thought of as the poor part of town on
the south side of the river. Friends joked about him paying the
"flat rate" when he walked into movies theaters without a ticket.

Inside the bar, Stuart was sitting at the edge of a long plastic table spitting tobacco juice into a bottle of beer. There must
have been about a dozen of us, high school couples, mostly.
The day before, I had driven home from university for the summer, car stuffed with garbage bags and binders. It was late April
and it was a Saturday night and I felt big from all those lectures
about the role of journalism in society. I strolled over.

"Wanna dance?"

He grinned and stood. "Sure."

It was a country song. I can't remember which one now. The
dance floor was just a square of wood lit by the DJ's red and
green lights. Stuart led me to it and held out his palms to two-
step. I took them. A chorus or two into the song, he pressed
the small of my back, drew my waist to his buckle and spun
me. When he pulled me in again, my chest hit his and he kept

me there, lifted me like that around a corner, around all the other dancers. This dance, how plain lustful. How I know it. Missed it, even, for even though Regina is a country city in Saskatchewan and even though most of my classmates came from farm towns and parties that ended with two-stepping, I did not go to a country bar in Regina. If there was one, I didn't seek it out. I'd managed to forge close friendships with girls whose backgrounds were most unlike mine—a feminist Polish immigrant from Edmonton and a Muslim daughter of doctors whose family immigrated to Moose Jaw from Sudan via Oman and England and Toronto. The three of us liked to spend our free time in our apartments or in a lounge downtown, smoking menthols and drinking merlot and talking about how women could be saved by narrative.

A world away from those ashes and ideals, on that dance floor with Stuart, I felt curtained by his blue eyes and ball cap. When the song was over, we just stood there for a while, sweaty and out of breath. He was handsome and sweet and, God, he could dance.

Soon, too soon, the lights turned on.

"Want a ride home?"

I nodded.

When he phoned two days later, the caller ID said HOW-ARD JOHNSON HOTEL. The same hotel that sat above The Doll House, a strip club that—after the Christian extremists protested for all nudey bars to be banned and sent the strippers packing—would later return to being the bar known as Gringo's, where I ran into Scott last night. Apparently, when it was The Doll House, it served superb steak sandwiches for $5.95. "I don't think we should... I just think... We're too... different," I said, still on a high from university, still seeing myself as "other." But the next night he brought flowers. And it was summer. *Just a summer*, I thought. Soon I was putting my bare feet on the dash of his Jeep on our way to rodeos, weddings, weekends at the lake, barbecues in his parents' backyard with all of his aunts, uncles, cousins, sisters, brothers and their babies. In the fall, we stayed together and saw each other every few weekends after I went to Calgary for my internship and then returned to Regina in the winter for my last semester. He came to our class graduation party and helped me pack up the next morning for Medicine Hat, for good. That summer, we bought a house overlooking my high school football field. He was kind to me and came home every night. Most of the time, our life was mostly fine and I thought I should be grateful. So I stuffed my dreams in the closet, like a graduation dress.

Erin sighs.

I can't stop repeating myself. "Nothing's wrong with Stuart and me, you know? We get along. His parents, I love his parents. Our friends. God, The Group."

It's them too. Last year Stuart and I had a New Year's Eve party with all of our friends. Jennies and Joshes. The women are teachers, retail clerks and receptionists. The men are mostly nostalgic hockey players who've become "riggers." I was wearing a black sequin top. My red hair, curled, hung under a gold hat that had said HAPPY NEW YEAR! I was bounding upstairs and when I got to the landing, I felt dizzy. I saw all the girls in the living room talking about houses and babies and Coach bags. I saw the guys in the kitchen, talking about their teams and eating steak someone had won in a draw. I was watching a movie of my friends in my house on fast-forward. Their voices faded and I saw heads, nodding and smiling and sipping. I saw these same heads in forty years nodding and smiling and sipping. I felt ill. Drunk on rye and determined, I tugged Stuart into our bedroom. "I don't belong here." My voice, trailing behind sobs, carried the air of an apology. "I just know one day I'm going to have to leave." The next morning my eyelids were swollen. A few others had heard, and then politely pretended my outburst hadn't happened. I just went on feeling out of place: drinking Baileys with the girls at the Irvine hockey rink; most days at my desk at *The News*, where I worked for a yellow-mustached editor who was not above running pictures of half-naked women on the front page; and when I was grocery shopping at the Co-op, debating between steak or steak shish kebobs, eyes lost in rows and rows of plastic taut around slabs and chunks and slabs and chunks of burgundy red meat. The knowing in me said one day I might wake up somewhere else. The follow in me wished I could just want this.

"Everything's fine with me and Stuart, but it just *feels* wrong, you know?"

I don't know why I keep telling this story: things are fine. In fact, doubt has been trailing us since the night we met. I knew even then that him being a good guy who loved me wasn't enough, but it became enough. And then, a few months ago, Stuart started ducking into Payday Loans and the bank's been calling about missed payments on his $36,000 Ford. He had to have that truck because all of his friends had big fat brand-new trucks. Had to have that truck even though he gets laid off several months of the year. My name is on the loan. He wants *things* and he wants *this*. Suddenly I want something else so much it hurts. But I don't know what it is.

And I don't yet have the language to express the part that just *feels* wrong. I know, deep down, I'm just as Medicine Hat as he is. I like drinking cheap beer from the bottle around a fire. I like golfing in the wind high above the river. I like witnessing cowboys trust their bodies to the bare backs of wild horses, and the raw, earthy smell of rodeo dirt. But I also like reading obituaries and watching *Question Period* at lunch. Stuart cheats at board games. Says "them" instead of "those" ("Them trucks are terrible on gas"). Calls his dad every time he has to make a decision. But he can two-step better than anyone. And I love how he flies his shrieking nephew in the air like a plane until the boy begs him to stop, and then begs for more.

"And last night—"

"*What* happened last night?"

I tell Erin not about Scott's sofa, but about what Scott said. I recounted the way he said "here," like it tasted bitter.

"Why does that bug me so much, what he said?"

"'Cause he's right."

Scott is right. Erin is right.

THE RULE
OF SEVEN

THE SETTING IS this: Sometime between one and two in the afternoon, Christmas Eve, one of those chain restaurants that appears local because the flown-in designer from Toronto went to the local archives to print photos. Nancy, the grizzly bear that was penned outside the CPR railway station as a tourist attraction until she sank her teeth into a boy's arm. The S.S. *City of Medicine Hat*, a 130-foot-long steam-powered stern-wheeler built by Scottish nobleman Horatio Hamilton Ross with no expense spared; it sank on its first run along the South Saskatchewan River after hitting telegraph lines submerged by spring runoff at Saskatoon. Charles Hatfield, the rainmaker who drew crowds from as far away as Denmark on word that, from a tower thirty-five feet above Medicine Hat, his precipitation-inducing contraption would yield rain clouds and plentiful crops. Before I left *The News*, Stuart and I would come here for dinner on Fridays after work and I'd hear couples scan the photos and say, without ever knowing the story, "Oh, now, is that ever neat."

I only know because even though I'd been blackballed by the editor I stormed out on (he read my emails and didn't like me pointing out that the mayor's last name had been misspelled in a headline, again), I was able to get a job at the sister paper in Lethbridge covering the weekend shift. To help me make a little more money, they've given me a book project that will mark Alberta's upcoming centennial and sell ads. So, I've been charged with reading 100 years of newspapers and then writing a page for each year about the stories that made headlines.

Today, the photos and the diners feel even more staged, like the ceramic Christmas scenes on old ladies' coffee tables. Smiling, happy people. Hungry from buying fat gold watches for their fathers and low-fat eggnog for Santa. The soup special is some kind of cheddar bisque. Scott and I are both spooning it into our mouths.

I told Stuart—asked, even—if he minded if I met Scott for lunch. As if last night hadn't happened. As if I shouldn't have just packed up then. And I was excited, turning the ignition in my frosted-up Nissan. As my little car bucked over snow piles across town to get here, my heart might have thumped with joy just thinking about the intellectual, philosophical conversation we might have.

"Good soup, huh?" says Scott.

"Mmm hmm." Hot soup dribbles over my chin. The chin he kissed. The plastic black boots he unzipped for me at the door. "Really good."

How peculiar, here we are. How backwards backwoods beyond, here I am. Here.

This meeting, it could be one of two things, or even both: a chance to do the talking we didn't get around to last night, and genuinely wanted to; and a kind of date, a way to see if there's something there.

"Did you know that Lethbridge had the second-highest number of cases of VD in Canada in 1944?" I ask. A few weeks ago I was at the library reading papers from the year 1944 for the centennial book. Each morning I lug a Safeway bag full of microfiche rolls to the basement of the library and spend the day with old ladies on genealogy quests and delinquents using the free Internet.

"VD?"

"Venereal disease."

"Oh."

"Yeah. Alberta's Social Hygiene Division—funny name, right?—it actually told Lethbridge, 'This is out of control. You're going to have to shut down your red-light district.'" My spoon rounds the bowl and I catch the reflection of my hair, my face. My stomach churns with a confluence of guilt and fluids— coffee, cheese soup, last night's rum, the aftertaste of cigarettes, the film of sin. My voice softens. "The Point, they called it, the red-light district."

Scott coughs. "Yeah?"

My cheeks burn. *Why did I just tell him a story about venereal disease?*

"Sorry. I don't know why I told you that. Oh, I do. I was working on 1944 the other day, yesterday, actually. That's weird. Hmm. Because you were in it. Well, *you* weren't in it, but your last name was. I came across an article about Lethbridge welcoming home its first English war bride, Mrs. Fred Wicks. Traveled all the way from England alone with her baby and just stepped off the train. Think it was February. Bet that was a bit of a shocker."

"Natalie, that's really cool."

"About Mrs. Wicks?"

"No. Well, yes. But the whole project. You're, like, writing the book on southern Alberta. Not a lot of people can say that."

In my mind's eye, the microfiche machine whirs and pauses on grainy articles. Fantastical stories. The 1927 cyclone that lifted the mayor of Vulcan's Buick and chucked it at the

Catholic church. The 1935 Coalhurst mine explosion that buried three brothers. Filumena, the rum runner's maid, hung at the gallows. I realize I don't think I've told Stuart a single story from the book. What have we been talking about? What did we ever talk about?

Sometimes, we make leaving happen to us.

"Yeah." A smile slips out. "I guess it is." In between the archive stacks, telling the stories of people long past, my own story, forsaken. It's so easy, slipping into the lives of others instead.

"Natalie, are you really going to stay here?"

"I don't... I'm not... I don't know."

I know it's odd, because of what we were doing mere hours ago, but right now Scott and I are not talking about the two of us. Perhaps because we know, with me here and him in Ottawa, it would take too much, too soon. And if I'm honest, the thought of being there kind of excites me, it does, but not because of Scott. If I go anywhere, I want to get there on my own.

I tell Scott this other story about a journalism conference I did, in fact, attend in Saskatoon. One of the speakers, an editor from Seattle, I think, told us that if we manage to find an editor who possesses seven of the ten qualities we admire in a person, we should be content with that.

"And she said, 'I apply The Rule of Seven to my personal life too.'"

I let my soup go cold. Look at him, looking at me. Me, so very eager. So needing plot notes. So needy.

"Maybe a seven is enough."

Those words, the ballad of my early twenties. How sad. How very, very sad.

Scott: "A seven? I won't settle for anything less than a ten when it comes to grades, or a race."

A political race? A running race? He participates in both. And no one has ever contradicted me about The Rule of Seven before. So I just stare.

"Why would I settle for a seven in someone I want to spend my life with?"

My throat lumps with the truth. Sevens: Medicine Hat, my wasting-away black-and-white house, Stuart. *Stuart.* Who might propose tomorrow morning.

HOMESICK

STUART WHISTLES CONWAY TWITTY while he shovels snow. The shovel grits and scrapes the sidewalk every three seconds. *Scrape, scrape, scrape.*

It's Boxing Day. Beside the bay window above him, I rehearse. When Stuart opens the door, I don't give him a chance to take off his coat or even stomp the snow off his boots.

"Can you come upstairs? Now, please?" My voice, so soft and in such cracked spurts I think it scares him.

It's like the opening of a soap opera scene. Silence. Heels. Eyebrows. The weight of what's to come. Except instead of shoulder pads, bouncy curls and wet fuchsia lips, I wear a greasy topknot, snotty nose and eyes blotched red with sorry. Plus, the setting is all wrong: our sofa has been clawed apart by the cat, and the rug is musty orange shag.

He reaches the top step.

"I have to go." The sentence falls like a leaf, gently, but going all the more.

"What?" The very blue of his eyes says, *Don't, don't do this.*

Stuart is now sitting at the opposite end of our beige

sectional. We'd had to move it to make room for the Christmas tree, a fake, eight-foot-tall evergreen. The lights haven't been on for three days. I haven't plugged them in since that night. If Stuart noticed, he didn't say.

But it was also Christmas, and so we were at my parents' house eating turkey and opening gifts, all eyes on the white-blond pigtails of my four-year-old niece, pretending we're not pretending at something. If there is another way for a stepfamily to be, we don't know it.

And then we were at his parents' house, eating turkey and opening gifts. Wrapping paper and ribbons and bows buried our socks and the entire living room floor. His mom took pictures with her new digital camera, her first ("One, two, three... Oh shoot. Have to do it again. OK, there we go!"). And each time one of us took a step, wafts of plastic displaced the tang of scrambled eggs. On the red skirt of the tree, a velour-robed electronic Santa swiveled his hips to a muffled holiday song. Stuart flew his nephew like an airplane and the boy shrieked when his ears nipped past the angel. All of them, how perfectly happy. I sat on the sofa, legs crossed, thinking, *This is what I'm leaving.* This real family, whole and loving. They invited me in so completely, even hoped someday Stuart and I would give them a little girl with red hair. *Will they forgive me?*

"Stuart, I need to leave." I will use the broken-record method. I learned it when I was ten, at school, when they introduced a say-no-to-drugs program and the acronym was DARE, and I can see us all against a brick wall in our pink-and-white DARE t-shirts, too large, swallowing our skinny legs, lined up in rows, *yes, please, tell us more.*

"What do you mean, you have to leave?" Stuart squints. Like he's got soap in his eye.

Guilt shoots up my stomach, clings to my ribs, rubs, like tumbleweeds against a fence.

"I just have to go. I'm not supposed to be here." It wouldn't help, to tell him. And anyway, that's not why. Why is I can't marry him. Why is I have to quit this city. Or I might forget this, get stuck, this time for good.

"I'm sorry." If not now, maybe never.

"What does that even mean, you're not supposed to be here?" He pegs his words in the air like darts. His fingers, so pale against the arms of his black jacket. "I don't get it. You're telling me you just woke up this morning and decided you're leaving me?"

"No." *No, Stuart, that happened two days ago, but I didn't want to wreck Christmas.* I've been bawling ever since. He probably thinks I'm just getting my period.

"Jesus, Natalie." He takes off his hat and runs his fingers through his hair. Like a tourist, hot and lost. He is surprised, I believe, that he is not surprised at all. "This house, we own it. You were just talking rings."

"I know. I know."

And I would have gone down that aisle, after that ring. I would have. All my friends were.

I'd wanted the princess cut, a square stone and white gold. Had hoped for, then dreaded, a proposal on Christmas morning. Stuart didn't ask me to marry him. He gave me golf shoes. There was no ring in his truck. "I just have to go and I need you to let me."

"Is our life that bad?" Stuart's voice rises. His cheeks redden. "Because I thought it was pretty good."

I think he thinks he should have bought that ring. Should have watched the news with me. Should have feigned interest in the indie film about lesbian moms in Greenland.

Stuart gives a glare. I look away.

"So what now?" Stuart's eyes turn to Maddie, our cat. She was one of the things I bought, just like the sectional we were sitting on, to put buttons and bows on a dress I didn't like—my house, my life. "Huh?"

"I don't know." I haven't gotten that far. All I have is my little car, a few hundred bucks and the fire of a redhead with an affection for taking the long way.

I turn to face the street and the tree.

Snowflakes fall as the sky darkens. The tree's bristles suddenly look so perky and rubbery. Each one stands straight, in a row, in order. The branch will never wilt or fade. It took me an hour to pull all the boughs out of the box and spread them symmetrically. But they're too pretty, too perfect. Next year I want a real tree, a Charlie Brown tree. Branches missing, bristles yellowing. I want to be able to smell it and know that it's alive.

WILD ROSE
COUNTRY

I LOOK BACK.

In the rearview mirror, I see Stuart leaning against the garage in a white t-shirt, dirty icicles above his head. Eyes tracing my tire tracks. I see the house, all the more of what it is. A white box with black boards trimming six windows. I see my mom, slamming the truck gate on my mattress. And across the street, the edge of the football field, smooth with snow and somehow as lost as me. Far beyond the field and hidden by neighbors' houses is my old high school. Seven years I walked those bone-white tiles, and each day with a grin. *I'm going to get out of here,* I thought. *And one day you'll say you knew me when.* On graduation night, Zora, one of my best friends, had sobbed into my hair-sprayed curls. "You're going to leave me," she cried. "You will." That was six years ago.

Now Zora is waiting for me in a half-empty basement suite in Calgary. It's the closest big city, the first city most of us move to. It isn't far, but it is away, enough for now.

It's been four weeks since I broke up with Stuart. After that afternoon, I moved into a bedroom upstairs and stayed there, reading Paulo Coelho and Gabriel Garcia Márquez, while he spent most nights in the garage, tinkering with his truck and drinking beer. We agreed to share the house until I was ready to move.

I turn left.

My mom, following me with the futon and everything else I couldn't fit into my little car, is still in the driveway. She convinced my stepdad to lend us his truck even though they're not talking. He'd pulled up that morning while we were hauling boxes out of the house, slammed the truck door and yelled out for her.

"Peggy." His voice, harsh, like March winds.

When I was a little girl, after they got married in the living room of the house that would fit all six of us (our three and their three), I complained to my mom that Wes was mean for not letting me keep wild kittens or for making me sacrifice old toys to the dump. She'd say he didn't have it easy growing up, you know. Wes's German dad, also seemingly unfeeling, died when Wes was a boy and they mostly ate foods of dough or potatoes for years, and then an older sister who'd saved him from drowning in a half-frozen pond, a sister he'd dared to love, died of some kind of cancer when she was eighteen.

My mom peeked above the two laundry baskets of books and shoes in her arms. "Yeah?"

"Keys." He threw them on the hood, then got in her car, an aging Buick. It was one of many vehicles she'd had since meeting Wes at The Alamo when I was five. Back then she drove a yellow boat that was always breaking down or running out of gas.

"Wes!"

He waved her away.

I went toward him, to say goodbye. *I'm moving, you know.* "Bye, Wes," I said, and I caught the shadow of my seven-year-old self, scared of him yet wanting that hug. "Thanks for—"

He waved me off too. "Bye."

I don't know it yet, but they're talking divorce. They're talking about a man named Wayne. They're talking about fifteen years of being *so fucking cold*.

And I don't know why adults always fight in the open when you're too young, and then hide it when you're old enough to hear it.

Perhaps because of this, this separating, my mom is one of few who understand why I need to leave. Medicine Hat. And Stuart. The others asked why. *Why, why, why*. When I couldn't answer, they smirked. Now, as I wait for a light by the Co-op and think, *Come on, come on*, their faces spin inside my head like markers on a game show wheel. *Why? What are you going to do for work and stuff? Why? See, and I like Medicine Hat. Couldn't imagine living anywhere else. Why? What about Stuart? What about the house?*

The light turns green. My foot tips off the brake.

Medicine Hat will always be here, honey. My mom's words, spoken weeks ago when I said I wasn't sure, when all the what-ifs were strangling me. What if I was supposed to marry him? What if I can't make it anywhere else? All I have is questions, more questions and something like homesickness. Except I won't feel right until I've left.

THE
NUMBER ONE

T HE TIRE FACTORY. The fertilizer plant. The drive-in. My beat-up little car putters up the Number One. Speeding, then slowing.

My gut says, *Go, go, go.* I almost married the wrong man and started growing old. And yet leaving feels like a bat trapped in my chest, beating its bony, leathery wings against my lungs.

That line. How did it go? *The fear of suffering... A heart never suffers... No.*

My car barrels over to the far-left lane without a signal.

"Tell your heart that the fear of suffering is worse than the suffering itself. And that no heart has ever suffered when it goes in search of its dreams."

Three months ago, I devoured Paulo Coelho's *The Alchemist*, a novel about a shepherd who deserts his flock to find a distant treasure. In his moment of doubt, the universe tells him the truth about fear and suffering. Those pages, I read them secretly. Stuart wouldn't have understood. My friends—a lot nicknamed The Princess Pack after dressing as the crowned Disney characters one Halloween—they wouldn't have understood either.

A few girlfriends have left Medicine Hat, but the ones who stayed were the ones who stayed. Even for those who left, *The Alchemist* would have seemed too "out there." At least I think so. Most of us come from long lines of farmers and Christians; "fate" and "magic" are not in our vocabulary. Maybe all the more, the shepherd's story, it became my moon.

The hours afterward felt as if I were in limbo. I woke beside Stuart in the brown-orange carpeted basement room where Grant and his brother used to play stick hockey. I dreamt all day of the highway. Getting on it, once and for all. Because unlike most who leave small towns and never come back, I could leave—for university in Regina, an internship in Calgary and even a dude ranch in Kananaskis one summer. My problem was, I kept coming back. Then I got a real job and my name was on a mortgage and someone I'd grown used to was on the other side of the bed. I stopped wishing on the night sky.

The cab. Scott's palm, open in the middle seat for me to take. The meter's red, blinking numbers. This dash. This steering wheel. This highway, heading north. Barely going the speed limit.

I roll down the window. The chill sweeps my cheeks and the front window fogs. I gaze at the fields. Prairie grasses poking out of the snow. Spines of the hills, just yellow. My face, cold. But I like listening to my tires, spinning over snow and gravel. White noise, it is, against the voices in my head: *Didn't think I'd see you here. You were just talking rings. You walk out of this newsroom, you can forget...* The soap-opera-ness of it all, my mind is hitched to it.

Now, of course, now that I'm fueled by my dramatics and finally going, nearly gone, I need to stop and pee. I'm afraid, though, that if I pull over here, already... Somehow my mind paddles away from the accusations, to scenes of all the times I've peed myself, laughing, and there have been many: on the trampoline of a Mormon friend, age seven; in the cafeteria in front of the entire school, laughing at a simple boy flirting with my friend, age eight; at Zora's kitchen table, a silly remark while four us of were eating Velveeta cheese noodles, age fifteen; in Zora's kitchen, when she couldn't find the lock to her Ikeda lock jeans (a terrible fad of the mid-'90s that involved a tiny padlock that shackled to a clasp in the button area and from which a brass chain loop dangled), and she had to pee her pants and I did the same, also age fifteen. (She found the lock in the morning, in her front pocket.)

Instead of pulling over to relieve myself, I shove my purse off the emergency brake to root around for some matches so I can smoke. Always, at least, there's smoking. But looking down, I glance at two photos I'd almost forgotten on the fridge.

The first is of my little brother, Tyler, and me in the Victory Lutheran Church parking lot just before the wedding of our older stepbrother, Kevin. In a few minutes, I will burst into tears in the receiving line as I hug Kevin, who is just twenty-three and marrying the mother of his two-year-old daughter. He'd wanted to be an artist and now he would manage a department store, buy a bungalow. I was twenty, almost the same age as his wife, whom I adored, but I was suddenly overcome with sadness that he would now stand at the edge of life, like a fence. My dress is black, and my red hair, gleaming in the afternoon light, is there and not, like a sunrise. Tyler is still lanky, and younger than me, in the face. I remember him like that, and like he was at six, or five. His cheeks, always with a sheen of dust. His eyes, his brows, tipping into a secondborn's question mark, *Should we?* His legs, bruised from boyhood and skinny, *like a Biafran*, said the women. Always just a leg behind me, leaping from dirt hill to dirt hill. Ours was nearly the last new house on the block, the edge between Ross Glen and a gray-faded farmer's shed, and they'd dumped hundreds of hills of dirt between our backyard, the farms and the highway—for more. More houses, more basements, more Nintendos, more fake Christmas trees, more trampolines, more Alpha-getti cans, more beds. For these houses are mostly filled with *blended* families (as if it were a treasured recipe's step that produced us rather than rotten circumstance and a lack of choice in mates), and so there must be enough squares inside the house to store and separate all those bodies, that stuff, the kids like us, who couldn't breathe under that watch, that tension like tar, always it reeked of tar and fresh paint and just sawn two-by-fours around there. So we fled, forked out with sticks in the dirt our own streets and houses and cats. Built stink bombs and forts and frog gardens in wagons. Whatever the land, always its people ate waffles on school days and there was no fighting. Or we played at the day things went to shit, and we spat *goddammit* and *chrissakes* and *sonofabitch* until our tongues hurt.

But my brother and I, at least, save for the odd brawl over cereal toys, we stuck together. We were like soldiers, lost in a fog. We lamented the ghostly land of *Usedto*. We treaded lightly, clasping blistered hands, sometimes blotting the other's blood, or tears. We plotted. We often nearly wet ourselves, in fear at stunts, in laughter. We knew without swearing it that we would never betray or break the other's heart.

Brothers and sisters, they can have this most uncomplicated kind of love.

In the other photo, my dress is short, blue polyester, and I'm wearing tan, knee-high pleather boots. My friend Stella is on the left, in a similar dress that's peach, boots black, blond hair. Our giddy smiles. Our skinny arms around Kimmi, in the middle. Kimmi, her brown square-dancing dress, the cowboy hat with a veil stapled to the back. An inflatable mustached man waving from her knee. It was her '60s-themed stagette. Soon we would be singing "Delta Dawn," the version Tanya Tucker sang in 1972.

Soon half the married or engaged women there that night would be divorced. Or wishing for it.

I steer with one hand. Blow my nose with the other. My friends, as far away now as that night is. They think I've lost my mind. Maybe I have. Maybe I have.

The sun's glare turns the snakes and paddies of tar into streams and ponds. Over and over, I expect splashes. Instead, my tires glide over the hardened tar. An illusion of the sun.

This highway, I was only ever on it twice with Stuart. Once on our way to a group ski trip, during which I threw a drunken tantrum over a board game dispute and went to bed early. Once to Radium, where Stuart feared the hippie man who lived in a treehouse with goats would emerge while we ventured through it with other tourists. The only other place we went together was Elkwater, a lake not far from Medicine Hat where we water-skied and camped. Stuart always drove, tapping the steering wheel as he bellowed Conway Twitty songs like "I'd Love to Lay You Down."

The ditch. A distance sign I miss. A bouquet of pink and violet flowers wrapped in plastic and roped to a fencepost. Someone died here. Someone died here and she probably would have been happy just to be alive, just to breathe and be hugged. Never mind have a good man who loves her or a five-bedroom house.

I tip a cigarette over the window and watch it bounce on the road. Tumble twice, embers flickering, then stop. I can't see it anymore. Instead, I see my shadow, pacing on the edge of the ditch where my car broke down two weeks ago. It happened somewhere near here.

I was on my way back from looking at places in Calgary with Zora. My car was going about eighty miles an hour. Then, nothing. Just coasting. I rammed the gas pedal, tried pumping. But the car kept drifting. Eventually, it stopped. I didn't know what to do. My mom wasn't home so I left a message. My brother wasn't answering his phone either. Even though we had been broken up for weeks, I called Stuart. His dad, a mechanic, drove almost two hours to find me and fix my car. He lifted the hood with already blackened fingers. Flicked his thumb a few times and let down the hood rod.

"Fuel pump was loose." He stood there, one foot on the white line as passing cars blew our hair.

"Sorry." *For this, for what I've done to your son.* How do others do it—pick up and carry on, heels spitting rocks on once-famil-iar faces? Do the faces forgive?

He shook his head. "Don't worry about it."

I got in the car, turned the engine over and cried, from some place in my stomach that churned regret and guilt and fear until I was nauseous. I saw flashes of Stuart in the middle of the garage with a case of beer at his feet and the half-burnt-out lightbulb illuminating his face.

Back inside my car, against the hum of trucks, my mom phoned back.

I answered, sniffling.

"Sweetie, what's wrong?"

I told her about breaking down and Stuart's dad driving out.

"What am I doing?" I sobbed. "What if I never find in-laws like that again?"

Stuart's mom took me garage-saling on Saturdays and his nephew called me Auntie *Natawee* and the Tenney house was always, always, erupting with laughter and dishes and horsing around. In fact, I remember his dad talking about how much he loved coming home from work when their four kids were little. "Can't imagine a quiet house," he'd said. "Nothing better than the sound of little feet." Growing up, my family's house had the hush and chill of a funeral parlor.

"Oh, honey." My mom paused and let me cry. "I know. I know."

THE SUN, TRYING. The road, quite empty. Except for us. Twenty-five miles from Calgary, just outside Strathmore, my mom catches up. Pulls over, ahead of me, and her face swivels like a doll's. She waves at me, smiles. The smile of pageants. She won Miss Congeniality in a beauty contest when she was studying nursing in The Pas. She grew up more than 240 miles away, in Thompson, Manitoba, a desolate northern town not far from the lodges of polar bears. It was named after John F. Thompson, chairman of the Inco nickel mine where my father was working in the summer of 1972. My mom and dad met at a burger joint run by a Chinese man named Q. My dad was nineteen and he had long hair. My mom was seventeen, and she had this smile. She grew up wearing mukluks, washing dishes with her sisters and spending Sunday mornings in the second pew at St. Lawrence Roman Catholic Church. The Allens filled an entire pew. My mom was born smack in the middle of seven children, and so she became a fixer, a peacekeeper, a nurturer amidst the giggling of the little ones and the barking of the older ones and the clanking cutlery of their nine and a few more—friends were often invited, but there could never be thirteen (bad luck), so Grandma Allen would send one off to find another child to join. Those sounds, that house, they must have filled my dad like chicken broth. He had grown up in a quiet house, where you might hear the horn of a kitchen chair at dawn, the call of a long-eared owl at dusk and in between, people spoke only of the weather, as it related to crops, in passing. And it had been that way for a long, long time, ever since my grandmother caught sight of Jerzy, my grandfather, carrying the limp, blood-soaked little girl from down the road. *The tractor. The tractor was running and she . . .* If the neighbors came to forgive, it didn't matter. My grandmother Halina's guilt outweighed the tractor, the house, the farm. It left her crippled, cold, a mute. So that she rarely rose from bed and never left the house again. She wished, I imagined, that the guilt would just sink her after all. By the time she died six years later, they say her hair had turned the gray-yellow shade of hymn pages and hung all the way to the floor.

My dad still had shoulder-length hair when he and my mom were married on a July afternoon in 1976, after my mom spent all morning soaking in a tub at a neighbor's house to get away from the chiffon and questions. In the first few years of their marriage, she waited for a baby, but a baby would not come. Doctors said she would never conceive. Endometriosis. Then, eight days after their fifth anniversary, at two o'clock in the morning on a Sunday in July, following the sort of Prairie summer storm that lit skies and scared dogs, I was born. My brother, Tyler, who arrived eight days after my second birthday, was still a baby, still toothless and wide-eyed and clapping, when the babysitter strolled into my mom's office and said she had something to tell.

Was I three or four when I first heard them fighting? Bastard, my mom yelled. And, You've got nerve. She must have just found out, or finally had the chance to yell. About Vicky. The babysitter who sang "You Are My Sunshine" as the afternoon sun dusted above my head, just before nap. He hollered back, frothing nearly. What was his defense? She was eighteen. Dark, curly hair. She let me have a sleepover at her apartment once. My bed was the bathtub. My nightie, one of her t-shirts. I might have loved her. My fucking goddamn fucking secretary's daughter, Mom screamed. I stood on the chair, shouted, Stop it, guys. They caught my face and took a breath. Said, Sweetie, sweetie. And started again. *You...*

Then, he was gone.

I prefer to think of my mom not in the kitchen with mascara-stained cheeks slamming a pan on the counter, but in her high heels and pantyhose at her office. Or even at that beauty pageant with a white sash across her big fat heart. A few years ago,

I framed her black-and-white eight-by-ten contestant photo. It doesn't show her best feature, her gray-green eyes, which she frequently takes off the road. My mom drives carelessly; she never thinks anything bad could happen.

She signals and sails onto the highway. I follow.

And it strikes me, that I was desperate for a big, loud family the way my father must have been. That I found one, and had to give it back.

The flowery, purple fabric of my teenage twin bed knocks against the truck rail when my mom swerves to miss a brass floor lamp rolling over the dotted line. Someone else is moving today.

WITHOUT MEN

THIS IS WHERE I live now, a few doors down from the neon orange TUNE-UPS sign of Alberta Oriental Auto Service. And from a Wal-Mart, a Vietnamese noodle house and the Rusty Cage, a bar that's dark but for the blue of cigarette smoke. A few blocks away, the trendy 17th Avenue, its bars named after numbers, its amputated panhandlers, its stuff shops selling wooden expressions such as PEACE and LOVE. Like displaying the word would make it so.

Zora and I share a front step with Paul and his wife, a couple we believe could be Greek. Our four-plex basement suite is below theirs. Paul, our landlord, pretends to be pruning a bush as my mom and I begin to move in, along with Zora and her mom, Lois. We each catch shadows of his wife, a heavy woman with dark hair, in the front room window. Wondering where the men are, I suspect, as we ferry mattresses, televisions, saggy garbage bags, pans, a kitchen table, a computer and my sectional (seven feet tall, brought in standing upright). We take a cigarette break.

"Well, this is a cute little place, girls." My mom uses the word "cute" all the time. She rolls her sleeves up to her elbows, arm hairs glistening in the sun. It's the first day of February, but it nearly feels like May.

"Yeah," says Zora. She sits down next to me on the stoop.

Zora found it last week. She had been living with a friend in McKenzie Towne, a neighborhood so much to the south of Calgary that it pretends to be its own village. It even has a cartoon-looking town square with faux old-fashioned street signs, a block of shops and a clock at the entranceway. Zora doesn't mind McKenzie Towne being cheesy. She just doesn't want to spend an hour driving to college every morning anymore. If there is anything Zora resents, it's a lack of sleep. I discovered this on our first sleepover. Zora's mom, Lois, tapped on the door not long after ten in the morning and Zora screamed *Don't!* so violently I wanted to call my mom to pick me up. Zora would never speak to anyone but her mom like that, and only on matters involving sleep, but I didn't know that at the time.

"I'm just glad I get to sleep in," she says. This place is a fifteen-minute drive from Mount Royal College, where she's studying criminology. "And I get to live with you." She squeezes my arm.

I stare at her and see the friend I fell in love with when we were twelve. Zora, the makings of Lois—Danish, always smiling—and *him*.

She calls him The Co-Creator. Not George, not Dad, the Irish-Indigenous man her mother fled from when Zora was just six weeks old, swaddled, ear-splitting screams with colic, allergy to milk, knowing the vibration of danger. She inherited his high cheekbones, an intolerance of alcohol, skin that tans to the color of tobacco, his donkey laugh, says Lois, but not his fists. Zora never looked for her dad.

From Lois, she inherited narrow green eyes, broad shoulders and blond hair that bleaches in the sun. In ways of the heart, Lois indulged her. In ways of the world, Lois pushed her.

At eleven, Zora could baste an egg, do a load of delicate colors and recognize the sound of a failing engine in their blue Ford Escort. But she sucked her thumb when no one was watching and expected Lois to say yes when she asked for things. She has always called Lois by her name, not Mom.

The day we met, Zora Nilsson and I were both wearing Guess jeans. Mine were brown. Hers were red. Her hair, cut in a bob, was dyed orange. Between her two front teeth, she had a gap the width of a pencil. It was the first day of French class and three rows ahead of me, a terrific sound erupted from Zora, her laugh. Her hoarse voice amplified in laughter, which reached volumes and lengths that were shocking in a girl. At the end of her fit, she wiped a tear with her t-shirt and saw me staring at her.

For the first few months of our friendship, I watched her in awe, as if I were a farm kid who had discovered a giraffe in the barn. We were ... so different. I whispered. She yelled. I did the jumping jacks in gym class. Zora told the teacher to stuff it and sat on the floor. I was afraid, going to Zora's after school, that her bus driver would shout at me. Zora was afraid to be alone. We got into trouble, told secrets and lies, and laughed until Zora choked and I peed. It seems wise to me now to move in with the kind of friend who used to make you wet yourself. As girls, we had dozens of sleepovers, mostly in the bunk beds of her little gray house in Riverside. I stayed at her house as often as I could; it was so loud and carefree and messy, so opposite from the stale, frigid white halls of my house on 7th Street.

And now this is Day One of our permanent sleepover. I'm glad for that, mostly. The coals of me, they need Zora. Her disregard for rules, her insistence on having a good time. When we were thirteen, we stole Lois's motorhome and drove through Riverside, smoking Lois's Number 7 butts, listening to "Bette Davis Eyes" and wearing tracksuits and lipstick to look like moms should we pass a police officer. At fifteen, we dropped acid and broke into Riverside Pool in the middle of the night and swam in our t-shirts until Zora's got caught on the barbed-wire fence, half her ass and wet underwear dangling under a streetlight (and me, trying to help, legs crossed to avoid dribbling). We took taxi cabs to bush parties and paid with dimes.

Right now, I need Zora. I need her to make me laugh, help me forget what the world thinks I'm supposed to do.

"I'm just glad you two are living together," says Lois, eyes watering. She is often on the verge of tears.

My mom rubs Lois's shoulder and chuckles. "Yes, that makes me feel better, knowing you two are together."

She and Lois first met as Zora and I became friends, but now they're friends too. They also share clients, my mom being a social worker and Lois being a care worker. Today they're wearing matching, thick-heeled, white runners and pants with narrow legs. They both have the tired look of middle-aged single moms who have had enough, of bad hands and bad unions. And yet they carry hope around like keys.

Lois wipes her nose, stuffs the tissue in her purse. "I think we moved in just fine without any men." In truth, we had a few minutes of help from Lee, a bartender Zora met working at a pub called Woody's a while back. They might be together. A couple. Or couple-ing.

"That's probably a good thing because it's not the first or the last time, is it?" says Lois.

We all laugh. We don't want to think about another move just yet, but, yes, one of us will move again someday, without men. Save for the on-and-off appearances of Lee and with Wes about to officially part ways with my mom, at the moment, there isn't a promising sign of any kind of dad, husband or boyfriend to be had among any of us. But we're all used to doing everything without them. Growing up in the dawn of divorce,

Zora and I were among the majority of kids in Medicine Hat (or was it just our circle?) who either never saw or never knew their dads. My brother and I saw ours sometimes at Christmas and in the summer—when we'd go for walks in silence along the river, or to a pool hall, where he'd try to teach us to play with the laws of physics—but for most of my childhood and teenage years, I knew him only by the dark, deliberate strokes of his signature on a check. I don't even know his birthday.

What will happen to us, us children of parents who fucked it up and walked away? Will we marry better, or not at all? Or will we take it just as lightly, signing marriage certificates on hot June afternoons in $6,000 dresses knowing it takes the same, a few pen strokes and a line of credit, to call it off?

"No, probably not," says my mom, probably tallying, in her mind, all it will take to separate from Wes. The signatures. The boxes. The Jenga with last names. The shocking cold of starting over, again. She tries to slide her lighter into her front pocket, but it's too tight so she stuffs it in the back.

Because of her seemingly lackadaisical approach to marriage, as a teenager, mine was diagnostic, almost mathematical. I understood the odds and ramifications of getting it wrong. I told myself, when she was tipping away her anger in that rocking chair, or when I was waiting at the phone for him to call, that I would only marry once—not because I wouldn't divorce, but because I wouldn't want to. But I understand now, how it happens. Someone loves you. You think it's enough. It's enough for other people.

What would our grandmothers think of all of this, this slipping in and out of doors and beds and dreams?

My aunt Diana was already eleven weeks in my grandmother Grace's belly the day she kissed Cecil, my grandfather, outside the church. He was in his uniform. She was in a long coat and heels. In 1996, as their fiftieth anniversary and the late Diana's birthday approached, my grandmother, a devout Catholic, may or may not have willed herself to death at the thought of her children doing the math about the dates and realizing their eldest sister had been conceived out of wedlock.

I think my grandmother Halina willed herself to death as well. I don't know if she had been happy before the tractor accident, but I suspect she didn't have time to contemplate it much. She'd married a fifth son who wouldn't inherit any land, and it's likely she spent sixteen hours a day on her feet feeding cows, milking cows, fetching water, boiling water, baking bread, sandwiching bread, feeding children, bathing children, washing clothes, mending clothes, fixing plates, cleaning plates, whispering prayers. *Praying, praying.*

The women and men I am descended from, will I catch their madness, their zealousness, their wandering eyes? I wonder, and so I keep these worries a secret, even from myself. Even from my own mother.

Only in recent weeks and at age fifty has my mom taken up smoking. You can tell too. She barely inhales. Over the next few months, as the divorce between her and my stepfather becomes final, my mom will act more and more like a teenager. Her catchphrase will become "I'm fifty. I can do whatever I want." Today, though, she's still my mom, and she slides her free hand over my hair, looks down at me and winks.

Our mothers—for so long, we see them only as that, a being at the other end of the cord, the cradle, the dinner table, the telephone. And then suddenly, both of us, women.

AFTER OUR MOMS leave, after we fill our first garbage bag with pizza boxes, after we root through suitcases for sheets that smell of other homes, Zora and I pass in the hall.

She wraps her arms around me. "Night, Nattie-do."

I smile, teary with thanks. With fear. With happiness. Yes, happiness.

There's a pause. I think she's wondering if she should say something. About the breakup.

But this is what I need, a hug. "Night."

Soon, I'm crawling into my new bed, my old twin bed. The mattress is as wide as my pillow and already worn in the shape of my body. Why is it so unsettling, sleeping on the bed of your childhood? I picture teenage dreams dressed in ruffled prom gowns at a party crashed by the goblin-like figures of adult fears. The tension between what could have been, what is and, now, what could be.

What now?

I listened to my gut about getting out of Medicine Hat, and now here I am, twenty-three, in a basement suite with my best friend, starting over. I feel so little, flung into the ditch by the wind of everything I know. And yet I'm warm and tingly with the breath of a voice that says, *You're going the right way.*

STRANGERS

FIRST, I WILL learn how to do laundry in public.

The bells on the back of the door scrape against the glass when an older man totters in with a blanket reeking of fish stuffed in an orange yard bag. I am reading the HELP WANTED ads, trying to talk myself out of applying for jobs.

A few weeks after Christmas, I made it to the year 2005 with the book project and dropped off the last of the microfiche rolls at the *Lethbridge Herald*. My work with the book was done and my final check was in the mail. In my haste and shame, I didn't ask Stuart to sell the house. Naively, perhaps, I even left my name on the mortgage. And so, I have about $700 to my name and no sign of future income.

The man with the blanket only asks about the weather, and soon I am babbling. About Medicine Hat. About leaving. He asks what brought me out here and I say I don't know. A truth and a lie.

"Starting out's never easy," he says, soiled fingers on his kneecaps, matted hair draping from his Shell hat. He introduces himself as Ernie. Tells me about leaving his family and Manitoba with his wife forty years ago, for the promise of work in Alberta. "No," he says. "But it gets better. Don't worry about that."

Eyes clinging to the lemon-yellow floor tiles, I nod. Since I left Medicine Hat, it's like I'm smelling the world with a dog's nose.

How is it that strangers can leave you less lonely?

I wonder, too, if the universe is parachuting people and books into my world at the very moment I need them, or if they would have been right there all the while, and I'm just starting to find my way.

I scribble a star next to an ad for servers at the Barley Mill downtown. In the Prairies, the tallest object as far as you can see is a scraggy, leaning cattle fencepost, and it feels as if your whole life is laid bare for the sun and all to witness, for you to know. Downtown Calgary, with its glass skyscrapers and clogged one-way streets, seems an exotic if practical place to wait out my next move.

MARRY
KETCHUP

TWO DAYS LATER, Megan marches toward me with a tray of half-filled ketchup bottles. She sets the tray on the counter. Around the bottle tips, the paste has dried and thickened. Inside, behind the label, clumps of sugar painted red.

"Hey, before you help do roll-ups, can you marry these?" says Megan. Her hair is dark and shiny, the shade of a fly. She's shorter than I am, younger too. But her walk and her voice—like a doll's—make me feel smaller.

Marry ketchups, marry ketchups. What? "Ummm."

"This is what you do," she says, stomping back over to the condiment station. She pours a near-empty Heinz bottle into a full one. "There. Now they're married."

She wipes her purple fingernails on her apron and stares at me, willing me to begin. She's high on pot, hasn't graduated from high school, and she's showing me how to marry ketchup. For all she and the others know, I'm as dumb and unmotivated as the walls, and this kills me, even more than filling condiment bottles.

It's my first week as a waitress at the Barley Mill, a pub that stands at the edge of downtown's shiny towers, in the shadow of a Sheraton hotel. Not far from the Bow River, it's housed in a red, two-story wooden building masquerading as a logging mill. A waterwheel on the outside spins and spits out water when a switch marked Wheel is flicked on inside. It's an homage to the Eau Claire and Bow River Lumber Co. In the 1880s, logs drifted downriver from the Rocky Mountains and into these mills, which turned the wood into the timber that became the walls and floors of the Prairies. The Barley Mill's second floor is made of lumber from the original Alberta distillery. Otherwise, the Barley Mill is an imitation of something historic, but it fools a lot of people because of all the wood. On the floor, the tables, the walls, the beams.

Its fragrance is wood. And dust. And the parade of perfumes worn by the servers. And the dry breath of men who want, the suits who work in the head offices of oil and gas companies. Many have never been to the derricks—those black, grasshopper-shaped structures that dip down and drill oil—or the unsullied sites where men plunge metal into the earth to prepare its disembowelment. These men work in fluorescent-lit offices and sit in meetings. They are more accustomed to the sounds of this restaurant—waitresses calling each other "sweetie," ale glasses clinking and steak knives scraping plates—than they are of the squealing sound of the Prairies being sucked dry.

And I think about our great-grandfathers, fleeing the old country with pockets of seeds and coins, knotting cloths around their soles, hoarding twisted nails for shacks, feasting on rabbit and bread peppered with the droppings of mice. And what would they think of this, this pretending, these towers, these *men*?

I'm marrying ketchups as quickly as I can, trying not to spill. *Ketchup is viscous. Viscosity: the resistance to flow.* I was good at memorizing science definitions in high school. Mr. Barrie's science class stages in my mind. My sixteen-year-old self is slumped over the desk where daydreams streak across the football field past the window. The bars of fluorescent light above us sting my eyes and I hear Mr. Barrie, a tall man with a pointy nose, bellowing: "Don't make things harder than they are." Another one of his aphorisms echoes now: "Wherever you are, you got yourself there."

I rub the bumpy, peeling ketchup bottle labels. The glass is still strong, shiny. The thick paste slides, slowly and in blobs that break open, then fall faster, from one bottle into the other. When the bottle's full, I can't tell which ketchup belongs and which doesn't.

Footsteps thud all the way up the stairs. I turn my head to see who it is and my hip pokes the ketchup tray. One bottle drops, and then another, rolling, crashing. Ketchup splatters my legs, leaches my feet.

"Nice one." The busboy, hands on the railing, pulls himself to the top of the stairs and lands in a stomp. He surveys the damage—shards of glass, ponds of ketchup—and smiles. "You really made a mess."

I'm left to clean it up with stained, rotting cloths from the kitchen's laundry basket.

An hour later, I drift to my car scraping with a key the ketchup rooted underneath my nails.

The air is cold. Wind smacks my face and tosses my hair. I squint, searching for my car in a massive parking lot. Shouldn't be too hard. Mine's the only one more than fifteen years old. When I spot my roof, I jog to the door.

"For fuck sakes."

Scratch marks zig and zag around the keyhole. Résumés are strewn across the backseat. A Dixie Chicks CD, opened with the disk still inside, was chucked onto the dash. They took nothing. Nothing to take. Maybe that's why they slashed my tires? Jagged cuts of rubber ripped open.

I lean against the car, my head and arms folding over the roof as if it were a pillow. I stand there for a while, sniffling. Thinking, *If I were in Medicine Hat, this wouldn't have happened.* I'd be strolling down the meat aisle or watching *Trading Spaces* on the couch.

I search for my cell phone in my purse, a black hole of pennies and bits of tobacco. *Good thing your purse is organized, Natalie. This would be excellent in an emergency.* My mind's narrator imagines that scene making the news. I see my mother on television screens, saying, I don't know. Maybe if she could have found her phone in time ... maybe she'd be here now.

After tossing the purse on the cement, I excavate the contents like a child tearing the wrapping paper of a present. When a man in a trench coat and tie walks by, he barely looks at me before he flicks the car-finder button on his keychain. I'm on my ketchup-stained knees, bawling and rooting through a fake leather purse.

I'M MARRIED

I DRINK. AND I wake up drunk. And there he is, sitting on the edge of the bed, Zora's bed. She's out of town. Was it my idea? I glance at a collage that had been in her bedroom since she was a girl—photos of her in a white dress at age two, her on a rocking horse next to Lois—and then back at him. His hands cup his mouth, and he sighs.

We met last night at a bar called Melrose. There was a table of us, and then he winked at me. We stumbled out of the cab and up to my front door, his fingers sinking under my jeans, under my underwear, under my self. I stopped, smiled, let him.

He grunted. "You are . . . something."

And we went inside.

I'm naked now, naked as his shaved head and those stocky hands.

He looks back at me, blinking, still under the sheets. "I'm sorry."

I sit up. Above my head is Zora's map of the world with yellow-tipped pins sticking into all the places she's been—Denmark, England, France, Thailand, Laos. Places I can't quite imagine are real, despite her paper flags and photos in front of castles and beaches. There couldn't possibly be a girl like me in Copenhagen right now, naked, dry tongue, next to a stranger.

"I've never done this before," he says. "I'm, uh... I'm married."

I take a breath, fix my eyes on the lint of the duvet cover. I can't see or feel for her. Can't see anything beyond the door. In a sad, strange way, I am merely intrigued: I've always been the cheater. Nearly every boyfriend I've ever had, followed by a confession and a quick departure. In my mind, I line them up like soldiers: Paul whose dad was a paraplegic. Alex from Saskatchewan who was my first. Joe the comedian I met in Kananaskis. Stuart. I've inherited this cheating, this leaving. And, in fact, I think now, this is what led me to Scott's basement. I forced myself there, to make me break it off—with Stuart, with Medicine Hat—not for once but for all.

He eyes the floor for his jeans, collects the stuff of his pockets and leaves.

FLOODED

B Y THE END of the month, I dent the front end of my car in a parking lot. I break my phone and have to use a two-pound, decade-old one with the *Jurassic Park* ringtone. I fall down the stairs at work carrying three plates of hot wings and barely blush.

I receive a neatly folded letter that says, *Thank you for your application... Unfortunately...*

I had applied to a master's degree in communications program at the University of Calgary. I don't really want to get into PR or become a professor, but I need an anchor.

Being a reporter again doesn't look likely. I dropped off my résumé and some articles at the *Calgary Herald*, but never get a call. Pretty sure I've been blacklisted by the yellow-mustached managing editor of *The News*. I can't freelance any agricultural stories for *The Western Producer* anymore because in Calgary, also known as Cowtown, there are no cows. Every time I try to dip into that world again or find a job there, I half hope I won't get a call. I don't know why. Maybe I'm not enough right now to do such lofty, public work. Anyway, it doesn't seem as if the world wants it for me right now either. So, for the last four months, I've worked as a waitress, wearing cleavage-bearing tops and bringing assholes steak and beer. One of the suits started winking and calling me Scully, the red-haired FBI agent from *The X-Files*. Sober the next day at lunch, he pretends he forgets. The Barley Mill, it was only supposed to be for a little while.

Zora and I are fighting about dishes and laundry soap and her "boyfriend," Lee, who helped us move in the sectional. Lee lives with his grandpa and he says he's twenty-nine, but he's balding and won't let Zora see his ID. Says he has to wear his hat, even when they are... you know. Lee tells people it's his truck, but it's Zora's, and he uses it to give rides to other waitresses. I know because now he's bartending at the Barley Mill. And I heard he left work the other night in Zora's Dodge with Tammy. Tammy: big breasts, big brown eyes, beautiful smile, part First Nations, just left a bar called The Unicorn. The kind of girl you could fall into hoping her caress could right you, make you good.

I lock myself out of the four-plex for an hour when I go outside for a cigarette without a key. And I think I'm going to be shot when a man walks up to me outside my building and ominously opens his black leather jacket. But instead of a gun, he pulls out a pigeon. Its red-orange eyes blink and its feathers, shades of gray with scarves of green and purple around its neck, look greasy.

"Here," he says. "Yours?"

I shake my head.

"This is the bird of someone, I think," he says, surveying the block. "Whose?"

"I... I don't know. I don't think it's anyone's bird."

In the end, we give the pigeon to the wife of my upstairs landlord. Even if she can't speak English, she seems to understand the predicament and waves at the man to pass her the pigeon. An hour later, the stench of steaming bird descends through the ceiling vents. She's baking the pigeon.

The pigeon, it almost made it. Until we all got in the way.

WHEN I TELL my aunt Cindy about my spell of misfortune, she stomps and slaps her thigh. Laughs like a Muppet, all tonsils and hair.

"Someday this will all be funny. I swear," says my aunt, the only relative I have in Calgary. We're in her kitchen because all I want in the world is a grilled cheese sandwich and there is no cheese or bread at my house. It's Zora's turn to buy both. Because we have opposite schedules, Zora and I know each other only by the TV's last channel and what kind of noodles have glued in pots.

While my aunt has been flipping my sandwich, I've told her everything except how I feel: awake, a stranger, sorry, unknotting, bad-lucked, found out, *lost lost lost.* That's what I know right now. That, and I might have a bit of melancholy. If it weren't for horoscopes and cigarettes, I wouldn't want to wake up. I tap my pack on the counter and my aunt nods.

Outside, along her fence, the smoke curls after her kitchen window. When I was about fifteen, we were having Christmas at my grandpa's house in Lethbridge. He'd just passed away, but we'd all gathered at his house, a house he'd only lived in for a year or two with a second wife, a Mormon named Iris who had been friends with my grandmother before she died. Sometime between dinner and our tradition of opening one Christmas Eve gift, pajamas, I lit a cigarette in the downstairs bathroom. Afterward, I stepped out in the hall and I heard Aunt Cindy talking to Aunt Donna.

"Do you smell smoke?" Aunt Cindy said, sniffing the air.

Aunt Donna inhaled. "I do."

"Is it Dad?"

Grandpa smoked. I remember the amber ashtray at the kitchen table, the transistor radio, his long, freckled bony fingers, not unlike mine.

"Could be left over," said Aunt Donna. She held the idea on her tongue a minute. "From before."

"No. No, it's Dad."

I said nothing. Aunt Cindy would later tell me, when I moved in with her family while I was doing an internship at a TV station in Calgary, that she believed that every time she smelled cigarette smoke, it was a sign from her dad, from Grandpa. Saying, *Hi honey. I'm here. I love you.* Often, when I lived with her, she'd stumble out the back door, nose first, and tear when she spotted me and my smoking. "Oh, it's just you."

Why do some of us sniff without rest for hints, traces of passage?

The last time Aunt Cindy smelled my smoke at her house, four years had passed since her visit with Clairvoyant Kim, a medium who told her my grandpa had woken her up just after five in the morning the day of her appointment with my aunt. Clairvoyant Kim told her my grandpa said my grandma was in the room when he died, and she sits on the bed of each of her eleven grandchildren every night. I've felt her. I feel her and something else, something just as warm and right as resting my head on her chest when I was a girl. So does my aunt.

Back inside, at the center of her kitchen, Aunt Cindy slides the ketchup toward my plate. "Here you go, hon."

I take a bite, savor the butter, the bread, the cheese. Study her kitchen. You can tell a family lives here. Red and blue plastic cups perched on the counter, letters from school posted on the fridge by lopsided alphabet magnets, two toy cars dumped on the kitchen table.

My eyes reach for the ceiling, to still tears. I know there are people in the world with *actual* problems—lost limbs, missing children, dying wives—but I'm miserable and I want to blame somebody.

"You know, no one tells you that your twenties are going to be awful."

All these unfortunate incidents, they're not punishment. They're not signs I should go back, though I did wonder that. No, they're signs I need to keep moving.

My aunt takes off her oven mitt and rubs my arm. "I know." Her fingers are cold and now she's crying too.

I stare at the gray tiles of her floor. "You're not supposed to say that. You're supposed to say, 'They're not *that* awful,' or 'Oh, it will get better.'"

She holds her breath awhile, then sighs. "Well, it might."

MY PALE, FRECKLED cheeks sink into the couch as the rain pelts our windows. Like grasshoppers crashing against a car on a farm road.

The Elbow and Bow riverbanks are swelling. Thirty thousand sandbags have been planted to keep the water from spilling over onto Calgary's streets. Deep freezes are bobbing in basements like corks, the zoo had to move three moose to a ranch and stagnant pools of water have spawned millions of bloodthirsty mosquitoes. We are flooded.

I need help. The heart, it hushed I should go and so I did. But now, now I can't hear a sound.

Oh, Natalie, what are you doing?

I drink. I drink and I seek the company of undeserving men. A twin who is a headhunted oil executive not yet thirty. Calls only after midnight. A hockey player–academic whose erect penis resembles a toothbrush. Never calls.

I saw a reflection of my old self for a second. The day the *Lethbridge Herald* agreed to publish an article I wrote about Aunt Donna's book, a collection of stories from people whose lives changed with the help of just one person. I wondered, *Is there one person who will help me?*

Maybe because it's spring, maybe because it's been a while, but when I see my aunt's olive smiling face, my byline, the possibility of that text triggering other, better stories, I think, *I miss all of that.* What I don't miss is being forced to phone perfect strangers at all hours to get quotes about their wrongdoings. Or turning up at the tracks along the coulees and police scrambling to cover the body so my camera won't catch those stony eyes. Or ringing up the family of a farm girl whose car swerved off the gravel road. And what I'm starting to see is it's not the news I want to write, it's stories. True stories. For now, though, I will peddle ale for tips and try to drink less of it myself.

I was on call for work this afternoon, but it's raining again. The suits don't like getting wet.

My mind drifts back to another flood, to Riverside. Zora, Stella and I are thirteen, standing on the banks of the South Saskatchewan River in tank tops and ponytails, pointing with plugged noses at cow carcasses and trees taller than basketball nets. Within hours, the baseball stadium in the Flats became a lake, the water nearly spilling over the ten-foot-tall outfield fences. We knew we were at the edge of something bigger than us, and all we could do was to gape at it.

The rain stops. A tear falls.

I need help.

Gil. I'll send an email to Gil.

GOODBYE, ZORA

GLANCING AT THE flight board for the eighth time in two minutes, I realize I should have asked questions. About visas and contracts and pay. About getting picked up from the airport, what teachers wear and where I'll live. But I didn't. The only thing I know about Thailand is how to spell it, and I need to keep it that way for now.

Seven weeks ago, as charcoal rains brushed away the sun, I turned on my computer and wrote to Gil. He's a family friend and he used to be the registrar at Medicine Hat College before he retired and moved to Arizona. In the first two years of my journalism degree, he helped me get into classes that were full and out of ones I would have failed. I told him I didn't get into that master's program, but thank you for your reference. I told him I know he's not in the field anymore, but I need help. I told him I don't know what to do: I can't go back to Medicine Hat and I can't be a waitress forever. What should I do?

Gil replied: Sounds like a good time to do some traveling. He still had some friends in Thailand, mostly former students from the late '60s when he taught at a government school for boys.

"I have an idea," Gil said. "Why don't you go and teach English in Thailand?"

I hadn't thought about travel or living abroad as a way to solve feeling lost, mostly because it wasn't in my vocabulary, although a long time ago, it seemed now, I naively imagined myself becoming a war correspondent. Now, though, I've been given this chance to go far, far away. And as soon as I saw Gil's words, I knew this was what I needed to do.

A few days later, I was contacted with job offers through Sompan, one of Gil's former students, and Narunand, a fellow teacher. They don't get a lot of applications from women— something else I should ask about. I spent mere minutes debating the options: a private elementary school in a Bangkok suburb or a university in the center of the capital. The university gig meant I would get to teach English for mass media, and because this is loosely tied to journalism, the job resembled hope. Plus, I like the sound of it, "I teach at a *university*." I don't know how to teach, and I add this fact to the list of things I can't think about just yet.

I suppose I also like how this will sound back home, so gutsy and unusual. "Yeah, man, she lives in *Thailand* now."

I accepted the university job and called my mom. Her voice was breathy from running to the phone. She was outside on the deck, smoking, when I called. I told her about Gil and Thailand and the job. She almost cut me off: "What do you need?" My mom knew I had to go. Quickly.

Now, at the airport, holding a suitcase I'd borrowed from her and a plane ticket she paid for, she is teary-eyed. She keeps gazing at me as if I were a baby.

In the three weeks between my announcement and today, everyone has been asking if I'm scared. I say no. That would mean I have something to lose or that I know what I'm getting into. I don't. But I do get the sense I'm being guided and I let myself follow my feet. I'm going Somewhere.

Getting ready for it felt good. I sold my Nissan for $500 to someone Stuart's dad knows. I got a passport with the signature of the blind paperboy's lawyer father, and I bought some reading material for when I arrive: a Thai phrasebook, having just realized I'm going to a non-English-speaking country, and a Lonely Planet guidebook. One of the girls at the Barley Mill said I had to have one; I had never heard of Lonely Planet before, this being my first time abroad. Zora is the only person I know who has been overseas. One year ago, Zora had opened a linen photo album of her trip to Thailand with Lee (who hid his passport from her in their guesthouse rooms so she wouldn't see his birth date). The four of us were in my freshly painted beige basement living room with Stuart, drinking beer out of the bottle. I glanced at her glossy pictures—a sweet-looking Thai boy in a yellow t-shirt soaking wet from the river, Zora sweating in front of the fingers of a centuries-old banyan tree—and then back at the hockey game. "Do you want to look on your own?" she asked. "Oh no," I said, sick with envy and not wanting to see what I didn't want to see. "I'm fine."

Now, as my head turns to the security lineup, I spot Zora charging around suitcases under the fluorescent lights. I wait for her in my green khakis and white hoodie, a poor choice for sloppy me on a twenty-two-hour flight. When she's close enough that I can smell her—baby lotion and fabric softener—I hug her. And I can't let go. Strands of her sun-bleached hair stick against my face and I think about some of the other things I didn't want to think about. *My dear friend. I won't see you for so long. I wouldn't be leaving if it weren't for you.* Zora, who taught me how to tell the world to stuff it and do what I want to do. If she hadn't held my hand out of Medicine Hat, where would I be? All these years, she's held my hand. And I don't know why. But she has. A sniffle.

Zora pulls back, her tanned fingers on my shoulders. "Don't cry," she says, and starts to cry herself. So we stand there, darting each other's wet eyes, which makes us cry all the more. Finally, we wipe our cheeks and noses, and she clears her throat.

"OK, Natalie." Zora takes a breath before doling out her instructions. "Get out of Bangkok right away. Just head to any damn island you can get to. Everyone says don't take a *tuk-tuk*, but I think they're fun," she says, hands surfing with each sentence.

I nod, one eye on my mom, sauntering over to the Departures/Arrivals screen. She's talking so fast. What's a *tuk-tuk*?

"All I know is *sawasdee* means 'hello' and they kind of do this thing with their hands," she says, pressing her palms together at her chest, bowing just her head.

"Thai people are so nice. You just smile and they smile back. Most of the time you have to bring your own TP." (Toilet paper.)

"Oh yeah," she says, reaching into her purse. "I have something for you."

Zora hands me a little black plastic bag.

I pull apart the handles, but I can't see inside so I reach in with one hand and feel something a little bigger than a thumb and cold, like the bottom of a lightbulb. It's attached to a cord. In the corner of the bag are two spiky, gel-ly bits I assume are meant to jacket said electronic metallic bulb.

"Zora!"

"Shhh," she says, index finger over her mouth. "Can't get 'em there. You'll thank me later." Zora will defy anything, even vibrator laws.

My mind drafts a headline: *Canadian Woman Jailed in Bangkok for Vibrator Possession*.

I might not see Zora for a long time. She still has another year of studies before she finishes her degree, but Lois has promised to gift her an around-the-world trip after graduation. If I'm still in Thailand in the spring, Zora says she'll come see me.

She's staring at the tarmac. Her green eyes, glossy and still, study the landed rear of an airplane. She watches the passengers getting off the plane, nibbling on her necklace pendant, a Danish grandmother's grandmother's. I've always admired her knowing just where and who she comes from. Who she is. With my grandparents, there was so much unsaid, so much they wanted to forget. As for me, as poet Joy Harjo wrote, I have yet to "unfold me to myself."

"You know what I think about, Natalie? I think about all the people on that plane and all the places they just were that I didn't get to be. I think about how many people had to have sex to create all those passengers. It's a lot."

She sighs, for herself. "Wish I was going with you."

"Me too." *Me too.*

PART II
CITY OF
ANGELS

September 2005–January 2006

NIGHT ONE
IN BANGKOK

THE STREET IS dark but lit by neon. Three in the morning nearly, must be. I see beer bottles and Styrofoam containers lining sidewalks like plate scrapings in the sink. Hippies, heads swaying, singing Bob Marley's "Redemption Song." Sunburnt girls. Thai boys in skinny jeans and girly haircuts, flip flops scuffing the concrete. A middle-aged lady mumbling to herself, pushing a food cart topped by big metal bowls. Signs stacked on signs stacked on signs. For suits, for bars, for a Starbucks. For a 7-Eleven, an Indian buffet. But no guesthouses. And no sign of New Joe's, the somewhere-above-squalor guesthouse Zora recommended.

At the airport I told the cab driver, New Joe's, the guesthouse. I told him Trok Mayom, the lane it's on. I told him Khao San Road, the big street beside Trok Mayom that all the backpackers know. I told him Khao San Road three times, and on the third time he said, "Oh! *Thanon Khao San.*" But his smile—frost-white against his police sunglasses and reeking of Red Bull—didn't last. "Cannot. This time," he said, pointing at his thick brass watch, "road closed." I got out my map, but he swatted off my fingers. "I take you not far. Then walk."

The map. I need the map, but if I get out the map, they'll know I've just come. So I walk, suitcase wheels humming and grating over broken sidewalks.

The farther I go, the faster. Past a girl in dreads and a bikini top doing a hula. A couple in rags French-kissing. A sign. *A guesthouse sign! Please, please have a room.*

Suitcases teetering, I toddle up the steps to a window. Behind it is a Thai boy sitting on a stool, cheeks yellow under a dangling light. Flicks his hair back and stares at me.

"Do you have a room?"

His eyelids look heavy. His voice is a yawny whisper. "One person?"

I'm tired too. Please help me.

"Just me."

"OK. I can." He lifts a key from a rack and passes me a paper.

My tongue, raring to babble, about the cab and the flight and Zora at the airport and even my cat. Instead, it issues thanks.

"Oh, thank you. Thank you."

He lifts the key off the rack, holds it at his thumb. "150 *baht.*"

A little more than $4. Cheaper than New Joe's. I don't know if that's good or bad.

Turns out it's bad, in the way four walls can weld and make sixteen square feet. I don't care. I'm just so glad to be still somewhere. Somewhere far from home.

"HOME," A
FUNNY WORD

ER EYES ARE swollen, too tired for this hour, for conversation, for us.

One night at work, in the weeks before I left, Lee told me about her. About ladyboys. Guys who dress and live as girls. And still, I fight staring. At her frame of six feet. Her red dahlia lips. Her strut, so studied.

"Yes?"

She's a foot away from me, inside the covered restaurant with a menu blocking the sun from her face. I'm sitting in the sun at a patio table along Khao San Road, just after sunrise. She is either not pleased about being awake or she is not pleased about being awake to greet yet another country naïf.

"Can I please have a coffee, please? Black please?" My voice is too bubbly, even to me, for this hour. She must be the first to serve so many of us, just off the plane from tawny wheat fields splayed for days, where great-great-grandmother's bones are buried under a poplar, where people dress just one way or the other.

Ponytail swinging, the waitress carries over the coffee, sets it on the table without a word. It tastes like a cleaning product.

As I lean back in my plastic chair, the sun warms my skin. I already have sweat stains at my armpits and my hair is nearly dry. With all the unknowns ahead, I barely slept, but when I woke I did manage to have something like a shower despite some confusion in the bathroom: two identical, handheld, white rubber rods dispensing water, one close to the toilet, one farther away. No one told me about those.

The hour is just a little after seven o'clock, and almost no one else is up. When I left the guesthouse, there was a cluster of backpackers zigging and zagging down the road behind a long-haired Thai man collecting people to get on a bus, probably heading south to the islands. They thumbed backpack straps digging into their bare shoulders, hunched forward and waddled, heads down, like caravan slaves in the desert. Now, a hefty Thai woman with wet hair and boxer shorts barks at a little boy and girl, twins maybe, as they skip down the street in their school uniform, a white shirt and blue bottoms with black shoes. Two guys, still drunk from last night, sit down beside me.

"Just cheat on her." The voice is Australian, and it belongs to a short young man with bloodshot eyes.

His friend is Thai, I think, and not as drunk. "I don't want to."

"I cheat on Pui. She's naughty too." He knocks the drink menu stand on the table. The server asks what he wants. "*Bee-a Singh, khot nung, yai, sai nam kheng.*" Singha beer, one big bottle, with ice.

He can speak Thai. This doesn't faze the ladyboy. She glares at him too. Insects in her face, we are. Just days ago, it was me, dealing menus, cursing the universe and drunken men.

"Yes, but I like my girlfriend. She is a proper Thai girl." His chubby fingers light a cigarette.

"You just can't do any better." The Aussie turns to me. "What do you think? If he decides to marry his girlfriend, shouldn't he cheat on her first?"

Cheat. The slush on the windshield of the cab, our knees on the soft velour seats, Scott's arm reaching out for the change. The clink of buckles. A pause. A nod. The cold door handle at home, at dawn, still dark. Lies. *Everything's fine.* I look up, solemnly. "I don't know."

Two cats circle my table. One is black with green eyes; it has a patch of fur missing from its left hip. The other is white with a brown spine and yellow eyes, one of which is half-closed and oozing pus. Its belly is round and saggy, too saggy and thick for such a skinny cat. A tail sweeps my ankle, and I shiver.

"More feral cats in this city than rice, I swear." The Australian, short and possibly handsome and certainly cocky, says this to me.

"Feral?"

"You know, wild cats, alley cats."

"Oh, feral. We say *fee*-ral."

The waitress knocks the cats on the bum with a broom. What is it that's making her so cranky? Is it the hour, or something else? What was she like when she was five? If it's so awful, why does she stay, or is it naive and privileged of me, to think we can all just walk away?

A phone vibrates, is picked up, is tossed back down. A joke, and then laughter.

The Aussie studies me. "Where ya from?"

Medicine Hat, my hometown in Alberta, the address of secrets and cheats, big trucks and the world's tallest teepee. It would sound like Saturn. Calgary, the first city I fled to, was just a short stop in between. "Home," a funny word.

"Canada."

I plunk my Lonely Planet guidebook on the table and open a page in the Bangkok section under the heading "Tailors." It says something like "Common scams usually involve those wily *tuk-tuk* drivers who deliver customers to shops that pay commissions..."

"Just arrived?"

"Yeah." I root through my purse for my cigarettes. His question, it dawns on me: No one knows me. *No one knows me here.*

"How long you staying?"

"A year." I exhale into the sky. "Not sure."

I've signed a one-year contract with a *rajabhat* university, a kind of polytechnic school. After that... I don't know.

"Well, I've been here three years and this is my mate, Top. He's always lived here, but he went to international school because he's a rich little mama's boy, aren't you, Top? That's why his English is so good. Our girlfriends are friends and we're on a bit of a bender, aren't we, Top?"

Top says he wants to go home. His mom calls. The Aussie asks if Top's mom likes him. Top says no. His mom thinks the Aussie is a bad influence. I walk inside the restaurant and find the waitress powdering her face at the till. I pay my bill and leave.

I walk down the road to another patio, order another coffee. The server smiles as she sets it down. I smile back.

I take in the rousing street. Shop workers sweep their floors. A barefoot, mustached man bends over along the gutter to pick up cans and bottles. Store gates rattle up, revealing leopard-inspired luggage and floral-print bikinis. Men arrange tables of "Asian art"—hand-carved wooden flutes, black dragons, red kimonos for babies (apparently anything Asian will do). An Indian man drags a sign that says Tailor, Suits in 25 Hours. On the sidewalk, metal shelves rise, become stacked with CDs, t-shirts, sandals and silver jewelry.

I spread across the table my map of Bangkok by Nancy Chandler. She's an American artist living in Bangkok whose rendering of the city looks like a ten-year-old's treasure map: handwritten names in all caps, places marked by their actual shapes and watercolor-like purples, blues and yellows.

Choking down another sip of coffee, I light my fourth cigarette of the day and take an inventory of myself. I know where I am, on one road in the middle of a massive city. I'm wide awake but my eyeballs, so very sore. I went twenty-four hours without sleep before crashing in a moldy dive and woke to the same startling truth I'm pondering now: I felt tugged to the other side of the world, and I want to know why.

NO WIND

TWO DAYS PASS in Bangkok and I barely leave the backpackers' ghetto. This area, I'll learn, couldn't be less representative of the real Thailand. On Khao San Road, everything is for sale.

Little boys peddle plastic flowers and pencils. Twentysomethings wave them over like they would a nephew. The boy rushes up to their tables, sets out his pencils. The pencils roll between beer glasses. The boy rests his elbows beside the tourists' hands, dimples and dirty chins perched on wrists. The tourists play around with the boy for a while, ask him how much, to count to five, to spell his name, to say the tourists' names. They think the little boy likes them, that they're friends. The little boy stuffs the bills into his school uniform shorts and skips off to the next bar, to a foursome of skirts.

Hill tribe women, grandmothers from the North who move to Khao San to work, drag their feet down the road and as far into the bars as the owners will allow before yelling "*Bai*!" Go. The women wear the colorful stitching of their people from head to toe, and babies across their backs. Their arms and hands and shoulders are lined with their wares: beaded necklaces, metal bracelets, wooden frogs that croak with the stroke of a stick.

Middle-aged women, mothers and heavier women flip street meat cooked in woks on wheels. Shrimp balls. Spicy sausage. Pork kebobs. Their pigtailed daughters sit on plastic stools, eating the night away with fingers stained by the juices of chickens and pigs.

A toothless old woman in white sits, legs snaked on the sidewalk, rocking, gums bleeding onto her chin. Or so you think. The red is really just the juices of the areca nut. Her brittled fingers are cupped, pleading.

I'll never forget her face, will I?

Barefoot men, whose hands are as dark as their eyes from the dirt, hunt for drops of beer and bits of rice on square Styrofoam plates. They smell as if they sleep in blankets of rotting plantains and dregs of beer.

You can't see anything beyond Khao San Road by looking up. The buildings are six stories tall, covered in signs and the laundry lines of people who live here. *People live here.*

The road is no longer a road but a market, umbrella- and tarp-covered booths selling CDs, fake teaching certificates, spring rolls, the telling of fortunes, fisherman pants, turquoise stones, silver jewelry, Singha beer t-shirts, the braiding and dreadlocking of hair, beds you can be escorted to by massage girls, *tuk-tuk* drivers trying to get you to go somewhere, anywhere, with them, right now.

At each step, the pungent odors of old urine, vomit, stale beer and sweat rise from gutters and lanes. In the tiny alleys almost hidden from the main road, such as Trok Mayom, where I found New Joe's, newcomers keep their noses plugged.

At every corner the same song, "Zombie" by The Cranberries. Eleven years old, this song, and it's played like it just came out.

AT DUSK, KHAO San is thick with the kind of makeup that's ugly and cheap, tough to breathe through.

Men lift the green rain tarps. Bars on wheels offer "buckets" sloshing with Coke, Red Bull and SangSom (a revered Thai rum distilled from molasses, forty per cent alcohol). Around the buckets, friends shout as they count to three and slurp from straws, grinning at each other and the disappearing liquid. The girls who pour, trying to sell more. "Spec-ee-al cocktail for you. We no ID." They nod as if to say, *It's true!*

Buckets may be the reason there is always at least one guy, shoeless and drooling, passed out on the concrete the next morning.

Thai girls in skintight beer-logo dresses stand outside the doors of clubs where men and women, but mostly men, find the Thailand they were looking for. Inside, the girls throw back their long, long black hair. Shove their little-boy-like asses against hands and legs and crotches. Stop, pleased, when they're finally offered a drink. You can see the same men— white-haired men, chubby men, barely men men, ugly men, father and son men, and married men—holding hands with the same "girlfriends" all week.

Ladyboys parade themselves: penises and pink miniskirts, headbands and mustaches, high heels and leg hair. They're looking for love, or a living too. The neon signs glint on blond dreadlocks, sweat-soaked tank tops and Crocs. The backpackers, guitars in tow, try not to gawk at the fried crickets.

Near the end of the road, a man hollers, "Ping-pong show for you?" He wants to take you to a place where strippers perform tricks and he takes a cut of your cover charge. Of course, during the day, he wants to take you to a tailor. "Nice suit for you? Cheap, cheap."

A shoeless little girl whose eyes look too big for her head pokes a plastic windmill against your arm. She wants you to buy it, but the spokes won't spin. There is no wind.

A SONG CALLED "NATALIE"

O N AN OVERNIGHT train to the south, through my bunk's tiny window I take in the rusted tin tents, children chasing wild dogs, the setting sun. In the morning, a sea of mangroves. Later, a blond German girl who talks a lot, an awful lot for someone who speaks English as a second language, waits with me, for the bus to Krabi province, along the Andaman coast. I have a little less than four weeks left until I start work, and so, before meeting Sompan or anyone from the university, I've headed to the South. Soon the German girl and I are splitting the cost of a long-tail boat to an island called Hat Rai Lei, surrounded by limestone cliffs patched with alabaster rock and green fur. The cliffs, sitting at the beach's edge like the dimple of a smile. Now I know awe.

Later, alone on the beach with a bottle of beer, I hug my knees, grasping sand with curled toes. Rocking. Staring, at a cliff quite close to the stars. The cliff face, lit by the moon, a projector for Canada: my mom quivering as I folded down her arms and stepped toward Security without a word; the street I grew up on in Medicine Hat, with the crab apple trees I climbed

and the yellow coulee beyond our back fence where I wandered as a girl. The cliff. Feeling warm all over. Knowing I'm
where I'm supposed to be. Right here, just like this. Harmony,
in waves through my body like the fleeting moments after an
orgasm. Weepy, even, shaken.

I'm going to find myself, whatever that means.

But where I find myself about twenty-eight hours later is
on the sand with a man from Ireland who has been teaching
in China.

"Their skin is so soft," he says, of the girls in Asia, as if that
were the only reason he needed. He tells me, before or after, I
can't remember which, that he wants to marry a girl like me
someday. Before or after, I can't remember which, we are at The
Last Bar with the German girl and I spot a familiar silhouette.

Big breasts, big brown eyes, big, beautiful smile. Tammy.
Barley Mill Tammy. My legs, as if in a lake, or a dream.

"Tammy? What the heck are you doing here?"

She turns and, with doe eyes, says, "Natalie? Oh my God."

What are the chances?

She is at this bar, holding a tin for ice. Behind her, at a sit-
on-the-floor table, is Lee. With his big teeth and ball cap. *Rat.*
Sees me too, I know it. But I stay here and he stays there. To
speak would mean we'd both have to admit things started
with Tammy when he was still with Zora, and all that drama, it
would be just too heavy for this island, thick with humidity and
traveler's delirium, even at midnight. Lee goes on talking, tall-
tale-telling, probably. And that's fine and I'm not tattle-tale-ing
to Zora. They've been broken up for a while now, and sometimes you just don't need to know the truth.

THE NEXT MORNING I leave with the German girl for Koh
Phi Phi, an island shaped like a pair of lungs. Hours after dusk,

an Israeli man who has just finished his army service seduces me with a song called "Natalie." Made up, probably, but well delivered, at least.

"I will sing for you."

"OK."

My brown tube top dress makes being outdoors—aside a path that leads to all other bungalows, where we met minutes earlier—easy. Our only instruments are the moonlight and a single green plastic chair. Each time I rise from his waist, I see the rounded roof of the island mosque. Most Koh Phi Phi residents are Muslims, descendants of fisherman who are proud of the mosque they built, once surrounded only by coconut groves. They have always cherished their place of worship, but since the tsunami their souls feel an incredible tug to prayer, even the first five a.m. call. Blaring on loudspeakers, the muffled, ancient song drowns the Israeli's groans.

My sex, the sex for sale in the tourist districts—they're not so different, are they?

HELLO
HELLO

LITTLE GREEN BUSES without doors, teetering around corners in the rain. A family of four, including a swaddled, sleeping baby, scooting past us on a motorbike. Police officers in rain ponchos blasting traffic whistles.

I'm in the sedan of Sompan, one of Gil's old students. We're at a red light on the way to meet my new colleagues, including *Ajarn* Nand, a professor who once taught with Gil. My bottom lip has been wedged between my teeth all morning: I have no idea how to teach. None of this, the teaching here and the living here, seemed real until today. But where I had to sprint wearing blinkers like a racehorse to get here, now the list-maker and the looker-upper-of-things in me needs to plan for my classes, all six of them, all without textbooks, just course names and some an outline. I have no business teaching Business English.

The light turns green and we pass a block crammed with photos of a middle-aged man who never smiles.

"Sompan, who is that?"

"Yes. This is our king," he says. His English is formal, soft against the thunder and a dark, rainy season sky.

Vendors sit on stools beside portraits of their monarch's face: life-size canvases of the king with his wife; ones of him in white regalia; one in safari clothes kneeling on dirt with a camera around his neck; one as an old man in a golden robe, waving a stiff hand from a white balcony, leaning down so close to a decrepit peasant woman that his nose nearly touches her sparse, spiky white hair and her crooked fingers.

"Thai people, we love him very much. Like a father."

Sompan grins and nods at me in the rearview mirror. He spotted me under a forest of signs on Khao San Road. There was some confusion about how he'd find me because I was now staying at one of three Sawasdee guesthouses on the block. When I spotted him, raindrops dotting his pressed jeans and black loafers, it was easy to tell he didn't belong around here: his skin was unmarked by wrongdoings or the sun, and as we walked past a massage parlor whose women called out to him, he confirmed Khao San was unfamiliar: "Most Thai people do not go here." Before that, though, we exchanged greetings and then he pointed at the sign for my guesthouse. "In Thai language, *Sawasdee* means 'hello.'"

Sa-wat-dee. That's how he said it, with a "t" instead of an "s" in the middle. In 1939, in the face of world war and in a bid to unite the country—all of its regions and all of its races, from the Siamese to the Chinese—the government changed the country's name from Siam to Thailand, made the alphabet simpler, created pronouns that no longer distinguished gender and status, and issued a decree asking people in all provinces to use the same greeting: *sawasdee.*

The word drifts from my mind to my tongue, echoes it, silently, the way Sompan said it. *Sa-wat-dee. Sa-wat-dee.*

Outside, the drizzle turns to sleet.

We pass a pair of elderly, chubby monks crossing the road and a street corner where three old men sit on low stools under a shop awning smoking and moving black pieces. Chess, I think. For a moment, their faces are blocked by the black diesel smoke of a *tuk-tuk,* those three-wheeled taxis Zora told me about. A teenage boy with cracked heels and boxer shorts carries three boards of lumber over his shoulder.

Soon we're standing in front of *Ajarn* Nand in the lobby of a hotel located on the university campus. Until I find an apartment, I'm going to be living a few hundred feet from the building where I will be working for the next year. During that time, I will also be called *ajarn*, the title used for high school and university teachers. *Ajarn* Nand's real name is Narunand, but, like all Thais, he goes by a nickname.

"*Sawasdee krub,*" says Sompan, bending his head to *wai* to *Ajarn* Nand. Hello.

"*Sawasdee krub.*" *Ajarn* Nand returns the *wai*, palms briefly raised to the face, no bending. The *wai* is the Thai bow. Every time they greet someone or receive something, they press their hands together at their chest, fingers almost touching their nose, and bend just their head. Thais bend their heads lower depending on the age and status difference. Being older and having once taught Sompan, *Ajarn* Nand is senior. He's a little man with dark skin, syrupy eyes and thick lips.

Shit, I forgot to wai Sompan. If I wai Ajarn Nand, will Sompan be offended I didn't wai him? Shit. I should have read the etiquette section of my guidebook a little closer. I'll just smile. I'm good at smiling.

"Hello, Nat-a-lieee."

"Hello. It's nice to meet you."

Ajarn Nand speaks with Sompan in Thai. My eyes wander the walls of the lobby, quiet except for the heels of a woman behind the front desk. If it weren't for the Thai staff, as erect and polished as palace soldiers, I could be anywhere. The hotel exists in part to give students studying hospitality a chance to have some firsthand experience with impolite foreigners who forget they're in Asia and want everything, language and meals, to be just like it is back home.

Sompan departs, waving as he walks out the door. *Ajarn* Nand looks me over.

"Good, good. You look like a teacher, uh-huh. That's good."

I smile.

On the way to the Business English office, he tells me about the old days with Gil, how Gil said I was such a good student and would be a good teacher, how they always need teachers but they usually only get men. *Ajarn* Nand asks about my trip to the South. He tells me that's where he's from, Surat Thani; he and Gil, which he pronounces *Geel*, taught in Nakhon Sawan. A few years ago, Gil emailed to friends and family a story he wrote about his time there. On a day trip to a nearby village with three students, two drowned in a river. One boy's parents wanted Gil dead; the other boy's mom saw the pain in Gil's eyes and took his pale, clammy hands in hers, tanned and warm. "Do not worry," she said. "Sometimes people die and there's nothing we can do. It is *duang*." Destiny.

WHEN *AJARN* NAND talks, I'm drawn to his teeth, fat and white. His speech is croaky and laced with "uh-huh." As we meander around the detached campus buildings, all outdoors, students and staff stop to *wai* him. With each one, he smiles and returns the *wai*. *Ajarn* Nand jokes with his colleagues until they laugh.

In the university courtyard, my mind shrinks his voice to take in all of this. The heat, the plants, the perfume of a greenhouse. Geckos scaling picnic tables. Girls in black miniskirts with long, shiny hair. Tinier, I think, than when I was a child. The teachers, mostly older women with short hair, thick glasses, suits of stiff Thai silk, they walk with calculation, like queens. A parking guard's whistle rings and stops, and rings and stops as a blue minivan decorated with the university emblem wiggles down a road between buildings. Most buildings resemble houses, houses with intricately carved rooftop casings, wooden shutters painted yellow and tall teak doors. On the ground level, the door is open to a crowded classroom where students are rehearsing a classical Thai song on the carpet.

Ajarn Nand notices me watching a girl playing an instrument with a long, narrow body and an oval head. Something white, the tooth of an animal, maybe, plucking the strings by a finger.

"We call it *jahke*. Like a crocodile, because of its shape," *Ajarn* Nand says. "The strings are made of silk."

Without looking down from her teacher's gaze and while sitting on her side, in a skirt, with a cloth covering her knees, she plucks. The *jahke*'s hum is hushed by a violin as skinny as its bow and a bamboo xylophone, sloping in like a prairie valley. The song sounds like morning, like wanting.

"Thai love song." *Ajarn* Nand backs away from the classroom. "Very beautiful, uh-huh."

Not now, but still, with the persistence of ghosts and crows, I will look for it, love. My ten.

Ajarn Nand leads me to a three-story stucco building where the hallways are filled with upside-down umbrellas. It's rainy season and it's bad manners—or is it bad luck?—to bring a wet umbrella into the classroom. Three girls slide across the floor, each with a cell phone to her ear. At five feet six inches and 130 pounds, I am a giant amongst a sea of dolls chattering away in a language I can't understand.

My throat clamps on two thoughts: *I have to teach here*, and *I have to live here*.

Walking through the corridors, students gawk and giggle when they see me. My heart pounds at the mere thought of being locked in a room with them for more than an hour. I imagine myself on the first day of classes, standing behind a lectern. My tongue stumbling. My cheeks, pink and hot.

WHEN *AJARN* NAND swings open the door to the Business English office, it's as if the lid has been lifted on a chicken coop. Women jump, flap their arms, scurry.

"*Ajarn* Nand!"

He saunters to a wall with his hands in his pockets, bashful at their enthusiasm. He used to teach in this department, but now he does translation work somewhere else on campus.

The women flock to the front of the room, *wai Ajarn* Nand and then stand together, nine sets of brown eyes blinking at me.

Ajarn Nand gives me a big grin. "Nat-a-lieeee, I would like to introduce you to the BE teachers. This is *Ajarn* Som, *Ajarn* Mee, *Ajarn* Soon, *Ajarn* Nok, *Ajarn* Sinn, *Ajarn* Aw, *Ajarn* Tida, *Ajarn* Fah.

"Everyone, I would like you to meet Nat-a-lieeee."

They whisper and smile and some come forward to shake my hand. They ask how I am and what I think of Thailand.

"It's very... warm. And the people are *so* nice."

Why am I so very awkward?

The women cluck and coo and usher me to a couch. Song, the secretary, brings me a coffee, acidic but warm, at least. I choke down the first sip and fake a smile. The second time I raise my cup to my face, the handle slips from my fingers.

Coffee splatters across my shirt, a sheer lavender blouse now soaked and sticking to my skin. My face stings even though it's dry. The teachers pat me and the floor and the table and the couch with paper towels.

Then AJ, the American I am replacing, walks in with three students trailing him. My shirt looks like a rotting grape. Coffee steams on my neck and I have to stand, introduce myself and shake hands with him.

"Hi. I'm Natalie." It's freezing in here, the hairs on my arms are standing up and my erect nipples have moused their way to the tip of my shirt. "Nice to meet you."

He surveys me, shivering and stained. "So, how are you making out so far?"

"Couldn't be better, really, as you can see." I smile, and as my eyes leave AJ's face, I notice the teachers' faces, still with shock, tight with politeness. Staring at me, as if I were standing there topless.

SHE'S BEEN AROUND THE BLOCK

I MENTION NEITHER THE coffee spill nor the Israeli man in my first email home, though I do include the blond German girl in my brief account of what I've been up to for the last month. I don't know what keeps me from telling more. Maybe home is crawling off, like a turtle.

For the first few days at the hotel in Bangkok, I barely leave my room. I don't know where I am, where to go, how to get there, what to say. I'm alone. Alone in a land that could not be more different than where I came from. Growing up, our only trips were to the Cypress Hills to tent between lodgepole pines, and to Havre, Montana, where my brothers and I bought odd chocolate bars and gawked at the photos of bare-breasted women glued to the walls of The Eight Ball, a bar that's part of the mall. That, until now, was what I knew of culture shock.

I'm also a klutz. And bad-lucked. And I've seen *Broke-down Palace* and *The Beach*. I'm afraid if I leave Bangkok again, between now and when I start work next week, something will happen on my way back. So I have penned myself in the Dusit district.

In my little world is the campus 7-Eleven, its packaged raisin rolls and instant spicy soup, the 100 *baht* ($2) I spend on food each day. The outdoor hotel pool, where I take off my towel as close to the edge as I can. The male swimming-lesson teacher, rather tall. The little boys and girls in wetsuits, the mothers sitting on plastic loungers in pants and button-up blouses, a barefoot pool boy, staring.

The teacher, happy to have a chance to use his English, yells across the pool, "Can I help you?"

"I just want to swim?"

He waves me in as if to say, *That's fine, go ahead.* In their eyes, even though back home my bathing suit would be a modest, Hawaiian-inspired two-piece, I might as well be naked. I've noticed it already, that there are two Thailands: The tourist districts where everyone wears sandals and tank tops, where bar girls on swivel seats bark out to the street, to suitors, "Love you long time." And the rest of the country, where women wear shirts that reach their wrists and collarbones, buckled loafers that shelter toes, and skirts that sweep past knees. Where women run schools and offices and restaurants and multigenerational households and say quite little. Those women, I later learn, would never go in the water. Not like this. I last four minutes.

Instead of swimming or exploring, I nap. I read this golden brochure from the National Gallery of Bangkok, and give myself over to Thailand's art and its ways and its storied past. I lose myself in the ceiling, knocking my knees. Maybe instead of being brave and fast, maybe *I* am only crawling away from home, like a turtle.

One block. Go one block.

How is it we can lunge over a hump nearly the length of earth itself, and then stagger on a strip of sidewalk? Shouldn't we be fearless after crossing oceans and continents and cultures? Maybe it's the streets—the higher probability of stumbling, even on a small scale, often—that daunt us, halt us. And I guess it never is a lunge so much as series of moments in the air, off solid ground.

One block.

My mind recalls a book, *Who Moved My Cheese?* My mom gave it to me to read when I was having doubts, about leaving. Two days after my car stalled on the way home from looking at places in Calgary, she left *Who Moved My Cheese?* in my mailbox. It's a fable written by a doctor to help people handle change. Two of the book's main characters, Hem and Haw, are running out of cheese. Haw thinks they should enter the maze and look for new cheese. They can always come back if they're wrong. Hem's too scared to leave the old pile. Haw decides to go alone, and in his search, he finds dead ends but also enough crumbs to keep him going. For his patience and persistence, Haw is rewarded with a mound of cheese the size of a city. At points when he feels lost, like giving up, Haw asks himself, "What would I do if I weren't afraid?"

Natalie, the mouse did it. The mouse.

One block.

A red gate nine feet tall surrounds the hotel and the university. Layers of rectangles are etched in it, no spot or corner faded. The sun is bright on this side of the road. The back of my neck sweats. On Thanon Ratchawithi, the quiet fades. This is the main entrance to the university. Beside the gate, a girl stands behind a wheeled glass cooler of watermelon, pineapple and guava. She hacks at the pineapple, then slides its pieces in a plastic bag with a wooden stick. Beside her is a fried rice lady, a stationery lady, a school uniforms lady, an earrings man with a mat on the sidewalk, and a woman selling cell phone sacks adorned with buttoned eyes. The sidewalk, a sea of black and white: black skirts, white shirts, black pants, white socks, black hair, white teeth, black phones. There is no side for coming or for going. Everyone is in a lump together, squirming like worms in a jar. Halfway down the road, the sidewalk is almost bare. A man on a stool hammers the heel of a man's leather shoe. A seamstress sleeps, head down next to her antique machine. As I pass, her eyes open. She swats a fly with her hands and returns to her slumber. At the end of the gate, a psychic traces the lines on a girl's palm. The girl nods in wonder, ears perked, I guess, for notes of love. So universal, the language of love. Still following the gate, I'm now on Thanon Samsen. A shirtless, chubby hobo with curly gray hair sits cross-legged on the ground. I try not to look too long at the tattoos of Thai letters between his nipples. He studies the sky and smiles. A lady in green with a wide-brimmed bamboo hat sweeps leaves.

The hobo, the seamstress, the sweeper, the guards—they are my neighbors now. Already, I wonder if they will come to know me, and nod at me in the afternoon as I pass by. Already, I want to be *with* them.

Ahead, I catch sight of little boys in blue shorts and white shirts racing ahead of their mothers to open the heavy doors of McDonald's, and inhale the whiff of salty French fries. Back home I was the sort of tree hugger/reformed vegetarian who occasionally ate Big Macs in Wal-Mart. To smell and see this one sign of home, even one I am supposed to oppose, is like running into a childhood classmate.

At the third corner of the fence is a small public garden with curved concrete benches and four trees. To the left, a basin of water emits the odor of sewage. An older man with a chipped tooth holds a fishing rod over the rail. Two boys squat not far from the man's feet and draw with sticks. The man lifts the rod and a fish the size of a cell phone appears, flicking water at their faces. The boys squeal and jump. The man drops the fish into a plastic bag and dashes across the street, one boy at each knee, grinning with the rod over his shoulder. I picture them later, chewing the little fish like chicken wings. The boys' eyes sparkling. The family, whole, in love.

The rest of the day I smile at anyone who will look my way. I forget, for a little while, that I have to teach my first class in eleven days, that I don't have a backup plan if I get fired.

SHOOTING
AN ARROW

T HE SMOKE OF roasting squid, the tinny jangle of "Hotel California," the swarm of teachers shuffling me onto the planks of a restaurant along the Mae Nam Chao Phraya.

It's my first real Thai meal with real Thai people. The teachers are taking us out to welcome me and thank AJ.

While two servers in aprons and flip flops assemble a table for thirteen, the teachers jabber and joke. *Thai words. Thai words. Thai words.* I bite my cheeks. I'm nervous about all of this, the faking I will have to do with the food, the talk of teaching. I've been assured my students will have already had years of English instruction, though only some, if any, from a native English speaker. There's a good chance they'll understand a fraction of what I say. I just have no idea what to say.

Behind us, the sun sets, paints the sky pink. The river below, for its fishy smell and choppy tide, looks much more like an ocean. If there is a bank, it's hidden by sun-dried wooden houses and restaurants like this one, perched over the water's edge on mossy stilts.

AJ leans toward my ear and covers his mouth with a hand.

"You shouldn't wear those pants."

"What?" I think he's joking, but he doesn't smile when his breath falls away from my ear. "My pants? Why?"

I thought I looked nice. I'm wearing a buttoned-up yellow cardigan and white, wide-leg pants with high heels. I got the pants for a wedding two summers ago when all the dresses in the stores were fuchsia, which clashes with my red hair. A gay salesman, the first I had met in Medicine Hat, found me almost in tears in the change room. When he returned with an asymmetrical brown-and-teal top, and this pair of white pants, I wanted to hug him.

"Well, you can see right through them."

I twist my neck to see my backside, a view I hadn't taken into consideration earlier. They're not quite as solid as I'd like, but they're not transparent. It's not like they can see cellulite.

"They'd never say anything, but I know they're talking about it." His voice is loud, lecturing, and there's a chance he's trying to help, but he's only making me feel worse. Maybe he feels like he's been here long enough that it offends him too. And maybe I'm still discovering how formally "proper" Thai women dress.

AJ's head rises when a man I haven't met makes his way to our table.

"Hey, Ek. How's it going?"

Ek, a tall man with a large head and spots around his nose, nods and glances at him. He answers facing away from AJ. "Fine, thank you. And you?"

"Good, good. Yep, still have about fifty essays to mark, but I'm almost on my way out."

"OK. OK, everyone." Song, the secretary who speaks near-perfect English, is appointed to make announcements. She stands at the top of the table, now extended the full length of the restaurant deck and dressed with plastic pastel plates. "Please sit."

I hang back, waiting for seating instructions and contemplating a way to transport myself to the table so that only the river sees my hind end until I'm in a chair or it gets dark. I don't know if the pants complaint is valid, but I don't think AJ would've brought it up otherwise. Plus, the incident with my coffee-spilt, sheer shirt is still a bit fresh in our minds, and the Thai teachers might now be wondering if I'm actually a Russian hooker (common in Thailand, particularly in the nearby city of Pattaya) and how they're going to get rid of me.

I end up at the bottom of the table across from AJ and *Pii* Som. *Pii* Fah is beside me. *Pii* is the honorific title for someone older than you. Tonight's seating choices reveal an unspoken system. The teachers with the best English have to sit closest to the foreigners. The others dread speaking with us, even though they have master's degrees in English and teach the subject at a university every day. This only seems backward to me until I introduce my tongue to the unfamiliar, lyrical sounds of the Thai language.

"Do you like Thai food?" *Pii* Fah asks. She is wearing a blue, fitted Thai dress and dangly balls of earrings. Her hair is long, tied half-back; bangs are backcombed. *Pii* Fah is always winking and smiling. I wonder if her cheeks tire, or if a lifetime of kindness has primed the muscles of her mouth.

"Yes, but I haven't tried very much yet." I speak slowly, as if I were talking to my uncle Greg. When he was nine, he got meningitis. He lost his hearing and learned to read lips. Went on to father a redheaded girl born just eleven hours ahead of me.

"Can you eat spicy food?"

"A little." This is a lie. The spiciest thing I have eaten to date is hot salsa, by accident, and it was promptly coughed right back out, of my nose.

"Good. I hope the food is not too spicy for you."

I glance at the river underfoot and envision myself secretly tipping curry bowls into its choppy waters.

The Thai teachers are flipping through the menu, deciding what to order. I glance at its lines, its letters, winding like rivers and forming never-ending words. Sometime between 1277 and 1318, King Ramkamhaeng invented this alphabet. He needed letters that would express the joys, hopes and history of his people, the Tai. Believed to have once lived south of China's Yangzi river and migrated, in groups, down the Golden Peninsula, the Tai came together for a cause: their own country. After a battle with the Khmer in 1257, the Tais captured their first capital. It was a resplendent, religious land on which they felt a sense of belonging. It was called Sukothai, Dawn of Happiness. And its alphabet would dance.

My chest throbs at the sight of it, these letters, these sentences without spaces.

Pii Fah detects my twitchy eyes. "Oh, you don't have to order. We will eat all together and share."

"Yes, Thai-style," says *Pii* Som. "Everyone eats together."

She is little too, with waist-length hair and oval glasses perched on a Chinese nose. Most of the teachers and many Thai families are actually Chinese, descendants of the traders who profited from Bangkok's days as a port village.

This city was once entirely under the Gulf of Siam. Over centuries of monsoon seasons, the river carried dirt from farmland to the sea. Mud banks rose above the waterline, mangroves took root and the lungfish moved in. Each year the river left more soil and silt. Farmers planted rice on the delta; stilt houses sprang up. King Rama I chose the east bank of the Chao Phraya because he could erect a palace surrounded by water that the Burmese could never invade. On April 21, 1782, he laid the city pillar, a ceremonial act following the birth of a new Siamese city. The pillar was made of *chaiyapruk*, the tree of victory. It stood alone without images of gods. There was no shrine or pavilion for it, just a roof to protect it from the rain and the sun.

Back then, if asked where they lived, most Siamese would have said, "Mae Nam Chao Phraya." When an American doctor wrote home of Bangkok in 1835, he said, "Half the population is afloat." He told about a little girl, Luck-loi-nam, child of the waters. The girl was advertised as Bangkok's amphibious infant. She wanted not her mother's breast milk but the river's water, and at age one couldn't walk or talk but, at her sister's side, treaded water, gurgled like the sea itself.

Somehow I taste the sea, feel hypnotized by the water, knocking against the boards below my feet. I try not to look like I might be sick. But it's hard, especially as the food arrives.

A sea bass wrapped in a banana leaf with its head and tail still attached is placed in front of me. Our eyes meet. The scent of garlic, lime and chilies rises from his pierced gut. Beside him is a large, tiered metal bowl containing a steaming red soup and several bobbing shrimp. The anatomy of shrimp—a food I'd only ever eaten at Christmas on a thawed, plastic tray—had eluded me until now. These creatures have black eyeballs, a jagged horn, long and short spiky legs, a thready antenna longer than the body, and a humped back of shells overlapping like petals.

My eyes, I suspect, so very wide.

More food follows: White rice. *Som tum*, a spicy salad of papaya slivers soaked in garlic and chopped chilies. A noodle-and-straw-mushroom dish dressed in oyster sauce. A bowl of mussels. A plate of glass noodles topped with pork and draped in bean sprouts, sugar, chili and fish sauce.

Pii Fah explains what everything is called, in Thai and in English, what's in it, how spicy it is, and plunks spoonfuls on my plate. I feel like a toddler at the adults' table. At the other end, the teachers eat and laugh. They don't notice me, shrinking and dreading. I can't stomach seafood. I'm a Prairie girl who won't eat steak (though I've happily eaten fast food burgers and often bought top sirloin for Stuart). A Prairie girl whose great-grandmother, upon selling the family farm, went to work in town slaughtering and skinning chickens at the Chinese restaurant. And yet I say yes to the shrimp soup, yes to the headed fish. When my plate is full, I wait and watch. Sip my water. Sip again. And again. As long as my hands and mouth are busy, maybe they won't notice?

As I observe, dishes are kept separate, even from the rice, which is spooned toward everything else, including the soup. The fork is not used as fork but as knife, edging food onto the spoon, pulling apart meat and noodles. The fork, I am told, is the assistant. The spoon is the boss. Only the spoon enters the teachers' mouths. Putting a fork in your mouth, to a Thai, is the Western equivalent of putting a knife in your mouth.

The country's first fork, a two-pronged utensil introduced at the court of Rama V after his trip to Singapore in 1870, had a nickname for the way it was used: *plaeng sorn*, shooting an arrow.

The utensils are made of such thin metal that in my mouth I'm sure I could bend one with my tongue, and I try. It's funny now, but I was enrolled in a modeling and etiquette class when I was eight. I remember the fancy table setting but knew, even then, I'd never need that lesson. These people won't have to fire me. I'll just starve to death because I can't orchestrate all of this, holding my fork sideways as a scoop. AJ is an expert.

"How long have you been eating like that?" I whisper.

He swallows a mouthful of rice and wipes his lips. "With the spoon?"

I nod.

"Awhile, I guess."

"So you know about the fork and you're sticking with the spoon?" I feel like I've heard this line on *Seinfeld*. I have, only Jerry's bit was about chopsticks. And it might have been on a stand-up episode on one of the four DVDs I brought from Canada. I've probably watched it nine times on my laptop already.

"Yeah."

"Do you think you're going to eat like that when you go back to the States?"

"Yeah." He looks at me like I'm stupid.

AJ actually has a degree in education (a bachelor's degree in any subject is all that's required of native English teachers; most come with additional certificates in teaching ESL). He lasted two semesters, an academic year, which is about the standard. The program is given a budget to have one native English speaker on staff every year, and most go back home as soon as their contract is up. They miss home, or they want to miss Bangkok.

"Really?"

He flicks back his brown hair, thick and long after a receding hairline. "It's much more couth."

I wonder if there will come a time when eating fish heads with a spoon will be natural, when I will think of this as normal.

And I missed the section about how in Thai culture, an empty plate is a sign of hunger, that your hosts will continue filling it until scraps of noodles dangle, soggy and cold.

Every time I take a bite, *Pii* Fah piles more food onto my plate. Despite an abandoned prawn that can't take his eyes off me, the *tom yum gung* (spicy shrimp soup) is my favorite. Instead of attempting to dissect it, which I imagine will end with a constellation of fire-orange soup flecks across my upper torso, and perhaps that of *Pii* Fah's, I leave the prawn to dance in the soup. I hold the liquid near my nose, let the lemongrass and chilies linger. The problem is putting it in my mouth. I almost choke on each sip because it's so spicy my throat tries to cough it up. My insides react the same way to the *som tum*. I love this salad, but its juices sear my gums and every membrane it passes in my body. I gulp water and clench ice cubes against my gums, but nothing helps. My tongue burns and my lips swell and my eyes tear.

"Natalie." *Pii* Fah tilts her head and touches my shoulder. "Are you OK?"

"Umm hmm." This meal, it feels longer than that time I got stuck dancing to a twelve-minute-long Meatloaf song with Cory Dumphrey in ninth grade. I can still feel his chin brushing my breasts, the hot breath of his chipmunk cheeks blowing on my neck.

Pii Fah grimaces. "Dessert will make it better. We will have mangoes and sticky rice. I think you will like it."

While I wait, digging fingernails into my palms, I watch *Pii* Sinn, the oldest teacher, wielding a toothpick with one hand and covering the act with another hand. In addition to utensils, Rama V also introduced toothpicks to his people. The wealthy once wore chains around their waists from which they hung keys as well as toothpicks and earpicks made of gold.

Three seats away, Ek coughs and raises his voice. "Natalie, excuse me."

He's a teacher in the department, but he's on leave, finishing his PhD. His wife, Soon, a tall girl with wide eyes and an unusually curvy figure, also a teacher, is on Ek's right. On his left is his sister, Tida, another teacher. They're all within a few years of my age.

Ek pushes up his glasses, thick and strung by an outdated, oversized square frame with rounded edges. He leans over his plate, down the table, and looks at me. "Did you ever teach before?"

His words swing past discarded shrimp tails, empty water glasses and cold rice. They hit my ears like a pebble. I flinch.

My throat cramps. "No."

Perhaps he's curious. Perhaps he's resentful. AJ told me that our salary, while half of what English teachers at private international schools earn, is about five times as much as Thai teachers make. The difference, he said, is because we need more motivation to get here and stay here, and because of the simple math: we must live alone in apartments in central Bangkok and likely eat out every meal since most apartments are without kitchens, whereas our Thai peers live with their families either in the city or in the suburbs, on land their families have owned for dozens if not hundreds of years.

"How will you know how to teach?"

Good question. One I have been blocking from my own head, one I hoped no one would ask. Ek's on the edge of his seat, waiting for an answer. Everyone is listening. This is the job interview I didn't have, wouldn't have passed. This is how that interview would have gone:

Q: What are your teaching qualifications?

A: I don't have any. (Technically. I wouldn't be qualified to be a teacher back in Canada, though I do have the required BA to get a teacher's visa here in Thailand.)

Q: Why do you think you can teach English?

A: I don't.

Q: What is your background in English?

A: I speak it. I used it to write articles about corn-eating contests and school council meetings.

Back in the real world, at this table, my brain breaks off from my mouth to scan and search itself for an answer. It comes back blank. Blank. Blank. Blank.

"Uh, well. I think, I think most people know how to teach from being a student."

Pii Fah's eyes coax and widen.

"Plus, I've been working on my English for a while now." A mush of spice shoots up my throat and I cough. "Still have trouble with my accent, though."

Only two teachers detect the joke and smirk. Ek nudges his glasses up his nose again. His eyes, sulking, part from mine. The teachers smile.

I'm saved, for now.

FIRST DAY
OF SCHOOL

———

THE LIST BEGINS like this: Duangrat Arunrungneethum, Apichart Bansatsriyaphod, Ratanakorn Pitsraran. Feeling flush and sick, I steal a glance at the door. It's still slightly open; a line of light runs along the row of students against the wall.

"Du-ang-rat Ar-un-rung-nee-thum." My temples sweat.

Whispers, giggles, creaking desks. It's cold in here, from the air-conditioning and the yards of ballroom-style curtains blocking the sun. Even the carpet is dark, a red with black flecks.

Blushing, I try the name again, slower. "Du-ang-rat?"

Silence.

Finally, a soft voice from the front row. "Oh, *ajarn*, not here. She is not here."

"Thank you."

The student grins and curtsies. Her notebook falls off her desk, as does the purse of the girl sitting beside her who tried to reach for the notebook. The commotion kindles a breeze of cheap perfume—vanilla and alcohol.

Name two of fifty-two. "Ratanakorn Pitsraran." My voice

rises like I've asked a question. They sense my unsureness, read it like a sign. No one raises their hand or says, Here!

"Sorry," I say, shifting behind the podium. "I . . . I don't know how to say your names." If I had talked myself into a cloak of confidence before class, it's now fallen off, left me dizzy and little and light.

Also, cursing this country and its last names. King Vaji-ravudh, the short, round-faced son of Chulalongkorn who studied at Oxford, introduced last names in 1913. Believing the use of only first names to be uncivilized, he began coining surnames for his people after starting with his own, Rama, the Chakri dynastic name to precede a king's reign number. Rama VI's edict said all his subjects had to have last names, and Thai law still says a last name can only belong to one family in the whole country. Which is why they've gotten so long and complicated. Thailand's strange and fantastical history, I fall in love with it. I think I could be happy living in such a storied nation, so different from home—only as old, we're told, as our great-grandfathers. And yet because Thailand is ancient and its list of laws long and complex, I continue making an ass of myself.

"Ratanakorn Pitsraran," I say, faster than before. Speed isn't the problem; it's syllable stress, and tone. Their language has five tones—five changes in pitch for the very same sound. Low, mid, high, falling or rising. For every tone, a different meaning.

Even in just those two names, I blunder the pronunciation so completely they can't even recognize the sound.

A boy at the back with buck teeth, glasses and a narrow waist stands.

"Thank you."

I can't be saying it that off.

I am. And the class will wait until next week to tell me I should call them by nicknames such as Snow, Apple and Noo (mouse).

Though I enjoyed the odd round of playing school, I was never one of those girls who always wanted to be a teacher. I much preferred being a student, being alone with a thesaurus. But walking into my first classroom on the first day of school, I had felt not this nausea or embarrassment or fear, but contentment. I had a plan, a plan marked by numbers, bullets, sub-bullets and brackets. I don't know how to teach, but I know how to make lists. I was the type of child who inventoried Halloween candy and scheduled my monthly wardrobe. My teaching strategy is to come to class with lists, backup plans and lessons derived in part from websites claiming Free ESL Lessons! My list for today, titled The First Day of Class Outline, has seven points. I'm ready to walk out on number one.

Thankfully, there are only nineteen students here today; the rest have skipped, the way students all around the world do on the first day of class. *I hope they skip all the time. I hope I never have to read that list again. I'm not reading that list again. They can put their own checkmarks beside their names. I don't care if they're not really here.*

"My name," I say, with my back to them and fumbling with a marker lid, "is Natalie."

I want to be cool and young. I am young—twenty-four—only a few years older than my students. But mostly I want to be cool.

The next two minutes are spent on Canada and how cold it can get. I use my arms to demonstrate that the hand above my head is Bangkok, at thirty-five degrees Celsius, (ninety-five degrees Fahrenheit) and the hand below my knee is Regina, Saskatchewan, in the winter, at minus thirty-five degrees Celsius (minus thirty-one degrees Fahrenheit; both Thailand and Canada use the imperial system). A girl shrieks at this news. As my voice carries on, I find I like their eyes on me. I find it's not unlike the false love of one-night trysts.

While one side of my brain keeps my mouth moving, the other side determines who is who. The brown-noser. The one who thinks she's smarter than me. The thick-hipped girls from the country. The gays. The *kathoey*s. Song, in her magnificent ability to anticipate and execute a translation, saw my gawking eyes during my first week on campus as two students walked by with hairy legs and heels. The ladyboys of Khao San, while unfamiliar to me at first, seemed to suit those bawdy bars. But here, it's daylight and we're on campus and these are not costumes and no one else gives them a second glance, and the fact is, this is still wildly different from what I know. Song tapped my arm and whispered, so close to my ear I could smell her bubblegum, "In Thai we say they are 'the third sex.'" "Ladyboy" is Western slang. Thais say *kathoey* or *phet thi-sam*, the third sex: someone with the organs of a man and the spirit of a woman. Broad shoulders, breasts. Hoarse voices, pink lips. All as welcome as the sun. I will come to understand that Thais have nothing but acceptance for the third sex because in their bay of beliefs—where streams of Buddhism, Hinduism and Animism meet—anyone could be or could have been a *kathoey* in another life. Karmic debt determines it when you are in the womb. Ancient scriptural texts even show the presence of and an acceptance toward a third gender.

Many of these students, I have been told, are here because they couldn't get into the good universities—Silpakorn, Chulalongkorn, Thammasat. These students want to work at the front desks of hotels, hand out pillows on airplanes. In Thailand, these are good jobs and you need a degree to get them.

"My name is Natalie and I like noodles." I write this on the board as I say it, underlining each "n" before explaining the rules to a field of empty, eyebrow-bent faces.

"Understand?"

Nothing.

I give two more examples, a Sara who likes sandwiches and a Jeremy who likes jogging. "It can be anything, a food or an activity. I don't care. It just has to be English and start with the same letter as your name. OK?"

Starting again, I hold my hand out to a chubby girl with burgundy glasses in the front row. The skin of her feet folds over her mandatory black, square-heeled shoes. She rises, twists her skirt down. There's a bit of chutzpah in her hips.

"My name is Wassana. And I like women."

My stomach caves, my lips *oooh* in an attempt not to laugh. The students laugh and I can't tell if they're laughing because I'm almost laughing, or because it's funny or because it's true.

Song walks in. "OK, ready for a picture?"

Just before I left the office for class, Song had handed me a piece of paper.

"Do not forget this, Natalie," she said, swinging her index finger as if I were about to commit a no-no. She dropped the paper—the class list—on the stack already in my arms and opened the door for me. Most of the time she is my other brain, my other set of hands. She is those things for other teachers, too, because she's a good secretary and because of Thai culture, which asks more of those who are younger or in lower ranks.

Song and I are the same age, though, and as soon as I'm less helpless, I hope she'll just be my friend.

"Oh, thank you, Song." My back was holding the door open to the hallway, to the morning sunlight and students. "Ummm... Song."

"Yes?" She spun in her slippers. A few of the younger women wear slippers at their desks. The flat, thin variety you see at hospitals and spas, mostly. One teacher's pair is a plush blue animal with plastic black and white eyes.

"Can you please, if you have a minute—if you don't, that's OK, but if you do—could you come to my classroom and take a picture for me? For my first day?"

She grinned. "Sure."

Thais love taking pictures, seeing themselves smiling on a screen. Proof of happiness. My request didn't seem sentimental to her, only right. She wrote down my room number on a pink slip of paper, then waved goodbye with it.

"See you soon," she said.

Now I'm standing behind the far row, against the peach-colored curtains and below one of four air-conditioners. Song waves at the students to squish together and they do, sliding elbows onto other desks, hair on to other shoulders. Wassana is closest to Song and appears all the bigger in the picture. She is surrounded by four rows of white shirts and black hair. I am so far away from the lens you can't see my eyes are green, but you can see my smile. In a black cardigan with the top buttons undone to reveal the tip of a purple camisole, a conservative, common look in Canada, I am showing too much skin. My red hair is tied in a tight ponytail, my bangs erected into a small hill with the help of bobby pins, and without any earrings I look like a squirrel. A skinny, nervous red squirrel.

SHE'S SO
BRAVE

AN ALBINO GECKO climbs the wall above my pillow. It pauses, swivels its head toward me. The gecko's body is bumpy, like chicken skin. Its eyes, black and blinking, watch me. *What do I do?* I want it gone. I scan the ceiling corners for holes. *How did it get in here?* I reach for my broom. *You can't use the broom.* I tiptoe to the bathroom. My fingers are shaking. Hair spray. I dig my thumbnail under the lid to pop it. The gecko's on the floor now, on the tile by the end of my bed. *I'm not going to bed with that thing in here. I'm not.* My finger clutches the nozzle. I crouch toward the gecko and it freezes, claws spread on a strand of red hair. My hair has been falling out. It's everywhere. I spray, aiming for its eyes. It tries to move, but it's blinded. It blinks and staggers. I spray. It tucks its head into its tail, coiling like a snake. I spray. It inhales. I spray.

I leave its pale, shrunken body there for three days.

ON DAY FOUR in my Bangkok apartment, I tell my mom in an email that this place is the size of her bathroom, maybe smaller. I can nearly touch all four walls by holding my arms out in a "t" from the center of the room. "Honey, I'm sure you're exaggerating," she replies. I am not, and in fact I feel a bit dishonest calling it an apartment. It's a room, a tiny room. *Pii* Sinn came with me to see it between classes the other day. I needed a place to live and this was clean and close to school. The hotel gave me sheets, white, like the walls and the door and the floor. The bathroom has no division on the floor between the toilet and the shower. Always, it's uncomfortable here: I fear I'm showering on pee and peeing in the shower. The showerhead itself is as small as the butt gun beside the toilet. The post-toilet wash is a custom I have forgone. I'm klutzy and know I will leave bathrooms with a dripping groin. I will also forgo the way Thai women stand on the seat and squat because most toilets are not the Western style; most are porcelain-covered holes in the ground. These toilets pose problems. I spend a lot of time worrying about not peeing on myself.

Worrying about food also takes up a lot of my time. Every day on the way home from work, I walk down the lane with a plastic bag of 7-Eleven junk: noodles in a cup and salted broad bean nuts. I haven't worked out how to order food yet and I'm scared of getting hungry. There are dozens of little, housefront restaurants near my place. Apartments don't have kitchens and because street food is so cheap and it's on every alley and corner, everyone eats out, all the time, even families that have houses and kitchens. Once I asked Song to write on a piece of paper the name of a dish I tried with her and liked, *gai pad krapaow*, chicken with holy basil on rice. But I lost that piece of paper. Even though my apartment is less than two miles from Khao San Road, there are no other foreigners here. No one speaks English. I pour chili flakes on my half-cooked noodles and stir the cup with a plastic, foldable fork.

Later I'll play solitaire on my laptop and smoke between rounds, kneeling on my bed and exhaling out the window. I could get in shit for smoking in my room, but it's the only part of my old life I still have, a rotten habit I intend to preserve because it is just that, something I know, something I can still do. Who do you rebel against but yourself, when you are far from home, one in a city of eight million? To sit behind this one-way mirror, where I am seen but not known, is liberating and beautiful. Not so the rain.

I can't smoke when it rains. I tried, but the smoke can't get out and it mixes with the moisture, filling my room as if boiling water had been poured over an ashtray. If I open the screen, another gecko or a cockroach could get inside. When it rains, the cockroaches race up gutters, skittering along ankles or bricks to reach dry ground.

Rain should really have a different name in Thailand. There is nothing gentle or pretty about it. It doesn't brush the world green and fresh. It doesn't fall or sprinkle. It plummets, in drops as thick as my thumb. Asphalt disappears. Everything on the ground—dog droppings and cigarette ends—rises with the rain, and with the heat of the concrete and fumes from cars, it reeks. Acrid and heavy.

It's almost the end of monsoon season, and in the last two weeks it has rained every day at the time of day that seems the most inconvenient: late afternoon, about four or five o'clock. As buses pause for grandparents, hands entwined with those of uniformed little girls and boys. As the fried banana lady outside the school gates dumps her oil. As families set tables in their front-room restaurants.

When the rain stops, and it stops suddenly, the walls are left a darker shade of charcoal.

At least here, in my new room, I can't hear the parking guards, blowing their whistles into the wet as if the drivers on their rain-soaked routes were blind. Recently, at one of the tourist stops, perhaps the Jim Thompson House, I saw a card made by Nancy Chandler that features a parking guard waist-deep in water, whistle in hand. Santa's red pants are rolled up to his knees, black boots in one hand and a yellow bag marked TOYS in the other. Fish swim beside the wheels of a *tuk-tuk*. It's from her holiday collection and it's called *Floods*.

"Flood" is a more fitting word. Sometimes I don't mind the rain, though. My eyes become lost in it like a campfire. The window is a screen for what's showing in my mind, clips from home: A Mormon friend at age nine towing a wagon full of frogs no bigger than belly buttons, found in a creek at the bottom of the coulee. Mr. M, a math teacher in one of those Cosby sweaters out in the hall. He called the school counselor when I came to class crying about Junie and her wrists. Carol, a cook I worked with one summer at a golf course. She wore fuchsia lipstick and had winged, yellow hair. If something was wrong, she'd take off her apron and hug us and hush us in her Newfoundland accent, "Make no wonder you're upset."

Aside from playing solitaire, I use my laptop to write patches of scenes about places I've been in Thailand. Later, at the office, I'll upload them along with photos to my blog. Someday I might even tell people the blog exists.

I don't have the Internet here in my room, but I think about it a lot, the emails I would write and the emails I get. My mom sent one yesterday. Says she can't believe how brave I am. Each time I send pictures, all the girls at her office gather around her desk, which overlooks the downtown Dairy Queen. They flick their big, blond-streaked hair and say, "*Gawd*, can you imagine?" "Not in this lifetime." They say my mom must be so proud of me. "She just grabbed that bull by the horns."

I think half the reason I came here was so people would know I did something scary. To see the look on people's faces, to say, "I lived in Thailand." But I wasn't brave. I was a coward, running from that dusty sofa and the lies. Without that night, would I have ever left?

Now I'm so far away I forget sometimes about that other world.

"You're so young, do it now, before you have kids." That's what some people say, but they don't mean it most of the time. Most of the time they can't figure out why anyone would move to the other side of the world, to a country where they eat rice three times a day and speak Thai, or else they can understand and it pinches them in dormant places. They wonder why I'm not doing what *we're* doing. *We're* applying for a homeowner's line of credit to do the roof, *we're* trying for a baby, *we're* going to Mexico. Before I left, this is how I interpreted those raised eyebrows and rippled foreheads.

I had to go. Because of what I'd done and what I didn't want to do. That's half of it. The other half, that tug... For a while, just believing there might be a bigger reason was enough. But I'm like a child. I don't want to wait and I'm starting to wonder if that was a lie I told myself too.

Do we tell ourselves a story so we'll have a script? If so, what happens when we get to the middle, and the protagonist catches up to the narrator?

I want to know why I'm here.

I brush my salty broad bean fingers on my pajama shorts and gaze out my little window again, now that the rain's gone. I can see a neighbor's laundry, yellow bras and t-shirts, hanging under a sheet metal roof and the rows of windows and green pull-blinds at the back of the restaurant two houses away. The man and woman who run it live above. Yesterday we all said hello.

The husband heard my heels and looked up, a knife in one hand and a fish in the other. I smiled. I couldn't look up too long. The road was uneven and I didn't want to trip.

He nodded and smiled back, fat cheeks shining in the sun.

"*Sawasdee ka.*" *Ka*, the polite particle women use at the end of sentences, and sometimes on its own as a verbal nod in conversation, like "uh-huh."

"*Sawasdee, krub.*" *Krub*, the polite particle men use at the end of sentences, and also to show understanding in conversation.

He wiped his hand on his red golf shirt and stepped down from the area where the fish are kept on ice, then cut and smoked.

His wife was standing in the alley against a pale green wall covered in soda ads and flashy Thai fonts. A blue apron covered most of her loose red-and-orange shirt and her black pleather pants. She was hunched over a counter pounding a pestle into a wooden mortar bowl the size of a basketball. The paste inside— garlic and chilies and fish sauce—was dark.

She heard my heels too and smiled as I passed her.

I smiled back. "*Sawasdee ka.*"

She gasped before replying. "*Sawasdee ka.*" She giggled and said something to her husband. I imagined his reply: *I know. Surprised me too.*

Down the alley, nearly all the way to the street, I'm followed by the knocking and twisting sounds of her pestle.

It will be the first sound I hear every morning for six months, the wife pounding her pestle. Thais, in the habit of naming instruments after the sound they make, call the mortar *krok*, pronounced *kruak*. The pestle was once called *sark-ka bua*, or *sark* for short. A household word for a household utensil, at some point *sark* became a vulgar euphemism for penis. Now, in the North, it's called *mai tee prik*, at pepper. Once, pestles were a mighty weapon. Enlisted men who refused to fight were branded cowards and bludgeoned to death with the pestle. This threat, of soldiers' faces turning to a paste of blood and bones in the mortar bowl, is said to have fueled the victory of a battle against Burma in Kanchanaburi, a province dense with forest and sugar canes east of Bangkok.

Pestles were not just for fighting and cooking on earth. Gods, too, needed these utensils. Villagers in Thailand's northern Mae Hong Son province believed a climber at the top of a mountain could hear pestles thundering into mortars. If you scaled a mountain, you could hear heaven. Their heaven is a place where divine beings can be found in kitchens, cooking.

At night, other sounds trickle out of the restaurant. Like most others, it doubles as a karaoke bar. Neighborhood men and government officials sip whiskey—Johnny Walker, poured from a shared bottle set on the table—or beer, also shared and poured in a glass with ice. They take turns singing the same songs, American country songs from the '60s and '70s. Neil Diamond's "Rhinestone Cowboy." John Denver's "Take Me Home, Country Roads." Their smooth, wistful voices rise to my room and I get used to falling asleep like this, to the sound of drunken men singing.

SAME SAME,
NO

S ONG'S EYES SCROLL across the page while I wait, curious. She had to open a locked, glass-encased cabinet to get out the thickest dictionary in the office for this. She knows there is a word. She just has to find it.

"Sorry, Natalie." Song doesn't think she's searching fast enough.

"It's OK." I shake my head. I'm leaning on the corner of my cubicle below a laminated picture of myself and the words *Ajarn* Natalie in English and Thai. Song is standing in front of me, in the middle of the office, in her skirt and slippers. The dictionary weighs on her girlish wrists.

"Aaah," she says. Her eyes light up. An index finger rises. "'Elastic.' In Thai culture, we think time is elastic. It can stretch."

Oh. Lesson: in Thailand, time stretches.

After two weeks of almost fifty-two students showing up three minutes, twenty minutes or an hour and ten minutes late for class, I confided in Song. I told her while I'm grateful attendance has picked up since the first class, my students are never on time. "Never. This is *university*." Who do they think they are? Who do they think I am? There's no excuse. Anyone can get to where they're going on time if they leave early enough. "I'm thinking of locking the doors after five minutes," I told Song. But she gasped. She said she didn't think that was a good idea. She said we're different. Who? I wondered. Song and I? Bangkok universities and Western universities? Foreigners and Thais, Song said, and then pushed a chair toward the dictionary cabinet.

I accept my students' lateness knowing that I have to, and not yet knowing what many go through to get to school: several journeys by bus and boat, some of which start in villages more than sixty miles away. I learn this much later, while sitting on a bench with a student, a young girl wearing a long, pleated black skirt rather than one of the miniskirts. Earlier that day she'd been huffy after running from the bus, then yawned all through class. After class, on that bench, I asked where she lived. As she recounted her route from a distant town, I felt a bit sick about insisting students be exactly on time. It was a small miracle they got there at all.

What I really need to know is I don't know anything about anything.

PET AND I are in the hall, half outside, and that silent, pre-photo tension chokes the air. My glasses and an attendance list dangle from my fingers. With Pet's head below my nose, I can smell her shampoo. She seemed nervous, asking as I was wiping the board after class.

Pet's friend waves at us to get closer, then peers into the viewfinder.

As she leans her head toward me, Pet's thick, black hair drapes across my chest. She has fairer skin than most girls, and stockier legs. She's so quiet in class that I hadn't heard her voice until today, with the camera in her hands. Beside her, I look so tall, so much older. So hopeful. Mascara-sweat smudges under-line my eyes.

In a surprisingly loud yet wobbly voice, the friend says, "One, two, three."

"*Ajarn*, thank you very much," says Pet, making a *wai* and curtsying. She's almost gushing. Nervous, she is, to be speak-ing English to me, one on one, and she probably comes from a village where she didn't see a lot of foreigners. To her, I'm something of a celebrity.

"Oh, I'm happy to." And I am.

In one of my first student-teacher pictures here, I sit in the middle of four girls in uniform. They're all posing as if they were models, staring at the picture taker and making the peace symbol. I'm glancing off to the side, but I'm smiling. And it's genuine, almost candid. Getting my picture taken with stu-dents, it almost convinces me I'm not so awful at this.

My camera-happy students don't care if I'm a good or even likable teacher. I'm simply a rarity. White. Female. Teacher. To them, my whiteness is my best feature. Most Thais want to be whiter. Pharmacies line shelves with dozens of whitening solutions, labels featuring pale beauties attracting the opposite sex. *More white. More white.* Movies and TV shows feature fair-skinned Thais, mostly half Thais who don't look at all like real Thais. If you're white, you're wealthy. You must be, anyway, or your skin would tan from working under the sun in a rice field or at a market. In a few months, I will go to the beach town of Hua Hin for the weekend. Before leaving a student will warn me not to come back with a tan. "Or else you will be ugly," he'll declare. I will tell him where I come from some girls start going to the tanning beds at fourteen, the darker the better.

Aside from being white, it's good to be me because I'm from Canada and my name is Natalie. Another girl from Can-ada named Natalie won the Miss Universe pageant, held in Bangkok, last year. She took the crown with a charming *wai* to the judges and now the Russian immigrant is Thailand's idol. Everyone knows her name, even taxi drivers. As soon as I say my name is Natalie, they say, "Oh, oh, Nat-a-li*eeee* Gleb-o-*va*!" I don't mind being associated with a beauty queen, even when they point out how much I don't look like her. "Same same, no."

AT WORK, I read emails I've been ignoring for weeks. Stuart's mom says this year's Christmas craft show was probably the best ever. We still keep in touch. I don't think about Stuart very often. I've forgotten, already and somehow, the fights about fast-cash companies and being jobless, about chew spit on the carpet and choosing the wrong wood stain. About passing up the kind of love you sweat with. This, I think, is how we know. We let go. Quickly. Quietly. Completely.

In an email from my mom, she calls me "sweetie" three times and says everything is same old, same old in Medicine Hat. My inbox also tells me that two of my dear friends are getting married this year, the one year I won't be in Canada. Stella, whose fiancé is best friends with Stuart, and Junie, who was with me at the bar the night I ran into Scott. And I wonder, just fleetingly, if I hadn't left, would I be next in line? And will they forgive me for missing their weddings, or will it not matter because these aisles—theirs to the altar, mine to International Departures—have already chuted us off in different directions, so that even if we should find ourselves in the same arena someday, it won't be the same?

Zora and I still keep in touch the most. She's about to graduate. Lois has kept her promise to give Zora that trip around the world as a present. If I stay in Thailand for a few more months, she says she'll come visit me.

I send a short mass email. If anyone needs a laugh today, I say, here is a story. In my Varieties in English class, I'm teaching a unit on slang. It's actually quite useless because some students still have trouble asking to go to the bathroom; they have no use for the thirty-one English slang words used to call someone daft. In one recent assignment, they had to create a short conversation between two people using some of their new slang words.

A: So, tonight, don't forget to pick me up to watch a flick with your new car.

B: No, I can't. I have a pain in my ass.

A: What is wrong with you?

B: Yesterday I had a fender bender on the john.

"THERE ARE NO accidents," a line from John Berendt's novel about Venice, *The City of Falling Angels*. I test it on my tongue: "There are no accidents." Everything—that fight with my editor, running into Scott at Gringo's, the ketchup and the pigeon and the man at the laundromat—happened for a reason.

Or did it? Why do we do this, hunt for signs, even after we're long gone?

On sheets damp with sweat and stale with smoke, I roll away from the concrete wall, cool against my back. I set the book on my night table and flick off my flashlight.

THE HUSBAND LEANS over the coal-fired grill, yelling at the wife while he flips two fish. Smoke shoots up, into his face. He waves it away, notices me.

"*Sawasdee ka.*" My greeting sounds soft, tired. It's Friday afternoon, the end of month two. I look forward to weekends, but I'm also wary of them. Sometimes, my hellos to the family are the only words that leave my mouth between now and Monday morning. In between, I take the bus to the markets and the malls and the parks and the temples. It's kind of thrilling at first, setting out for an unknown destination, happening upon it. But returning home, to the night and no one to tell it all to, sometimes that has the prickle of energy recoiled, like bounding down the stairs in the dark when you think there's one more step, but you're already on the last. Mostly, though, I like the solitude.

"*Sawasdee krub.*" Now he's bending over the sidewalk, hoisting a bucket of ashes.

He speaks. *Thai words. Thai words. Thai words.*

My eyes smile and I nod. I search his face for a hint.

He opens his right arm, points up and down the block. He's trying to show me something. The street? The restaurant? All I see is his gold, on two rings, on a bracelet, on the face of a watch.

Thai words. "*Falang.*" *Thai words.* He looks at me and pauses, neck stretched out like a duck over a palm of bread crumbs.

"*Mai kow jai.*" I don't understand. Anything, other than *falang*, foreigner. I wish I did. I wish I could sit down and ask for a Coke and some soup and ask them how their day is going. We could talk about the weather.

"Oh, *mai kow jai.*" *Thai words.* "*Falang.*" *Thai words.* "*Falang.*" He's grinning, his gray mustache curling up with his cheeks.

I smile wide, walking backward until I almost trip on their dog, sleeping on a leg of shade.

The wife, who had come out of the kitchen mid-conversation, takes a half step my way and her eyes, they reach for me. She speaks, and with rubber-gloved hands, draws a line in the air from the end of the alley to the restaurant. The only word I catch, "*falang.*"

I study her lips. As if I could lip-read a foreign language any better. My eyes reach back: *I'm sorry.*

She wipes her forehead with a blue rag. Sighs.

I take a few steps, eyes still locked with hers, then turn my head and continue home. The metal tips of my heels tick the concrete. The sound echoes through the street.

What were they trying to tell me?

I CAN'T TAKE
THE HEAT

I F I OPEN my mouth, I'll cry. He only said, "Hey, sis," and I
froze. It's been three months since I've heard those words;
suddenly I miss him so much it stings.

A staggered, scared bit of breath escapes my lips. I cover my
mouth.

"What's wrong?"

My brother, who played dress-up shoes and stole me gas
caps. Who sagged just like me after seeing our dad. Who followed me and trusted me and knew me. And still loved me.
Would never wrong me. I've loved you always. And fuck our
family is as fucked up as ever and I've left you there.

Another sigh. I wipe my nose with a sheet and dig fingernails into my leg.

"You're crying."

I don't want to put a damper on his Christmas Day. I didn't
think this would happen. My mom started rambling about the
snow and the tree and I saw her and Tyler and Wayne in that
little apartment. Three plates. Nodding and chewing and smiling. Christmases past. That we almost had an almost family for

a while, to outsiders anyway. Even if it was backward. There were no fists, no shouting. Just the damp and dead air of a cave, but a house at least. Four kids. Two adults.

My mom asked how my Christmas was going and I almost said, Fuck, you know what I'd like? I'd like to not have to answer questions about my family by saying, Well, my real dad kind of hit the road when I was three and my mom got remarried and he had two boys who lived with us so they were like my brothers and one of them even played school and My Little Pony with me, but my mom and my stepdad always seemed to be either yelling or not talking and they eventually threw in the towel so that's all off and now my mom's with another guy. Wayne. Owns the paint store. *Oh.*

Her leaving, it's different from mine. Or so I see it. I'm a daughter, canting about what's right and knowing more than her. Everything. Twice. And I know that you need to be on your own awhile, once in a while.

"It was a Saturday here, Mom, just like any other Saturday," I say.

Bangkok is thirteen hours ahead of Alberta, so they're about to eat turkey, and I've just woken to Boxing Day in Bangkok. "And," I told her, "it's 104 degrees outside." I didn't tell her I spent Christmas day in a girlie bar off Sukhumvit with two middle-aged men, fellow English teachers. My mom mentioned something about gravy, then passed the phone to my little brother and that's when I began to bawl.

"Why are you crying?" His voice, so gentle.

Not because it's Christmas. Frankly, having spent last Christmas about to break someone's heart and now with a family like this, I'm glad to be so far away. Maybe a bit of it is grief for our other family. Maybe it's sorry that I've left him to sit at that brand-new table, unscratched and unknowing of places. Maybe it's him.

Finally, I get a hold of my tongue. "I just... miss you."

There's a beep, and a voice saying I have 35 *baht* in credit left—less than a minute.

"Phone credit's running out. Love you."

"Love you too, Nattie."

My thumb presses END. They stay there, my thumb and the phone, on the pillow beside my cheeks, soaked and hot.

THERE IS SOMETHING else I miss.

Lately, pencils and pop cans have become phallic symbols. *Penis. Penis. Penis.* My mind taunts me. I am supposed to be finding myself, becoming one with the world. Instead, in Thailand, the land of smiles and sex, another night home alone. The idea of online dating is entertained. I never did it back home and I'd be ashamed to be doing it now (it's 2006), but there is no other way. I'm stuck in some kind of strange social limbo. I can't really spend time with the teachers after hours. Even if either party wanted to, I am seen as a bad influence. Western women, if you can imagine, are thought to be loose: they smoke and drink and live alone and spend time alone with men they're not married to. I know this in part because the only single teacher who lives by herself suggested I stay with her when I first moved to Bangkok, but her mother, up north in Chiang Mai, wouldn't allow it because she was worried I might rub off on her daughter, though for all she knows I am quite proper, and have been, a bit to my dismay, since I started work. There are no other *falang* female teachers on campus, or anywhere, as far as I can see. There is no one to date. The barriers of language and culture are too great for a relationship with the Thai males I'm in contact with (adolescent waterboys and aging academics), and the *falang* males who live here are generally an undesirable lot: old, overweight Europeans who prefer the quiet, if expensive, company of Thai females. The backpackers at the other end of old Bangkok are just that, tourists. I see myself as more of an expat now, have assumed the Thais' disdain for Khao San, its boozy, half-naked patrons, its overpriced beer and tacky trinkets.

When I create an online dating profile, I make only one request: must be taller than me.

Over three days I get no responses. *Those jackasses just want a tiny little Thai girl who will tell them their dicks are huge and their jokes are funny when neither is.* I shouldn't have expected much. Most of the men on the Bangkok part of the site are in their fifties or sixties, and specifically state they are looking for "a nice Thai girl." They're called sexpats, and they're not here for white girls from Canada.

Instead of giving up, I explore another dating website. And another one, and another one. The third site is actually a teachers' forum. In a paragraph-long post, I explain my situation—that I am in want of company but can't find company to keep—and ask: How does a female *falang* find dates in this country?

I get two responses.

The first says: There's a market in Banglamphu. If you get there early enough, you might be able to find dates as well as pistachios and cashews.

The second offers some advice, worded just so: 1) Munch carpet, 2) Buy a good vibrator, and 3) Call me.

After reading these three sentences at my desk between classes, I close my jaw and my laptop. Not that anyone here would know what "munch carpet" means.

The air-conditioner behind my head kicks into the high mode of midafternoon. Lost in its hum and a stripe of dusty sunlight on the floor, I remember a conversation I had with a friend in high school.

"Haven't you ever wondered?" she asked, a case of beer rat-
tling on her hip, a cigarette dangling off her lip.

We were sixteen and trying not to get our jean hems soaked
in snow as we tiptoed up the driveway to a house party.

"Yeah."

It was a Saturday night. We had already had two beers while
we were getting ready in her parents' basement. We were tipsy.
Inside, by the time a round of Sociables was over, we would be
drunk. We'd call out like wolves and scuttle into the bathroom,
arms linked. We'd giggle, whisper, dance in the living room and
then throw up.

"Don't you think it would be better to try it with someone
you trust?" she asked, exhaling on the last word. In the heavy
winter air, the smoke sauntered toward my mouth, an invitation.

"Yeah."

Reason, it fell over us like frost.

The pulsing white of my laptop screen. My fingers, circling
keys. Delaying typing what I'm thinking: *Thank you, but I don't
think I will call a man who uses the phrase "munch carpet."*

There is one last option. On a website called "Mango Sauce,"
a *Maxim* for men in Southeast Asia, I discover the Thai gigolo.
You can find them in the same sorts of little bars where you
find hookers in Pat Pong. Bangkok's biggest red-light district is
named after Udom Patpongsiri, who convinced his family to buy
a plot of land between Silom and Surawong roads for $3,000
US in 1946. Then, the area's roads were nameless. When Patpongsiri died fifty years later, the land, worth $100 million US,
was known in Bangkok and around the world as Pat Pong. On
this strip, in addition to knockoff handbags and sex by the half
hour, you can find the infamous ping-pong shows where white
plastic balls catapult from women's loins. You can also find
girls who will lie under animals on stage, and gigolos. According to the article, the gigolos wear numbers on their sleeves

when they're serving drinks. Every hour they ascend a platform and take off their shirts and suit jackets to parade in front of customers like it's a fashion show. You can order them, for a minute or a month.

The article's writer interviewed a teacher who has been visiting her gigolo every Saturday for the last year, spending half her small salary on sex with him. The teacher says Nohp makes sure she comes three times before he does.

Am I this desperate?

Yes. And no. Yes?

IN THE RESOLVE of daylight, a no. No, I won't pay for sex. I will, however, go on dates with strangers in a strange land. Here, so far from home, my vision and values are altered. And nonexistent here are the usual things that might keep one on the right track: a mother living six blocks away whose face you cannot lie to, an old high school science teacher you could run into at the Safeway checkout.

My Internet profile attracts about seven suitors, and I proceed to go on a series of first dates.

AL, DATE ONE.

Al says he's half Italian and half something else. He just said the country where he grew up but already I've forgotten. I was too busy staring at his hair, brown and chin-length. He likes to run his hands through it.

We are at a Starbucks on Sukhumvit, the hundred-block road where all the mega malls are, gigantic and golden. In his tailored tan suit and gold rings, Al belongs here.

He tosses his espresso into his throat in one shot and licks his lips. "Actually, it's too late in the day for espresso."

I nod. I've never had an espresso and I get the sense he can tell. Also, sweat is distracting me too much to talk. It must be 100 degrees and I'm wearing jeans and heels and a suit jacket. I want to look like a local, like I can take the heat. Perspiration dampens my eyebrows and every appendage covered by clothing.

Al tells me he owns a leather factory. He has a shop in one of the fancy hotels along the River Chao Phraya where you can buy custom handmade crocodile-skin shoes.

"Any size. Any color. You would not believe it," he says, eyes hooked on mine, waiting, I suspect, for a gushing response.

"Wow," I say.

Was it journalism that made me a listener, an observer? Or is that why I found journalism?

He eyes my bag, fake white leather, and my shoes, beige Italian leather, purchased forty-five minutes ago.

"If my business wasn't doing so well, I'd move. I prefer Milan to *here*," he says, hailing the street and the sky. He says he remembers Bangkok before blue jeans and cell phones. He was also here long before the skytrain, zooming above our heads.

"California wasn't bad."

Is he going to go through a list of the places he'd rather be living?

"Had some crazy times there." He infers relations with Madonna, a woman he says, "was wild." He shakes his head at the memory.

He wants me to ask more. Instead I sit at the table, smoking, blinking. I sip the last of my cappuccino, something Italians would never think of drinking at this hour of the day, he tells me, and he calls his driver.

"I'll give you a ride home."

I half hope for more. I half hate myself.

JOHN, DATE ONE.

He's sure I could never say his Thai name, so I can just call him John. It's easier for me. John also has a driver. In the backseat of some silver sports car, he tells me I look even more beautiful than in my picture.

"What are you doing with me?" he jokes.

I smile.

John's family owns a few companies. He lives alone in the penthouse above a mall that's home to shops such as Chanel and Dior. He thinks I might like his other houses too. He studied in London for a few years and he didn't want to move back. He likes "being Western." But his mother begged him to come back.

His voice sounds soft and wheezy, like Winnie the Pooh's. He says "you know" a lot. An attempt, I think, at impersonating a native English speaker. He's taken me to a European restaurant where men wear suits and the air reeks of sausage.

I try to keep food in my mouth while he talks. I focus on his fat fingers cutting chicken, his cheeks inflating and deflating, his little lips.

When we leave, he holds out his arm. I am to take it. He likes the way people look at us. Doesn't he know they think I'm like everything else of his?

NIT, DATE ONE.

Nit and I agree to meet at a movie theater that happens to be located in the same mall under which John lives. I'm waiting for him on the second floor, outside a Tony & Guy salon that charges as much for a haircut as I pay for my rent. He taps me on the shoulder and I turn around.

"Hey, how d'ya know it was me?" I ask. In the midst of four floors of Thais, my red hair stands out like a penny on a plate of nickels.

"Because of your picture," says Nit. He's confused. His t-shirt, just tight enough that his nipples and the curves of his arm muscles show. Nit doesn't look Thai, not in the body or the face. His facial features are entirely *falang*: white and heart-shaped with a raised, narrow nose. Nit's mom is Thai and his dad is Belgian. His mannerisms are American because he spent a few years in Boston by himself after high school.

Rolling on an ankle to seem shorter, I blink. "Nit, I'm kidding."

"Oh." He wipes the back of his neck and points to the escalator.

Nit says this is the best theater in Bangkok. "I come here a lot. They have couches and blankets and everything."

"Really." Against the volume of the mall, I can't hear myself.

I let him buy my ticket and while we wait in line outside the doors, his Puma runners tap the carpet. He swings his arms so his wrists meet in front of him, then behind him, as if he were warming up for a race and just waiting for someone to yell, "Go!" I peek at him out of the corner of my eye, squirming, showing himself off.

The movie begins and Nit laughs at the stupid Thai commercials for chocolate milk and a cell phone carrier, which only four-year-olds would have found funny back home. And the English subtitles are all wrong. All wrong.

AL, DATE THREE.

"I wish I could paint you, just like this," he says, mirroring my curves with his palms. He's standing at the corner of the bed with his fingers wrapped around his mouth. It's two in the afternoon and stuffy, even with the fan. We're in an apartment overlooking the river. When we came in, he hung his jacket in a closet already laden with a woman's things, a white blouse, a pair of khaki capris. He wanted me to see them. When we are done, he leans over, chest hairs grazing my bare arm, and whispers, "You are too impatient."

Next week I will see a picture of Al in the society pages in a newspaper's weekend magazine. He's at some grand opening, arms linked with his wife, apparently a sort of celebrity herself. And about seven months pregnant.

JOHN, DATE THREE.

The driver opens the door and John shifts to kiss my cheeks, the European way. Then he sits back and slides a black velvety bag under my fingers.

"Open it, my dear."

Nausea swells. Last week he gave me a Christian Dior dress he brought back from London. I've never even seen a Christian Dior store, never mind had an occasion to wear one of his dresses. The most expensive label I have owned to date was a $124 brown pair of Doc Martens I bought at fourteen with babysitting and birthday money; I hummed and hawed over them for almost two hours in the mall.

The gift is a black leather Chanel bag with silver straps. There is an ID card inside a zipper. The bag has an ID card.

"Beautiful," I say.

We end up in a quiet booth at the back of a sushi restaurant on Sukhumvit. I avoid the fish on rice and try to choke down the rolls as fast as I can, focusing instead on a dance recital routine from junior high. It's not the sushi. It's not even John or Bangkok—not now or on the other dates. It's their class. I just don't speak rich.

John asks about my parents, where I want to live after this, and the differences between men back home and here.

"Well," I say, "you're the only Thai man I've dated." Which is not a lie. Nit is half Thai.

"I see," he says, trying to stop a smile from spreading.

We go on to talk about Thailand's problems: a lack of literacy, little ones who don't drink enough milk and girls who grow up to support their families with the only resource they have or who get educated, then end up spinsters. Most Thai men, average working men, John tells me, make poor husbands. They're lazy.

"So, when you see these girls going for ugly old foreigners, you have to understand their idea of love. It's not the same as yours. To them, love is ... 'Can you take care of me?'"

So unrelentingly lucky are we in Canada. No tsunamis, dowries or bony cows. Just steak twice a day, thick blizzards, plastic car seats, one-ton dually trucks and soul mates lying in wait. And yet, I believe.

I squint, a cucumber roll squished between chopsticks mid-air. The rice pumps down my throat, followed by the seaweed and then the cucumber. I cover my mouth. "They can't be happy. They must know…"

"Yes." He takes a sip of his green tea. In his dimpled fingers, the porcelain cup looks like it belongs to a girl's tea set.

"Why don't you have a Thai wife?"

"I don't usually like Thai women, you know."

I don't know. I don't know if I really *want* to know, but this is one of the most engaging conversations I've had in a while. The most interesting part of living in another country is watching people do things an entirely opposite way to what you know. The next most interesting part is learning why.

When his car pulls into my parkade, John leans over. I turn my face to the window and grip the door handle. His collar, soaked in a cologne I kind of like, brushes my neck. I writhe. Underneath my dress, it feels like I'm wearing a wet bikini.

NIT, DATE FOUR.

This is my second beer since we sat down twenty minutes ago. I'm trying to get drunk. We're at an overpriced Italian restaurant. I'm eating pasta; Nit's having salad. He won't even touch the bread. Carbs interfere with his weight training. He's not really an athlete, though. Just wants to look like one.

Between bites, Nit tells me about his dad, who runs a hotel somewhere in the South, and his mom, a Thai who now lives alone, chewing coffee beans and asking where he's going, which is usually the gym or to the movies. Or so he says. I've seen the tattoo under his red t-shirt, the one that wasn't there the time before. Nit says it's the name of a Hindu goddess, but I think it belongs to a girlfriend: he rarely calls and always leaves before ten.

In conversation, he is like a grasshopper. One moment he's talking about getting his pilot's license; another he recounts dancing at a club and the girls who were all over him. Nit, thirty-one, doesn't work. He *just can't decide* what to do.

And yet of these three men, he is the one I've continued to see. Al, I stopped responding to his notes. I was the child of a philandering father, and I don't want to be the other woman too. After that last night with John, when I knew I couldn't pretend any longer and he started talking about a weekend away, I said I couldn't see him anymore. I thanked him for the dinners, offered to mail back the bag and the dress (both of which I later found out were fake) and wished him luck.

But when I can, even though I know something is off or missing here too, and even though life is not long enough for this, I continue to see Nit.

Two of the server girls are staring at us, giggling. I assume it's about our arrangement, me a foreigner, him a half Thai.

"They recognize me," he says, and gives them a wave. The girls squeal, stomp their feet.

Nit beckons me with his eyebrows and a boyish grin.
He wants me to say, "They recognize you from what?"

OF SCARVES
AND SHRIMP

THE WIFE WANTS me to say something too, or at least understand what she's telling me. She wags her hand for me to come forward, then disappears into the kitchen, bleating. I'm standing on the *soi*, confused. The scent of boiling rice fills the street. She left her mortar and pestle on its table. I peek inside the bowl and see a heavy red paste dotted with garlic slivers. I want to crush them.

Did she really want me to wait? We said hello as usual and then she started chattering.

She steps out of the kitchen and down to the *soi* just as I'm checking my watch. I'm almost late for my first class. Standing over me on a step, she holds out a small blue-and-white-striped plastic bag, and waits for my reaction.

I open the bag and pull out a pale green scarf. It's wide with danglies at the ends and iridescent horizontal lines every three inches. It's almost three feet long, and so soft it slips through my fingers.

The wife's sister now stands shoulder to shoulder with her. I think it's her sister, anyway. They look alike, except the sister has boy-short hair and smiles even more often than the rest of them.

They're blabbering on, I assume, about where they've brought it from. All I hear is Chiang Rai, a city even farther north than Chiang Mai, nearly at the Burmese border. The restaurant was closed on the weekend. That must be where they were, where they're from, Chiang Rai, and they got the scarf there, for me.

Tears start at the edges of my eyes. I take my eyes off the scarf, lift my face. "*Korp khun ka. Korp khun ka.*" Thank you. Thank you. I stretch the last words, trying to express how thankful I am. The Thai language doesn't have room for the practice of stressing sounds to convey emotions. It has too many tones as it is. If they can't sense it in my voice, maybe they can see it in my eyes, wet with gratitude.

Love drifts between our bodies. A fizzy invisible yarn knotted from her heart to her hands to her eyes, to my hands to my heart to my eyes. *There*, love says.

Beaming, the wife and her sister hold out the bag so I can slip the scarf back in.

I try to thank her again, this time with my face: *you don't know how much this means.* I say goodbye, good day, and turn on my heels, the trail of smoking fish and steaming rice fading behind me. Late for class, I scurry down the *soi* crying inside. She doesn't even know my name. I've never eaten at her restaurant.

Later, I hang the scarf over a chair in my room and inhale its scent. It smells like a grandmother's perfume, like love itself, and it's filling my room.

TOM YUM GUNG *mai sai gung. Tom yum gung mai sai gung.* Spicy shrimp soup without the shrimp. Spicy shrimp soup without the shrimp.

I've been saying it over and over in my head all day. I asked Song how to say "without." When I told her why—that I wanted to order spicy shrimp soup with no shrimp—she laughed and shook her head, "Not possible." But I think it *is* possible and I have to eat at the family's restaurant. I have to and I want to and *tom yum gung* is the only food I know they have that I like and that I can manage ordering on my own. I love the soup's taste, but I can't stomach the sight of the shrimp's eyeballs or backbones. Since others seem to love this part best, it makes sense to me to save them for someone else. I don't see that this is me being North American, wanting Thai food if I can have it my way.

Nearing the end of the *soi*, where in a few steps I will have to either turn my feet into the restaurant or carry on walking home, I contemplate abandoning my plan.

Maybe I'll come tomorrow. Tomorrow might be better.

Just let them feed you.

I need a family. I need people to wonder if I've eaten and pat my shoulder. Family: a group of people who may or may not be related, who may or may not live together and who may or may not love each other. Was I seven or eight when the counselor pushed my chair up to his desk, opened a shoebox of pencil crayons and asked me to draw my family? I was in front, alone. Mom, stepdad, Tyler and two stepbrothers behind me. He was at the edge, on his own. Looking back, I see what the counselor was analyzing. Looking back, I still don't know what family means.

My throat is in a knot. But I nod at the husband, walk in, under the awning. *OK, I am in the restaurant.* He stops chopping, watches me trying to work out where to sit. All of the tables are for four or six people.

I'll look even more alone than I am.

I pull out a blue plastic chair and sit down at a table near the back, near the kitchen. I set my work stuff onto the chair beside me and open my purse. I need a cigarette.

Thai words. Thai words. The dad is at my side, arms folded behind him. He's smiling, waiting for me. His daughter comes home from school and distracts him for a moment. He goes into the kitchen and I hear the wife. They're all squabbling. I wish I could ask what they were trying to tell me that day.

The wife peeks her head out of the kitchen, sees me. Smiles, wide, like only mothers can. Her hair looks pretty today, half back with a sweep of bangs across her forehead. I couldn't guess how old she is. She has teenagers, but when I was a teenager, my mom always smelled like pantyhose and needed to do her roots. She had crow's feet and purple bags under her eyes, both likely caused by me. The wife doesn't.

She steps toward me.

"*Kor nam* Coke. *Kor tom yum gung mai sai gung.*" My tongue feels jilted. It wants to include several pleases and thank-yous. *Kor*, according to my Thai-English dictionary, means "please bring." The Thai language, from the little I've studied it, is simple. Aside from its five tones, seventy-six consonants and vowels, and its never-ending sentences, free of spaces between words. But there are no articles, no prepositions, no tenses. No past or future. Just now.

Her eyebrows arch and her head tilts. She has trouble saying it too. "*Tom yum gung mai sai gung?*"

I nod. I know what she's thinking: Does this girl really know what she's saying? Spicy *shrimp* soup without the *shrimp*?

Still, she lifts a notepad from her apron, scrawls a line and dashes into the kitchen.

I keep to the edge of my table, smoking and staring at the wall, a Buddha shrine, pictures of the king, soft drink posters and banners in big Thai letters.

Four months in, the ritual, the pageantry, the honoring of gods and ancestors and other lives, it enchants me still. I believe it always will.

Thai words. Thai words. Thai words, says the husband, setting down an ashtray and a Coke. He stays there, at the side of the table, talking and pointing at things. He rocks on his heels and waits for me to nod.

I nod and sip my straw.

He carries on. As far as I can tell, he does the least amount of actual restaurant work here. He prefers, or maybe everyone prefers for him, to spend his time entertaining guests. Three men in green uniforms step into the restaurant. His attention shifts to them, cackling, cutting each other off, knocking the table with twiggy fingers. I'm trying not to look at them, or at the street, where my students could see me sitting here, by myself, smoking. It's quite acceptable here for males to smoke but not women, so I try to be discreet. Back home, in Medicine Hat, almost everyone I know smokes, and even in 2006, it's still allowed in bars and on patios like this restaurant, which has a roof but only one wall.

On my second cigarette and the middle of an exhale, the wife sets the bowl in front of me. Her palm pauses over the steam: it's hot.

I nod. "*Korp khun mahk ka.*"

I want to hang my face over the bowl for a minute, let its juices steam into my nose. Instead, I hover over it a little and inhale. Lemongrass, kaffir lime leaves, chilies, waft around straw mushrooms in an orange-red broth. I have to suck it off the spoon. Soup spoons are more like little ladles you're not meant to put wholly into your mouth. The soup stings my lips, warms my throat and courses through my insides, waking everything along the way. I choke on the chilies' heat. Gulping almost half the Coke, I set the bottle down quietly. I don't want anyone to think I can't take it. I love *tom yum gung*; I just need to get used to it.

When the wife comes back to my side, a rubbery straw mushroom lies on my tongue. She studies my progress and smiles. This is the first of dozens of bowls she will make for me. Her *tom yum* is my new chicken noodle.

"*A roy, mai*?" she asks. Delicious, no?

"*A roy mahk ka.*" Very delicious. After "thank you" and "hello," the Thai teachers taught me how to say *a roy*. The "r" is unrolled with the flick of the tongue, the "oy" sound carries, rises, then ends suddenly. Thais show they care for someone by feeding them or saying their food is delicious. In fact, instead of saying hello, they most often ask, "*Gin lao*?" Have you eaten?

The wife laughs. The sister is now beside me in an apron and rain boots. The wife tells the sister about me ordering *tom yum gung* without *gung* and points at my shrimp-less soup. The sister steps in for a closer look and laughs while dropping more ice in my glass. I feel them standing over me, as if their hands are on my shoulders, as if I belong. They retreat to the kitchen, clucking.

What compares to women taking you in with soup and laughter?

FEELING LIGHT FROM the family and their broth, that night I pray to God: *Please bring me a friend. I'm lonely and I need a friend.*

The next morning I'm yanking underwear out of the washer as quickly as I can when the apartment manager, a woman I simply call *Pii*, waves me forward, shouting, "*Falang, falang! Falang!*"

With my macabre imagination, I picture a white twenty-something male in a pool of blood, stabbed in the neck with a pen by a jealous Thai girlfriend, a student. I'll be asked to call the embassy and his mother in England.

I step out into the courtyard nervous about having left thongs and push-ups unattended since some of my students live in the building. *Pii* is rocking on her cracked heels next to a tall girl with legs like wiener-roasting sticks.

Staring at the ochre tiles, she brushes the sweat off her pale forehead. The baby hairs around her face stick out like bent broom bristles. When she lifts her head, our eyes meet and we smile.

"Hello," I say.

"Allo," she says. "You speak English?"

She resembles a pale, blue-eyed doe. She's also braless and her long, skeleton fingers look like they belong to an old lady. She's wearing a cheap skirt from the market, quite similar to the potato-sack fabric one I own.

"Oh. *Vous parlez français, non?*"

"*Oui,*" she says, and laughs, continuing to speak English while I continue trying to speak French. I was kicked out of French in ninth grade because I started coming to class high and giggly with a girl who was cooler than me. But I've always adored this language. In fact, when I was sixteen I went around spelling my name the French way, Nathalie. And I took up learning French again in college.

I laugh too—I am just so happy. I'm not sure why she's laughing.

We manage, between the two languages, to discover she teaches French at the university. My university. Her office is a few doors down from mine. She's been here almost three months. Somehow, we've missed each other, there and here, in this building, where she lives on the floor above me. She's from Paris. Her name is Cécile and we're having dinner together tonight.

If I could just stop smiling.

Cécile points to the top corner of the building. "I will go to my room."

My fingers point to the laundry room.

We part.

Pii stands back, arms crossed. Beaming.

When I get up to my room, I hang my laundry on the line above my bed and light a cigarette. A white curtain scrolls down a window in a room where the family lives, above the restaurant. *The family*. They were trying to tell me about Cécile that day when all I heard was *falang* and they kept pointing up and down the *soi*.

I perch over my little piece of Bangkok—the smoke of frying chilies rising through corrugated metal roofs—and exhale through the screen as if I am a fairy, sprinkling the neighborhood with the dust of joy. Everything looks brighter.

AN ANT IN
MY BED

"SOMETHING UNEXPECTED" IS the subject heading of Zora's email. That phrase, it's used only to tell one thing.

Zora is on week two of a six-month trip around the world, a graduation present from Lois. Right now, she's in Australia. She's supposed to be in the sun, but she spent yesterday at the doctor's office in Sydney.

She starts the email by telling me about all these awful things that have been happening to her mom. First, Lois's sister died, then her dog was diagnosed with diabetes and might have to be put down. A few days ago, Lois slipped on a patch of ice and couldn't drive herself to the hospital. Zora feels guilty she's not at home.

Then she says, "And I'm pregnant."

Oh my God.

"Yes, you read that right."

Oh my God.

She thought she was late from traveling and the time change. But she just took a test. And she saw a doctor. It's Drew's, her on-and-off almost boyfriend of six months. It happened about two months ago during a ski trip in British Columbia over New Year's. Of course, she didn't know that until now, two weeks after she set off on a months-long trip she had planned to take alone. There, in Sydney, after seeing the results, she was sort of excited, and then she told Drew. He was not excited. After all, they are still kind of young, twenty-five, and not in a stable, long-term relationship together, never mind ready for the stresses of keeping a small human alive and loved.

Zora. Pregnant. *Pregnant. Zora.*

I check the clock. Twelve minutes before I have to go to class. *What should I say?*

When we were fourteen-year-olds at the Top Hat Bingo day care, I was drawn to the little boys who liked playing tag and getting into general mischief. Zora preferred to rock and bottle-feed the babies. *She might be a good mom.* My high heels slide off my feet and thud on the floor, waking me from a daze where my teary eyes can't leave those words on my screen. What I've learned is, you just never know what you'd do in a situation until you're in it. And you don't know that that thing you've been wanting or not wanting is already a part of your story.

Eight minutes. My chest and my fingers get hot. I don't know what to say. She's alone, in Australia. I want to help her. Grow wings—heavy, white wings I can use to scoop her up and carry her to the sky. Sit on a cloud and sort this out together. Tickle her arm and make a plan.

Five minutes. I click REPLY. I tell her I don't know what to tell her. I know what I think, but that's different from what I can say. I tell her it sounds like the idea of a baby doesn't seem so bad to her. I tell her Drew's being honest and she has to consider what he's saying. But, I tell her, neither of us grew up with a father and we're fine. We are fine. *We are fine.* I tell her I love her and I'll love her however things turn out. And, PS, I tell her

I would live with her in Calgary, help her out when I get back. I want to, if she wants me to.

CÉCILE AND I sit in silence for a few minutes, sipping beers cooled by ice cubes. We inhale, ash our cigarettes and stare at the street. The restaurant is busy today. *Zefamly*, as Cécile calls them, shrieked and clapped when we walked up to the restaurant together. Having seen our separate faces every day for so long, they're practically glowing at the sight of us. To Thai people, happiest when surrounded by others, it's hard watching a girl eating alone, day after day. The family's restaurant is another place where Cécile and I didn't run into each other for almost three months, despite their attempts to tell each of us about the other. I butt my cigarette, trying to think of something to say to her. Two female students swagger on the sidewalk, their four-inch heels almost longer than their skirts, impeding any chance of walking gracefully. About half the girls break dress-code stipulations on skirt length, some shockingly so.

"*Les skirts du les eleves c'est très* short, *n'est ce pas? Mais les pense qu c'est suai*, even on the *kathoeys*."

Suai, beautiful. A word Thais use lightly and revere greatly. Next to having a belly full of rice, here, you want to be beautiful. The sentences I speak with Cécile are often like this, a vomit-purged casserole of three languages, two of which I have no business attempting out loud. Until I met Cécile, I only knew the necessities of Thai: Where is the toilet? (*Horng nam tee nai?*) Thank you (*Korp khun ka*). And Marlboro Light (Marlboro Light). But Cécile told me she was learning Thai, as well as English, and I realized my worries about failing or sounding silly could impair my ability to eat as well as be a friend. So I decide to refresh my French and give Thai a try.

Cécile tilts her head, squints her blue eyes. My sentence grinds through gears and pulleys behind her eyes. Words spit and sputter in my mind too. Sometimes I can feel it, even hear a little elf turning levers and laughing at me for thinking I could juggle three languages, though most people who are raised outside North America can do this as preschoolers. I love her language, though. To me, it *is* sex. And Cécile says the boys in Paris would think *my* accent was sexy. So there's that.

"*Oui,*" she says, smirking. She stands and marks a spot, not far from her nether region, to show me where her students' skirts end.

"I know," I say. We're looking into each other's eyes, giggling and understanding, for now. But there's a lot that goes unsaid between me and Cécile. Here, at the family's restaurant after work, we ask how each other's day was, and then quiet covers us like the sun. It's on the tip of my tongue to tell her about Zora, but it would require too much thinking and translating. It's easier, most times, to keep our thoughts to ourselves. We can stroll along canal bridges and smoke in the fug of old Bangkok's side streets together, but we cannot share what is in our hearts. Alas, just knowing we would share more is enough. For Cécile and me, having a warm body on the other side of the table is already more than we can ask for.

Between the family's house and the restaurant, a sandy-haired puppy with folds of skin draping its eyes waddles off the step. The husband shuffles over and drops a long bean in front of him. The puppy sniffs the bean, his tiny nose sweeping the green stem. He senses us watching and looks up.

Cécile and I coo. "Awww."

The dog must have had puppies. My chair legs screech against the ground as I push myself away from the table to see the stumbling puppy. I catch the husband's attention, and my eyebrows ask, *Can I?*

The husband nods, "*Dai. Dai.*" Can.

Kneeling on my skirt, I run my fingers through the waves of his fur, on his back, on his thin, smooth ears, on the thick bit of skin between his eyebrows. He doesn't flinch or dig his head into my palm. The puppy lies there, trying to chew on a now-shredded long bean. He doesn't smell like a dog yet. Cécile studies us from her chair, blowing smoke the other way.

The husband steps around me with a metal bucket of ice for another table.

"*Pii, cheu a-rai ka*?" What's its name?

He shakes his head. "Mairoo."

"Awww." I take one of the long beans from my *som tum* dish and wave it on the floor. "Here, Mairoo. Mairoo-oooo." His damp, black little nose follows the bean. *Dogs eat these?* He trips twice on the way to my hand.

The husband laughs. He calls the wife, the sister and his daughter over.

What is so funny? I try to find the answer on their faces, then turn back to the puppy. "Oh, you're so cute, Mairoo."

The family is in a fit. The mother wipes tears from her eyes. The sister slaps her leg. The husband nearly snorts and makes a face like he's proud of having made such a funny discovery. The daughter smiles like she's sorry for them, for me.

Pretending it's just me and Mairoo, I smooth the rubbery part of his paws. His wet nose tickles my arm.

ZORA AND THE ants keep me from sleep.

At first I felt the ant underneath my knee. Now it's weaving around my toes.

I've been battling ants in this apartment since I got here. They form convoys and snake from room to hallway to room, along ceilings, under doors, through holes. If I have left a crumb or even nail clippings on the floor, in minutes, a pulsing black line is leading to it. Last weekend I set a piece of butter bread on my night table while I went to the bathroom. I came back out, dropped a chunk in my mouth and sensed their little legs on my tongue, heads bowing along the insides of my cheeks. I spit up the whole ball on the floor and gaped as the ants continued to devour the bread, despite the force of the fall. I threw up and threw the ball out the window, surprised at my poise.

I'm too lazy to turn on the light and kill this one ant on my ankle. I kick for a few moments and hope he'll move to stable ground. Ignoring it, I imagine Zora and me walking down a Calgary street in the snow. It's windy so she folds down the stroller's canopy. The baby, asleep as can be, it's a girl with Zora's long nose.

Zora, who taught me how to roll cigarettes and steal motorhomes. If she could be a mom, I think, is growing up nearly over? How much time do I have? How easily that could have been me, in a pregnancy in a marriage in a house in a town, and sorry for it.

Shaking my face at the thought, I picture Zora, sitting in an Internet café, eyes rowing from the screen to her navel. Chewing on her necklace, debating what to do with this baby.

PART III
MAGIC ROOSTERS

February–November 2006

I DON'T KNOW

PARKING GUARDS' WHISTLES bleat and a raucous gecko calls. I'm supposed to be marking fifty opinion editorials about school uniforms for my English in Mass Media class, but I'm distracted by the sounds, and the chill of the air-conditioning on full blast. I want to check my inbox on one of the dating websites, but there are two teachers behind me who can see my screen. A few days ago I sent a message to someone called Bergundy13. In his picture, he was falling down a flight of stairs wearing a long, red leather jacket, a costume, maybe, for a disco-themed party. He had dark hair and brown eyes. His mouth was in an "o," either because he was really falling down the stairs or he was surprised to be having his picture taken. The one-line pitch beside his screen name says, "Canada to Thailand and nowhere in between." He lives in Chainat, a city north of Bangkok that's revered for its bird park and pomelo fruit. The only other information I have about Bergundy13 is that he's twenty-seven and a Scorpio.

In my note, I said something like, "Hey, another Canadian. If you're ever in Bangkok, we should meet up to reminisce about socks and loonies." Socks, forgone in this sweltering heat. Loonie, the name of our $1 coin. One of its sides features the winged loon, whose haunting call, in some parts of Canada, is the last and only sound you'll hear at night. We also have a toonie.

One of the teachers I didn't want to see my screen now has her head folded over her arms on her desk, eyes closed, nose whistling. Another teacher, Nok, walks out of the office talking on her cell phone, arms stacked with folders.

At my cubicle, I type my password too fast the first time. I have to enter it again and wait for the messages page to appear.

Bergundy13 left a note. He says his name is Noel. Talking about socks over a Singha beer sounds nice, he says, but he won't be around for a while. He's off for two months for the summer holidays, and next week he's heading home to visit family in Canada. He grew up in a small town in Alberta. "You've probably never heard of it," he says. "It's called Medicine Hat."

I choked on my coffee and sprayed my keyboard. I felt a little numb. That sentence, I must have read it at least five times. Eventually, I typed.

"I can't believe you're from Medicine Hat! I choked on my instant coffee reading your email... I was born and raised there."

I mouth his name again. *Noel.* My mind hovers and dives like a bee over the places in Medicine Hat we might have met. The dim, dusty gymnasium floors of high school dances. The coulee above the train tracks where we partied around bonfires. The food court at the mall, its tang of grease. The fluorescent-lit concession stand at the drive-in.

I type some more. "I don't recognize your name, and I can't remember how old your profile said you are, but we must know some of the same people. What high school did you go to? Who did you hang out with?"

The odds, what are they?

All those nights I wondered why I was in Thailand. The truth and pain of waiting slap me like oars. All those whispers, howling now, sailing me off. A sea of thanks and wants below.

I mouth his name, *Noel*. I read those last four words again and again: "It's called Medicine Hat." And I know.

THE DAY DRAGS, and I pass the time with the linguistic puzzle of how to tell Cécile about Noel.

I saw her outside our offices after I got the email. At first my tears scared her, but I was smiling too, so she was confused. "No, no," I told her. "It's good. I will tell you at the family's."

Now, at the restaurant, Mairoo has nested himself in my lap. His jaw grinds against my hip as he nibbles on the long bean I'm feeding him. His belly is sweating, but I don't want to move him.

"So, what is it?" Cécile ejects her words like she has just listened to a tape. When she isn't really practicing, I would give my bottom row of teeth to have *her* accent, sex parading as sound.

"Yes. Today, in a *courier-electronique*—is that how you say 'email'?" No, I better stick with English.

"*Oui.*"

"I received a message... from a man."

"Oh," she smiles and leans in, her bare, bony elbows making a shadow on the table.

Last weekend, sitting on pillows in the loft of Saxophone Bar, somehow, above the drums and despite the barriers of strange languages, we spoke about men. She told me about leaving Paris. And a man. Perhaps married to someone else. She misses the man. And what she calls *affection*, a polite word, I believe, for sex. Still, she is heartsick.

Every inhale, even still, is a reminder she breathes on streets he does not walk. Worse, that all this time, this distance, it hasn't mattered. Worse, that she would have him again. And again. Her eyes are sallow with it, wading, like the silt and twigs and shit at the shore. Waiting, but not ready yet for the tide to take her back, become lake again.

Thinking of her, her plight, I pause. But I've already started. So I continue. "He is in Thailand, but he is from my same town, in Canada. It's very small, but we don't know each other."

A motorbike skids past, dampens our ears. Its trail of exhaust, off like my heart.

"His name is Noel."

"Ah," says Cécile. "It's like you, like Natalie."

It's true. "Noel" is the masculine form of "Natalie." When I was about eight, I liked looking at the "Meaning of Names" section at the back of my special edition of *Webster's Dictionary*. The spine was the width of my palm, and the pages were dusted in gold paint so that from the side it looked like a gold bar in a brown box. I felt smart and special with it open on my bed and studied its insides, mostly the back, where the maps and lists of presidents were, particularly during my phase of infatuation with the United States. I remember my heart jumping when I found my name and it said something like "Natalie: the birthday of Christ. Masculine form is Noel, meaning Christmas."

I love Cécile, speaker of this beautiful language of masculine and feminine word forms, for understanding this. She squints, biting a finger, thinking about the rest. The unlikeliness of it all. Closing the curtain in her mind, I imagine, on frames of that man kissing her nipples, paving lanes on the wall with his eyes when he told her, texting her as she stepped on to the train on her way to Charles de Gaulle. "It's good, Natalie."

I feel flush again and my cheeks are sore.

NINE O'CLOCK AND still, it's hot. Four hours after my afternoon beer with Cécile and telling her of Noel, I wanted to see the sky so I slipped out of the building, through the tall, creaky metal gate and down the block. I lit a cigarette. None of my students will see me here in the alley. Two cats hiss. Four eyes flicker through rubble. An open window carries the sound of a Thai country song, of yearning and drums. I follow the smoke pushing and parting before the moon, try to rope a piece of the sky. To thank it. Noel and I are under this very same moon, just a bus ride apart.

ZORA. TIME IS running out and she had to make a decision, she tells me in an email.

"I'm going to keep it," she says. "And that's that. Drew might not be happy, but fuck him, right?"

Her note also says she's in Byron Bay, on the North Coast of New South Wales with two guys who have a camper van. She's going to keep traveling, at least for a while, and wait to tell Lois at the airport in April. She's changing her plane tickets tomorrow. Sometime next month, in March, after Malaysia, she'll be in Bangkok. Do I want to go to Cambodia with her for a week?

Do I? Cambodia, it's one of those countries, so I hear, that breaks your heart. Its landmarks are of another world and its people bony and helpless, like cattle. Plus, I'm meant to be working.

I don't know.

IF THERE IS a phrase I should know, it's "I don't know."

I have procured the services of one my brightest students, Thongchai, to help me learn Thai. From a well-off family whose home is sometimes rented as a set for TV studios, Thongchai is way too educated to be in my class. But instead of griping about the easy lessons, he helps his classmates and even me. When I decided to really try learning Thai, I thought of him. In exchange for my lessons, he asked, "Can you teach me to sound cool, really cool?" I agreed. This is Lesson One, in a café on campus close enough to the hotel pool to smell the chlorine. His longtime girlfriend, Wipawan, a girl from the South with curly hair, is perched beside him.

I try to ignore a bug bite on my calf and pose my first question. "Thongchai, how do you say, 'I don't know'?"

"*Mai roo.*" His words, as sharp as his white school uniform shirt.

I examine his lips, pressing and parting, then forming the "o" of a kiss.

"*Mai,*" he says, then points to his cheek, "*Roo.* This sound is more like an 'l,' *ajarn.*"

I try the phrase.

Thongchai reads my lips, listens to my tongue. He shakes his head. "*Roo.*"

It sounds like the "r" is being held, clicked or vibrated, then flung by the tongue like dirt.

I try again. "*Mai roo. Mai roo.*"

He's grinning, eyes widening as if to say I'm getting it.

"Oh God." My ink-scented palms brace my mouth. Mairoo, the puppy.

"*Ajarn?*" Thongchai tries to read my face. "Did you forget something?"

I tell Thongchai about the puppy. Mairoo, who trips all the time and likes to lick things. Mairoo, not the son of a *soi* dog, Bangkok's scarred and starving strays, but of a bean- and fish-fed house pet who has free rein over a restaurant. I thought he was such a smart dog, running toward my white legs when

I called out his name, "Here, Mairoo. Good boy, Mairoo." I remember the befuddled look on the husband's face when I asked about the puppy's name, and he replied, "*Mai roo.*"

SMILE

ZORA JOGS TOWARD me like a peacock with a limp. She has never been athletic and today a twenty-pound backpack is strapped to her waist. A Thai broom bounces behind her head, a fan of straw almost the same shade as her braid.

I am fifty feet away, under an awning. She's here. In my arms.

My chest caves, my face crinkles, tears fall. We stand like this for a while, panting on each other's shoulders. I haven't seen a familiar face in seven months. For Zora, it has been two. We step out of each other, wipe our eyes and laugh.

She chucks her backpack on the chair. "Jesus, do I ever have to pee."

Zora struts off, blond hair swaying, tanned shoulders arched, as Zora as ever. I am somehow now older than her, though in 1981, she was born in January, and I in July. On this street, this café, where I wandered on my first Bangkok morning, my chest was so tight with worry. But I kept wandering, and day by day, my worries fell loose.

When Zora returns to the leafy, quiet courtyard of a restaurant lined with white tiles and yellow walls, she tells me Singapore was boring and people in Malaysia glared at her.

"I don't know how they wear so many damn clothes. It's bloody hot," she says, fanning her tank top.

Explaining propriety in Southeast Asia, particularly the Muslim South, would be a lost cause.

"God, how are you wearing that?" she says, wiping her hands on her flowy black capri shorts.

I'm in work clothes, a white collared shirt and jeans, a luxury I am permitted now that classes have just ended for the summer holidays. We all continue clocking in, marking, prepping for next term. Teachers in other departments are a little more lax about their schedules, but not us, which is another reason why I hesitated to ask for a week off to go to Cambodia. When I did, though, they agreed.

To get to Khao San Road to meet Zora on my lunch break, I took one of those rollicking green Number 56 buses. No fans. No doors. You almost have to jump while it's teetering around the corner to get off because I don't think they even have brakes. But I didn't want to be late.

Zora sucks all of her pineapple juice in one sip, licks her lips and proceeds to tell me about a tall traveler from the Netherlands who kept following her—to breakfast, to the beach—because he was the kind of traveler who couldn't be alone. Traveling afar by yourself, it forces you into corners where, if you can muster even small acts of courage to make your way, you'll discover how extraordinary the world is, how capable you are. I understand now why some seek it and others forsake it.

"I didn't tell him I was taking the train to Bangkok."

She says it the way I used to: *Bang*-kok. In fact, Thais call their capital Krung Thep, a shorter version of Bangkok's ceremonial name: "Krung Thep Maha Nakhon Amon Rattanakosin Mahinthara Ayutthaya Mahadilok Phop Noppharat Ratchathani Burirom Udom Ratchaniwet Mahasathan Amon Phiman

Awatan Sathit Sakkathattiya Witsanu Kamprasit." The City of Angels, The Great City, The Eternal Jewel City, The Impregnable City of God Indra, The Grand Capital of the World Endowed with Nine Precious Gems, The Happy City, Abounding in an Enormous Royal Palace that Resembles the Heavenly Abode Where Reigns the Reincarnated God, A City Given by Indra and Built by Vishnukam.

It's the longest city name in the world. For the hundreds of years it was a mere fishing village and port for Chinese traders at the middle of the River Chao Phraya, Thais also called it Bangkok, Village of the Wild Plum.

"Christ, if I would have told him we're going to Cambodia, he would have wanted to come there too."

In a few days, we are heading to Cambodia's civil war–torn capital, Phnom Penh, and to the ancient temples of Siem Reap. In the meantime, she's going to stay with me, in my two-by-six-foot room on Soi Suan Aoi. I would give anything for us to be able to go out, get drunk, kiss strangers, eat street meat and reminisce about it all the next morning over American breakfast. Alas, my partner in crime is with child.

"Holy hell, am I tired." She yawns, sideways, revealing teeth I wish were still separated up top by a gap, like when we were girls. When she was fifteen, she had the gap filled in, then a surgery to remove her sweat glands, followed, years later, by eye surgery so she wouldn't have to wear glasses on another trip to Thailand.

The baby. She's tired because of the baby. At this table, a third heart beating.

Zora looks away, remembering it herself, it seems. I get the sense she doesn't want to talk about it now, but it sounds like Drew has come around. She will have the baby. They will live together. I won't be needed as live-in aunt, and of course, I'm both glad for them and a little disappointed. I'd already pictured us cooing over baby in the kitchen-sink bath, waltzing the huffing infant in the dark with sore arms so Zora could sleep, frying us French toast on Sunday mornings. From work at that day care and cousins and a niece, I know how wonderful and yet trying it is, taking care of babies. I know being an aunt is a pretty good gig.

"Where'd you get that broom?" I point at its lacquered bamboo spine. "You do know that's a broom?"

"Yeah," she says, craning her neck to see it. "I stole it from a guesthouse. I thought it was neat."

The bristles on Thai brooms are soft and fine, like little girls' hair. Too gentle, it seems to me, to drift dirt.

"Well, let me show you your new abode. You might need a map to find your way around my room, but the walls echo really well, so just shout if you get lost and someone will come find you."

Heaving one side of her backpack around a shoulder, she laughs. Zora has seen the pictures of my ninety-square-foot apartment.

"No, let me."

She shakes her head. "It's fine."

I block her hand, clenching a strap as she shimmies the backpack in place. "*Zora.*" I give her a look: *Please, I want to.*

To my surprise, she lets the backpack slide. I know in her mind she won't admit that it's because she needs help, needs me to be like the big sister for a while. She's telling herself to do this because I'll look funny carrying her dirty blue backpack in my high heels.

ZORA DUCKS HER head until her lips are level with the straw, and sips her iced coffee. "Where are the ones we took at that really big *wat*, when the monks came out at sunset?"

"Thought they were at the front." I file through the blue envelope of pictures. We just picked them up at a shop on Khao San Road. As dirty as this street is, it's good to be back. Cambodia shares a border and an ocean with Thailand, but that's all.

"Here it is." I hold on to the picture before passing it. It was late afternoon. Sweat streamed down my back. We were at the entrance of Angkor Wat, a breathtaking city of ancient temples carved from sandstone. Wading through tourists dressed in every shade of beige, we'd strolled over the canal just as the sun was setting. Maybe because the time-worn charcoal towers were now in the shadow of the sun and the jungle, the four monks in orange robes who sauntered toward the foot of Angkor Wat stood out all the more. It was as if they had been left in color while the rest of the scene was painted black and white. Cameras clicked. *Click, click, click.* Now, on a four by six print, the scene looks rehearsed, the teenage monks talking and laughing about nothing like catalog models. Finally, I hand the photo to Zora.

"Thanks."

Zora studies the monks for a long while. They fascinate her, these men, bald and celibate. I wonder if she wonders what they would think of her, of me. Us.

Zora doesn't look pregnant, not in person or in the photos in my pile. She's tanned and smiling, sunglasses atop her head, the way she's looked every summer since I have known her. I took all of the pictures. The Buddha bodies missing heads. The skinny, white-haired man playing the Cambodian violin on a temple step. The men in green uniforms with their shirts open carrying planks from a temple to the jungle. A little girl who waited with her baby brother on an old-fashioned bicycle, hoping her contrived smile would draw coins from tourists. A tree that had grown over the top of a temple, its roots crushing moss-covered columns.

My eyes are lost in a shot of Zora and me at the end of a day of temple tours, eating dinner in the city.

Songs and conversations from other restaurants along that main, dirt road danced around each other like leaves in a pocket of wind. The chairs were blue rattan with cushions marked by elephants stitched in gold. It was dark. The breeze blew my hair and the leaves on a palm plant. Three cigarette butts, bent and abandoned by ashes that had blown away, filled the center of an ashtray. Zora and I looked content, tired, like people who have just had holiday sex. Only we hadn't. Not that I hadn't been thinking about it, but sex was the last thing on Zora's mind.

"Oh, Rattana." Zora holds up a picture of Rattana, my motorbike driver, standing at the each of the Tonle Sap beach with wet hair and his t-shirt wrapped around his neck. A foursome of locals playing cards under a pair of umbrellas were teasing him. He didn't know Zora was taking the picture. I did. I was swinging in a hammock beside her, studying him.

"Yeah." My mind drifts back to Rattana.

On the way to the lake, a thirty-minute drive from a ruin, I edged myself toward the thick of Rattana's denim seam and rocked, to no avail, as the seat vibrated. He knew what I was doing and when we got off the bikes, he told Zora's driver—I guessed by Rattana's gestures, laughter and the other driver's disbelieving eyes on me—and my face, already flush from driving under the sun, grew red and hot. Rattana either forgave me or didn't mind. But I shouldn't have. My pressing, against someone I was paying and who was driving and had no say, it was just as assuming and desperate and imperial as the acts of those old white men I loathe.

Later that night Rattana "accidentally" got lost on the way to the hotel after dinner. "You want to meet my friends?" he asked. We were at a light. The drone of the cicadas in the trees was louder than his engine. He eyed me in his rearview mirror. I nodded. In a dry field between huts of houses, we sat with three of his friends, drinking rice wine and eating fish smaller than toes. And I saw my reflection in the glass, a girl brave enough to be here but still, somehow, too quiet to say out loud, what I really want. Aunt Cindy told me, "Someday that'll go away. Someday you'll stop giving a shit. Just watch." But I'm not sure. It's still as if I'm hollering into the wind.

"Speaking of which, have you heard from any of your boyfriends lately?" says Zora.

This is the most Zora and I have spoken in a while, in part because Cambodia is a jarring country, a horrible and beautiful world of its own, and in part because we have spent too much time together. The silence started when I whispered "Zora, *don't*" after she plunked her feet on the headrest before us, next to a Japanese man's ear, as our minivan crossed the border into Cambodia. "Don't tell me what to do," she snapped. Zora was crabby. The driver wouldn't turn on the air-conditioning so we opened the windows all the way for air, but that sucked the shale from the road onto our skin so our sweat was dripping red. Still, I couldn't let her leave her feet like that. Asians believe the head is sacred, never to be touched, and that feet are the bowels of a body, never to touch another person. Plus her feet stank and it was just rude. Anyway, she got mad and I got mad and we didn't say anything to each other for a few hours. She left her chubby, rose-tinted toes next to the Japanese man's neck.

Even while we waited to pick up the pictures at an Internet café, we were barely speaking. Zora surfed online and I spied on a Thai girl in the next stall who was making sexy poses in front of a webcam for a pale young man on the other screen. They said nothing for twelve minutes, their grainy faces suspended, shifting. And yet this is more than I can say for my love life.

"I have, actually," I say, more sad than proud of this fact. To three men, I type about things a couple might discuss if they were to actually see each other in the flesh. A man in Vancouver.

Nit, that half-Thai once-actor who, I suspect, counts me as one of his several girlfriends (a few dates in, he told me he'd been in a few Thai films). And Noel, the Canadian from my hometown whom I still haven't met.

"Noel sent me an email. He'll be back in Thailand next week," I say, thumbing the ashtray and recalling his note about returning with his brother and sister-in-law next month to tour them around the country. "But then he'll be busy for a month or more."

"And you really never met him? He worked at Earls. Remember going to Earls for wing Wednesday? He worked there forever. I knew Jon, his brother. But then I went to Hat High." Zora switched high schools two years before graduation in favor of a more active social scene on the other side of the river, where Noel and his brothers had gone to school.

"No. I mean, his last name sounds familiar, and I think I met Jon once at a party. Actually, I know I did. I can see his face. He had gorgeous blue eyes, didn't he?" *Had* because he died, a few years ago, of cancer.

"Yeah."

"And his Lee jean jacket." I don't know why I remember meeting Jon so clearly. My smile fades and I resume spinning the ashtray. "But no, not Noel. Anyway, he doesn't seem terribly interested. Probably has a Thai girlfriend."

"Well, if things get bad enough," Zora says, eyeing my thighs, "maybe you could just say, 'Hey, help a fellow Hatter out.'"

"*Zora.*" This is the pronunciation reserved for her blunt and embarrassing comments. I'm not sure I ever have the chance to say her name another way.

"Well, Nattie, cheers to us," she says, and raises her empty glass of iced coffee, eyes glistening.

"Cheers."

I wish I could make Zora stay.

HIS KEYS ARE still in the door as he holds it open for Song and Tida.

I'm already two steps into the room. It's on the fourth floor, a corner room, 215 square feet. All but one wall is lit by the sun. The bed is a double. The wood furniture is brand new. The walls still emit the tin of fresh paint. "I'll take it."

Tida, one of the BE teachers, gasps. "Natalie. Already?"

My approach to traveling, life and flats, as of late, is to take a running dive.

Song and Tida and I were on our way back to the university after a special birthday lunch for *Ajarn* Fah, held at a restaurant a few blocks away from campus. I mentioned that my lease was almost up at my room. Tida said she'd seen a banner hanging on a new building on her way to work. It's on Thanon Prachatipatai, the road that becomes Thanon Ratchasima, where the university is. The Chinese son of the owners was sitting on a bench, the soles of his blue Crocs tipped to our waists as we pulled up.

He opened the door to one of the last apartments left and I knew I'd soon fill it with the few things I have—a torn gray suitcase, the green scarf from the family and sun-worn photos puttied to a mirror. Bangkok is no longer the place I ran to. It's home.

Song and Tida ask about water and utilities and locks while I look out the side window at the gilded pagoda of Golden Mount, gleaming in the distance.

A BOY'S SOAPY fingers graze my gums. A chalky film pools on my tongue. The street, it's like a demonstration.

"Here." Song passes me a folded strip of Kleenex.

"Thanks." I'm bent over and wiping my eyeballs after three palms smothered stinging white paste from my chest to my forehead. Icy water smacks my forehead. I look up to see two more teenage boys laughing and running backward with empty buckets in their hands. The paste streams into my ears.

I have to smile. "So, this is *Songkran*?"

"Yes," says Song, still dry from the shoulders down.

According to the Thai calendar, which began with Buddha's birth 543 years before Jesus Christ, today is April 14, 2549 (not 2006), the second of three days celebrating the Thai New Year with a festival called *Songkran*. On how the New Year came to be a countrywide water fight, one story says *Songkran*'s origins began a thousand years ago as Thais gathered to celebrate the start of a new farming cycle on the fifth full moon of the lunar calendar. Scented water—a symbol of cleansing and renewal—was poured over the hands of their elders to pay respect and make merit.

Yesterday, in the office, a golden bowl filled with jasmine water and white petals was passed among the oldest teachers. *Ajarn* Nand ambled in, sat down and eyed my tobacco-stained fingers. My turn. I had watched Song lifting the bottle of a perfumed liquid above *Ajarn* Sinn's palms, pressed together and almost touching the water in the bowl. Song gave a long *wai* and passed the bottle to me. "Come on. Do not be shy," *Ajarn* Nand said. These teachers, they feed me. And I eat, like a sparrow at seed. I didn't understand the ritual but I knew it was special, both on its own and because they'd asked me to partake. I hesitated. I feared I'd drop the bottle on his toes or spill the water on the tablecloth and curse the BE department for eternity. Eventually, I tilted the bottle and watched the water trickle across *Ajarn* Nand's fingers and sift into the bowl. The fragrance filled the room. All was still. When the last drop fell, I raised my hands and made a *wai* to him. If my eyes hadn't been closed, they would have seen my tears.

Now I have to shut them tight so I don't go blind.

"Falang! Falang!"

A steady pelt of water hits my armpit, my mouth, my eyebrows. Fingers smear paste on my hair, my chest and my cheeks. Even my underwear is drenched. I glare and block hands, but I can't swat them all off. They want to get me, dig fingers into my skin, because I am white and tall and live in an apartment with a concrete roof? Or do they just want to touch my breasts? That's probably it, the breasts.

"It's OK, Natalie," says Song. She didn't know I'd be attacked. "Come here."

She pulls me to the sidewalk, out of the mosh pit of teenagers with water buckets and guns and bowls of muddy paste on their way to Khao San Road and the fair at Sanam Luang. Song, who sits with me on wooden benches for hours on end at the stifling immigration office every eleven weeks. Song, whose fingers warmed my shoulder the night of the *Loy Krathong* festival, the November night when Thais make a wish and release lotus-like floats made from banana leaves into the river. I'd asked the goddess of rivers to reveal why I'm here. My float sank, and quickly. Song said, "Maybe next year will be better, *na*."

Tonight, she passes me more tissue, then steps back to take a picture. We're still on Thanon Prachatipatai, two blocks from my new room. On this street the buildings, once homes to palace friends, are grand, three-storied, a soft yellow. It's midafternoon, bright, and the road has a veneer of wet. Everyone behind me is drenched, dripping soggy chalk. I half smile. In the shadow of drying paste, it's hard to see out of my left eye.

"What is this, this white stuff?" I ask, scraping a cloud of it from my forearm.

"To protect you. A kind of blessing. But, they should only do it here," says Song, cupping her cheek. A few weeks ago, she cut off all her hair, just because, she said, but now she looks less a girl, and more the teacher she wants to be. She is saving to go to Australia, like Tida did, to do a master's degree in an English-speaking country that's warm and to return as one of us. I know already, perhaps better than anyone, that she will be a good teacher: smart, firm, fair. These academic-minded women are so focused; marrying, if ever, is something they say they can do later. There is no talk of gentlemen, not ever and not today.

On the way to a street-side café in the *Songkran* battle zone around Democracy Monument (four yellow wings in the center of a traffic circle meant to mark the 1932 coup that led to constitutional monarchy), truckloads pass with water guns and barrels of melting ice. Under the restaurant's awning, we are safe for a while. A few feet in front of us, a man is selling red and purple bowls of paste powder. His son, a plump, naked boy of almost three, prances around the table, sucking on a pasty plastic bag. A ray of sunlight bronzes his belly and lights his white, chubby cheeks. How wonderful, to be a bare-bummed child at the feet of your father on a sunny afternoon. How different from that other New Year celebration, the one in the living room of the house I shared with Stuart, the spinning reels of friends—downing shots, chewing steak, talking shades of wall paint—that flared a spark of want for nearly a year before I actually left. It took a while, but here I am, a world away, white muck crusting around my ears and a bra growing soggy.

And yet I can't help but feel like I haven't completely arrived here. Or that some-thing hasn't arrived for me. That getting here was just the start.

THE THRONE

I'M NOT SURE I want to know her. Her posts are misspelled and nothing is capitalized, not even her name, pippa. But she needs a friend, and so do I.

Cécile moved back to Paris a few weeks ago. She didn't want to extend her six-month contract and left four hours after her last class, not even waiting for the deposit on her room. The difference between us was that she missed home, and I didn't. Still don't. (What does it mean when we don't miss home?) When Cécile was packing up to go back to France, I was in Cambodia, and through a final episode of miscommunication, we didn't get to say goodbye. Now, in a new apartment with wireless Internet, I spend nights in the flicker and glow of my laptop, online. Tonight I'm on a forum for *falang* women living in Thailand. My post yesterday asked members if they knew anything about Nit's tattoo, the name inked around his nipple. Which probably has more to do with a girlfriend than any goddess. The replies say they don't know as much about Hindi Buddhism (Nit's current thing) since most Thais follow the Theravada line of the religion, but I'm probably right: he's a cheater. A lot of girls gripe about being cheated on in this forum. Thai men are not a loyal lot, but they don't see it like that. They come from a long line of men who have always had more than one woman. King Rama V had thirty-six wives and concubines, seventy-seven children. Philandering partners are the top complaint on this forum. Next is being single, followed by thieving nannies.

Pippa's posts were different. The first one asked if anyone knew how to go about taking care of an unwanted pregnancy in Bangkok. The second post, which appeared several weeks later, asked if anyone knew if it was OK to do something about a second unwanted pregnancy so close to the first. In addition to wandering eyes, Thai men are known for refusing to wear condoms.

Pippa replies to my post about the tattoos and I recognize her name. A few emails follow. She tells me she has been in Bangkok for two years, working as a jewelry designer/exporter. She came here for Korn, her boyfriend, whom she met in the South on holiday. He studied art at Silpakorn University, but now he sells t-shirts on Khao San Road. She feels sorry for the girls whose boyfriends cheat. Korn never has. I tell her I don't have any friends. She says she doesn't either; girls never stay long enough. We agree to meet for a drink.

I EXPECT PIPPA to be blond and frail, dressed in something funky but professional, like a linen suit and chunky wooden jewelry. So when she heads toward me, wearing a denim mini-skirt and her dark hair undone, my hand covers the chair.

"Sorry, someone's sitting here."

She steps back, confused. "Natalie?" Her British accent chops my name down to two syllables, *Nat-lee.*

"Oh, sorry, Pippa." I stand. "Nice to meet you."

As I lean toward her to hug, she is still except for her head, popping out to kiss my cheeks. Her cleavage comes between us, along with her damp hair and the scent of a fruity shampoo.

A boy in a red shirt waits behind us, paper pad in hand. The café is draped in flowers, lace and pink, from the floor tiles to the wallpaper. It's the retro little sister of a bigger artsy bar around the corner. It feels like we should be having tea in a little girl's bedroom about thirty years ago.

Pippa inspects my drink, a half-empty iced coffee. "Can I have one of those?"

"Ice coffee, OK." The waiter, whose forehead reaches Pippa's nipples, bows and ducks out of the room.

"It's so hot," she says, tugging at the neck of her top.

"I would have thought you'd be used to it by now," I say, forcing myself to look at her eyes, little and blue, rather than her breasts. Too big, they seem, to belong to her diminutive head.

"Some things you never get used to, do you?" She pulls her hair to the back of her neck and places her bag, made of denim and torn near the zipper, on her lap. It covers most of her pale thighs.

"I don't know." I'm wearing jeans and a fake black Polo t-shirt along with fake suede flip flops. "I don't know if I could ever go back to being cold."

She crosses then uncrosses her legs. "That's true. The sun is nice."

Nice things. Nice things. What are some nice things we can talk about? Over the last nine months, I've spent so much time talking to myself—or superficially, in shreds, with Cécile—that I forget how to talk to Western girls my own age.

The waiter returns and sets down her coffee, the ice topped with a violet orchid.

"It's lovely how they do that, isn't it?" Pippa lifts a hand from the side of the stool where it had been and lifts the flower out of the glass. She rolls the stem between two fingers, spinning the petals.

"I know. Can you imagine how many this country goes through in a day? I went to an orchid farm a few months ago. It was like this enormous greenhouse, just filled with orchids. All orchids. Just for decorating drinks." I can't remember the colors of the flowers or even the smell, just the dozens of blank CDs hanging from strings above the soil to deter pests. Orchids, grown so easily here and so much a part of the Thai way, to make all things beautiful.

"That sounds lovely." Her body is hunched. Her voice is soft. "I should do something like that sometime. I never do anything."

Pippa never does anything, she goes on to say, because she lives here. For the most part, she deplores tourist activities and tourists. She doesn't spend time with anyone but Korn. She works alone, from home. There are always girls at the shop, the table and two walls where Korn and his friends sell clothes, but Pippa can't stand them.

"It's hard not to be condescending when you're talking to some of these girls who have just been back from Koh Samui for the first time and they talk about it like they're from there or something. And they're just so critical of how Thais are, or they think they *are* Thai even though they've only been in the country for, like, eight days." Pippa pauses, gazes out the window and spots just these sorts of girls thumbing through paperbacks at a book stall.

"But a lot of people don't know what it's really like here, you know, what goes on when you stick around for more than a month," she says, taking her eyes from the lane below back to the ice in her drink. "Anyway, I get really tired of talking to tourists."

Now she looks tired, older. I wonder what she thinks of me. Am I naive too? Pippa knows more than I do, but I think she wishes she didn't. And even though regret has tiptoed across her face, I also see the shine of someone who has been brave, who left. In my mind, I try on her life—her real apartment with a kitchen sink, her live-in Thai boyfriend, her business. Do I want that? Surely, if I stay, this is how things would go. And I think I do want that, more than what I left at least.

Dolly Parton's voice crawls out of a speaker. "It's 'Jolene'!"

The thunder of country music always reminds me of Stuart, but even more, of hungry hands and home. "God, I miss country."

"Do you?"

"Yeah." I'm blushing. She thinks I'm a hick. "It's just nice to hear something else. I think this might be the only bar that plays more than Jack Johnson and The Cranberries."

She nods. "Oh, I just block it all out."

This is what you have to do, if you want to keep your sanity and stay, at least around Khao San. The very things that enamor many on holiday—the lack of lineups at toilets, the lackadaisical pace, the rain, the elephants on the streets—become the things that make your skin crawl when you live here and you're sober and you're trying to get things done or get somewhere, through the crowds and the traffic, and you always suspect the taxi driver or the shop owner or the local you just slept with isn't telling the truth, intentionally or otherwise.

But Pippa can't picture herself anywhere else, ever again.

A couple in matching fisherman pants, the uniform of travelers in Thailand, slides into a table across from us. The girl's hair is tied up in a greasy, messy bun. The guy has his arm around her, leaning in to see the images on a camera she's flipping through. We hear its button beep again and again.

"Do you come here often, then?" Pippa smiles as she asks, skinny, spaced apart teeth hanging from fleshy gums.

"I try not to." I'm starting to get annoyed by the same things as her—tourists and shop owners who treat me like a tourist.

"But I have been a little more lately. I just moved and my building's not far away, so it's kind of easy."

"I'm here a lot more than I want to be too, because of Korn. They just work so long, and, like, seven days a week. If I didn't come here, I'd never see him."

Thais do work long rather than hard, and my ethnocentric mind once saw this as inefficient, and yet they always seem content, where, in my old day job as a reporter, I was often red-faced, fingers shaking, chest aching with pangs of anxiety.

My mind darts from an image of Korn working to an image of them in the bathroom. The wand. The stripe. The questions. Pippa, fraught, unsure. Korn, turning his head. Pippa wipes her temples.

It's not me and I won't be righteous. Because I've never been there. Ever since Calgary, or even that Christmas Eve, when I discovered I didn't like people pegging me as someone I was or wasn't without knowing why, I've tried not to judge a choice but see all the befores, the give-ups and the go-ons and the found-outs that led to that choice. Everyone has a story. Everyone has stuff.

"It's the sixtieth anniversary of the king's ascension to the throne." My tongue slows midsentence, trying not to get stuck. "Or something. Next week."

"Is it? I'm so out of it."

"Yeah. I just found out I get a five-day weekend because of it. Which is good because I really need to get out of Bangkok." I tell her I'm thinking about going to Koh Chang. It's an island still relatively undeveloped and far from the full-moon parties of the southwestern coast. I want her to say she wants to come along. Later, she does, knowing even less about me than she does about King Bhumibol.

In June of 1946, Thai people were told King Ananda was dead, that he must have been playing with his pistol. His younger brother, Bhumibol—eighteen and known to the public as Chaofah Waen, the bespectacled prince—accepted the invitation to become king. But for much of his reign, he would try to live like a country man. He built a one-man boat called OK Dinghy just so he could be alone. He took as many pictures of his people as they took of him. He planted seeds on farms and sought ways to make rain. He smoked sometimes, Lucky Strikes. He was a musician whose jazz compositions were played by the likes of Benny Goodman and whose saxophone could be heard on Friday nights along with the Aw Saw Band on the king's radio station.

Wall-length photos documenting his life as king form columns around street corners near Ratchadamnoen Avenue as part of the sixtieth-anniversary celebrations. Lights blanket the trees, a bulb for each leaf. Gold streams over intersections like a rainbow. Because the king was born on a Monday, associated in Thailand with yellow, on Mondays everyone wears what's called The King Shirt: a yellow golf shirt with the elaborate anniversary crest of gold, green and pink. For months, the entire country will wear this same shirt. I have one too. In fact, I bought a second knockoff at the market so Pippa and I could wear them while we party on Koh Chang.

A YELLOW LAMP strung from a mangrove bough, like the setting sun behind my hair. The sky, quite blue and getting so very dark. The ocean, tumbling toward us.

"Move this way a little," Pippa says, waving me to my right. "So I can get it in."

It, the lamp shaped like the sun. I lean over so its glow is even with my head. My smile is gentle. My eyes, off and away, give the illusion of candidness. My hair, wavy from the beach and the heat, blows across my cheeks and my chest. My left leg trails the arm of the chair. In a brown tank top and short denim shorts, all my bare skin shows gaunt under the light of the lamp.

"That's quite funny, actually," says Pippa, eyes fixed on the sun-lamp.

After an overnight bus trip and then a ferry ride, we made it to Koh Chang, Elephant Island, so named because from a certain angle it looks like the mammal, lying down and drinking in the waters of the Gulf of Thailand. Elephants are not native to Koh Chang, but they're on the island now, used to take tourists through some of its eighty-four square miles of virgin forest. No one lived here until the mid-'80s, when malaria was wiped out and construction bans were lifted. We are at the south end of the island, at the Tree House restaurant, suspended over the water like a pier. A fallen fork would land in the arms of seaweed. The floor and the furniture are made of sun-dried wood. The only thing that isn't wood are the ashtrays, plastic and green. I'm filling one right now.

Exhaling, I bend down to get my camera out of my purse. "I better take one of you."

Pippa wraps her hair around one side of her neck. "Oh, all right, then."

She leans forward so the camera won't see her stomach. Her cleavage takes shape under a black tank top. In the background, a shore of wet rocks and the water meet, a thatched and weather-matted roof's straw sways, and a mile of bush between this resort and ours makes that end of the island look empty. Pippa looks away, as if it were a candid photo.

A Thai guy in a red windbreaker and baggy jeans swaggers past our table, his eyes tracing the railing like he's looking for something.

"Hey, are you...?"

"Pippa!" He says her name Pip-*pa*. His heavy lips part and big, paper-white teeth appear. "How are you? How is Korn? I have not seen him for many days." He speaks with the sing-song cadence of his language and the formality of a student.

"Korn's good. Busy."

"My name is Nung," he says, his chest and mouth thrown into his name. "Do you remember me?"

"Yeah. I just couldn't remember your name. What are you doing here?"

"Oh," he says, taking one hand out of his pockets to rub his forehead. "No good. Bangkok, no good." He knows how to say what happened, I think. He just doesn't want to. We can only guess—a fight, maybe trouble with the police. He hopes that we'll feel sorry for him anyway, and we do. "But, however, I am here in Koh Chang selling my lamps for a while."

Nung points to all the lamps, our stand-in for the sun, a green cylinder-shaped one draped over a fence at the entrance and a big blue ball in the center of the place, below the Tree House treehouse. Everyone reaches up to touch it, the white plastic pieces weaved around each other and leaving just enough holes between their ends to let the light of a colored bulb filter out.

Pippa's face darts around the restaurant. "Those are yours? They're lovely."

"Thank you. If you want to buy one, I will give you a discount."

The "s" in discount is left out. My ear is always listening for these nuances, and now, as a teacher here, I understand that the Thai language doesn't force the tongue to entwine two consonants.

"I am here selling every day. I stay here, at Tree House."

Short but stocky with a wide nose and long hair, knotted by an elastic, Nung is attractive to me in some way. His build, his eyes, his lips. Willing Nung to look at me and failing, I stand.

"Do you know where the bathrooms are?" I ask.

"Just over there." Pippa points past the bar area. "It's kind of down a ways, but there should be a sign."

My eyes follow her fingers.

"Don't forget your sandals," she says. "You don't want to go in there with bare feet."

For a toilet that is essentially a hole in the ground, this is the prettiest one I've ever seen. A blue bowl lays at the center of four rock-laden cement walls. Seashells and plant stalks are placed around the flushing water (as with other outdoor toilets, you have to reach into a tub and fish out water with a plastic bowl to flush). It's dim, the roof is low, the ground is wet and it smells—of stale water and all the things human bodies dispose of in bathrooms. I take a picture.

On my way back, I pass twosomes and threesomes spread over their mats like toddlers at naptime, eyes lost in the sky, swaying to the slow, knocking music called trance. Pippa isn't at our table. She's kneeling at one nearby, talking to three heads whose faces I can't make out. It's dark now.

"Hello," I say, standing behind Pippa and leaning on a rail.

Pippa turns sideways to see me. "Natalie, this is—"

"Liliwen." A girl with short, curly hair, thick cheeks and bright blue eyes smiles at me.

"Sorry." Pippa covers her mouth. "I'm crap with names."

"That's all right," says Liliwen, setting down her drink.

"Hi," I say, then reach down for my glass.

With her hands directing me, Liliwen says, "And this is Molly and this is Yonni. Why don't we... do you want to join us?" Liliwen's eyes dart from mine to Pippa's. I glance at Pippa.

Pippa swallows her beer. "Yeah, we could do. Better than shouting across the place."

"Here, I'll just..." Liliwen reaches for a cushion from another table and moves her own over. Now she's at the end of the table. "Molly, could you—?"

"Yeah." Molly moves in next to Yonni. Molly has a strawberry-blond bob and freckles. Yonni has glasses, dark skin and even darker ringlets of hair that end at his ears. They all have British accents.

Pippa and I set our umbrella-dressed drinks beside each other. She sits sideways on her mat. I sit cross-legged with my knees underneath the table. They brush someone else's feet.

"Sorry."

Molly grins and shakes her head, then exhales away from the table, past Yonni's ear. Yonni's smoking too. He only made eye contact when Liliwen introduced us and now his eyes are fixed on his hand, tapping away on his jeans.

"Now, Pippa, you live in Bangkok. Natalie, what about you?"

Night falls and we drink. We learn that Liliwen, Molly and Yonni are teachers at an all-boys international school on the outskirts of Bangkok. Pippa and I will call them The Teachers. The island is filled with them. We dance to rasta and rave music along with the wind. We smoke and fall and do shots and shout, "What's that?"

I gaze at Nung, sitting by his lamp display, and hope I'll catch him looking at me. That doesn't happen so I walk up to him with an extra drink and ask him something about his lamps.

Later, his chapped hands hold my ankles as I climb the ladder into his hut.

In the morning, we begin again. I can see his face now, ponytail unraveling, forehead sweating, eyes bleating like he's angry, like he's trying to prove something. Our sweat mixes, makes us glide. His legs are just too smooth. Amidst the sounds of birds and waves, we hear two girls, laughing. "Look, it's shaking." The hut rocks on its stilts. Inside, Nung holds himself, short but round, like a tuna can. "Have you ever seen one like this?"

The next three nights on Koh Chang are the same. Days are spent on the beach with the teachers. Lying on the sand, I read Tom Robbins's *Even Cowgirls Get the Blues*. I feel like I could be friends with Sissy Hankshaw and her oversized thumbs. In fact, my party trick is to show people my double-jointed thumbs, bending them until they reach a 90-degree angle. Truth is, everyone loves underdogs, but not outsiders. Outsiders remind us there's another way.

On the ferry back, I meet a girl from Ontario who broke her leg and sees my book cover, the naked blonde straddling a goose crossing a blue sky.

"Aren't his metaphors amazing?" she says, shaking her head. She looks like a girl I used to play basketball with, a wannabe hippie who wore beige and parted her sandy hair in the middle. My mind drifts, to the dust of a high school gym floor, the bubble and chlorine of her hot tub the night of her twelfth birthday, the eight of us, flush, on the cusp of masking freckles with makeup, wearing boxer shorts over our swimsuits, wanting to not wake up.

"Yeah," I say. "I kind of can't believe I haven't read Robbins before."

So many things I wouldn't have known. Wouldn't have ever known. Wouldn't have.

Nung nods and smiles at her, like he knows what we're talking about. Nung is going back to Bangkok too. I'm not entirely sure if it's for me, or if he was thinking of going back anyway. But we are both on our way there now. And I must be doing this because I want what Pippa has. Or because I am incorrigible. Or because I can't say no. The girl looks at him, then me. Folds up her questions. This is the part of the relationship I get attached to. And this is the part that's apt to get me into trouble.

COCKROACHES
AND CANDLES

I FEEL SEASICK, STILL, or again, as I perch my feet on the foot slides and straddle Nung's motorbike. I sweat with the heat of the bike and his thighs against mine. As we pull out of my building's parkade, the security guard—a tall man with a tiny head—yells at Nung, pointing at the street with the mouth of his whistle. I think I hear the word *fon*, rain. Nung waves him off, feet paddling the bike toward the darkening sky.

A wind circles my neck. The first drops alight on my knees and dry in the next blink.

"Nung, it's raining."

He lifts his hand off the gas and flicks the air, the worry in my eyes. I can't see his face, but I know he's grinning.

Like Zora, Nung thinks I think too much. I have known him for about a month now. I suppose you could call him my boyfriend. He stays over most nights and drives me to school in the morning. I wanted him to get a taxi driver's vest so no one at the university will know I'm dating a lamp seller. In my colleagues' eyes, it would be bad enough for me to be alone (and worse) with a man I'm not married to, never mind a peasant.

Nung told me not to worry, the teachers will never see him. I am wicked, wanting to disguise him. I am young.

At a light, he turns his head to me.

"Do this," he says, motioning for me to put my arms around his waist. His face pouts and begs. "Please."

We watch each other in the rearview mirror. I shake my head, hands firmly gripped on the bar behind me, above the license plate. On the sidewalk, a fruit vendor cows under an umbrella while he pushes his glass-encased fruit cart. A wet sandal slides off his foot. Water streaks the glass. The pineapples and watermelon appear as a pink and yellow moss. Beside us, a woman in a nurse's uniform drapes a newspaper over her head and I imagine the ink getting wet, becoming dye, dripping all over her dress.

Now the rain is beating our backs. Like the other people on motorbikes, I glance at the sky as if the clouds could declare how long the rain would last. Soon our shirts are soaked. The water has risen on Si Ayutthaya, a main road on the way to Nung's house, near Victory Monument. Cars spray our knees.

"Nung, you can't—"

"One more street, OK?"

I leave it alone, for now, because Nung's machismo is seductive and because, in truth, I'm drawn to the danger of riding motorbikes in Bangkok. The way outlaws get there faster by breaking off from traffic, inventing routes. Trusting themselves and their bikes, firing around roads as if under chase. I drove a scooter when I was fourteen, and I rode through town with my jean jacket flapping in the wind, imagining everyone else thinking how cool I was.

Nung's tires get tugged as we weave through currents of water. Worried that if I turn my head or breathe the wrong way the bike will topple, I cling to his damp t-shirt. Only my eyes move, from white runners too big for someone as short as Nung to the policeman in a poncho blowing a whistle and eyeing us. Nung either doesn't notice or doesn't care about the officer's stares. His last girlfriend was British and for more than a year they ran some sort of business acquiring and then selling clothes made in Cambodia.

"Look," I plead, pointing at all the other motorbike drivers pulling over beneath the skytrain.

Stopped at a light, Nung balances the bike by resting a foot on a crossing block. In a week, he will get into an accident on Si Ayutthaya, not far from this corner. He will be on his way home from selling lamps near Khao San Road at two a.m. He won't know what happened. The bike will fall out from under him. He will crash to the ground and land on his ribs. Blood from his head will stain the pavement and mat the part in his ponytail. He will come to and think no one is around. Then a shadow, a boy, will appear and try to snatch his wallet. Unable to move, he'll cry, "No. No, don't. Please." Lights will appear. A taxi. The driver will scare off the thief, find Nung's phone and make two calls: one to emergency, one to me.

The light turns green. He drives at the edge of the lane, so slowly and in so much water that he has to use his feet as rowers.

"NUNG."

"OK. OK. But you will be absent for your appointment."

He heaves his bike onto the sidewalk in front of some shops and we look for shelter under their roofs. There are others here, a young mother and her son in matching boxer shorts, a teenage couple flirting with their eyes, and an old woman dressed in a dirty sarong, twirling a plastic bag of steaming rice. They take turns peering at us, wondering what the arrangement is. I used to get off on that, the looks. But it's starting to wear and I just want to tell them: I'm lonely and we sleep together and he drives me to work. Yes, it is selfish. But I've also drawn up inventory charts, and profit and loss spreadsheets for his business. I write English emails to his Belgian customers. I ask if he's eaten lately. We both give a little, take a little. Still, it's not right, offering just half of yourself, knowing it and staying anyway.

"No good," says Nung, hands on his hips, eyes lifted to the sky, dark like midnight.

Ignoring him, I turn away from the street to face a Chinese jewelry shop and a uniform store. *Why isn't anyone under the awnings? Idiots.*

We are on our way to Nung's neighborhood because there's a salon on a *soi* near his building where he can get me the Thai price. For most things, there is a Thai price and a *falang* price. The Thai price to have my hair straightened is 800 *baht* ($23). Here, most women have their hair chemically straightened in a three-hour reverse perm process.

I'm starting to resemble Thai girls. So skinny now, and quiet. Soon my hair will be long and flat as well.

I ran and I ran because I didn't want to follow, and now, here I am, a pale little redhead trying to be Thai. It should be easier, when we're far away, to be who we are. But it's not.

Sitting on a cement step next to a window of brassy gold and Chinese letters, I begin to roll my soggy pants and shake the water out of my hair. The rain and the fumes have left a film on my face.

Thunder stretches apart the clouds, sends down its showers.

"*Oi*," shouts the boy of the couple, clutching his girlfriend's purse. She smiles at him and they continue eating sausage on a stick, dipping the fleshy links in a dark sauce at the bottom of the bag.

A finger taps my shoulder.

I turn around to find the old woman, nodding at my neck. I search her face: *What?*

Her dark, brittle fingers climb the air around my shoulder.

I look to the left and right. Nothing. Then I feel it, shuffling up my spine.

Dozens of cockroaches are crawling out of a crevice in the cement steps I'm sitting on. My scream, as shrill and uninvited as the rain.

Nung, jumping to me, flicking the cockroach with his finger. Another, scaling my scalp. The black, bristly legs of dozens more, skittering away from the water, and up. Up my shoulder blades, my arms, my neck, my hair, my ears.

"Nung! Get them off!"

Every appendage twitches. Nung plucks cockroach after cockroach off my skin, throws them by their antennae, batting in the commotion. The Thais gather round.

I pant and moan, lips pursed in fear they could crawl into my mouth.

"Gone," says Nung.

I give my head a rattle.

"Really," he assures me, circling and surveying me.

When I open my eyes, I see the old woman, legs swaying, smirking.

AS I BEND down to blow out the candles, I realize Song can see the greasy crown of my hair. I didn't know when I had it chemically straightened that I wouldn't be able to wash it for three days. Plus, I lied to the hairdresser and said I'd washed it that morning. So this is day four and my part is almost dripping. My ends are stiff and smelly, of ammonia and woks.

Luckily, the scent of sulphur and candle wicks cloaks the room. There are six candles, and as Song lit them with matches, I remember the last office birthday. After *Ajarn* Tan's candles blew out, the wax barely melted, I made the mistake of shouting, "Oh, no boyfriends!" Somewhere in her fifties, I think—it's hard to tell on Thais, they hardly age at all—*Ajarn* Tan always wears lipstick, her bobbed hair tied half back with bows, and bright Thai silk jackets. She speaks with a bellowing voice that contradicts her diminutive figure and her age. "That is what you mean, that I have no boyfriends because I blew the candles?" *Ajarn* Tan's eyes pulsed. I thought I was being witty, joking about her—the head of our program and a spinster—having a sweetheart like a teenager. "Back home little girls say this," I told her. Post blow, for every candle still alight, a boyfriend. She took a breath and smiled. "It's all right," she shouted, tightening the scarf around her neck. "I already had a love of my life."

Today they are singing Happy Birthday to me. Classes are over for the day. It's late afternoon, and muggy. *Ajarn* Som, in a pale green dress, stands beside me. *Ajarn* Petch is away at another campus, but a few weeks ago she took me for dim sum in Chinatown, and then to meet the father she still lives with, who owns some of kind of Chinese curios shop. He looked ancient, like a tortoise—puckered lips, neck in twists, so slow— and nodded my way between clocks and stacks of newspapers. These women, beyond filial, and Victorian in their ways. So very, very at odds with the bar girls.

Other than *Ajarn* Soon, *Ajarn* Sinn is the only one who is married. Her husband works in one of the government buildings nearby. I was asked if I wanted to give a few English lessons to him and a colleague; often they ended up being too busy, but when we did have a lesson, he was so quiet and attentive, as if I were his elder and truly a teacher.

Ajarn Sinn's phone holder necklace, a gold-stitched butterfly on black cloth, dangles from her chest and over a chair at the other end of the table, which is meant for a boardroom but acts more like a family's kitchen table. Above its glossy veneer, we gossip, console students, drink instant coffee, read the paper and eat fruit off toothpicks after lunch.

They sing it a little differently, but the last line is the same: "Happy Birthday to you."

"Sa-mile," says Song.

A flash goes off and she scuttles to the other side of me for another shot.

Sucking in air, my ribs graze the elastic of my skirt. *Blow, blow, blow* them all. I bend farther, hair falling. In Song's first picture, you can't see my face. The candle flames extinguish, become smoke. All but one.

"Natalie, there is a boyfriend, I think," says Song.

The others snicker. Flushed, I hover over the flame and blow and blow and blow again. The flame blackens and the wick smokes. I reach for the knife, resting on a plate of leftover pineapple slivers. In Thailand, you must cut your own cake, and this seems right to me now. You get yourself from twenty-three to twenty-four, in a car on the Number One, on a jet with a one-way ticket, in a taxi at two in the morning. And then you get yourself from twenty-four to twenty-five, on Number 56 buses, Marlboro cigarettes and hope. The knife slices through the chocolate-covered strawberries, white icing and stacks of chocolate before scratching the cardboard square under the last layer.

"Here, *Ajarn* Sinn. This is for you." I pass her the first piece.

She stops tucking her shirt in, holds her palm out for the glass plate and thanks me.

Twenty-five. Almost one year ago, I boarded a plane to Bangkok with little more than guilt, Zora's gifted vibrator and a cloud of maybes bobbing in my chest. I wanted to be telling the truth the next time I said, "I'm happy."

I bite my lips as I pass slices of cake to Soon and Tida. These teachers, they call me little sister. My thoughts are in Thai. Pippa, Molly and Liliwen, my friends. This country, it set itself out for me like the tracks of a train. It took a while, but I finally feel like I live here, like I know where I'm going.

Eight days early I opened the birthday package my mom sent. Inside the box were all of my requests: two bags of ketchup chips, some Hanes boy-cut underwear and a box of Kraft Dinner, which I will have to make at Pippa's or Nung's since I don't have a stove. My mom will be glad to know I had a cake. On my eighth birthday, my mom was filling up our minivan with gas before driving me, my little brother and at least five bathing-suit-clad little girls out to Echo Dale, a man-made lake near the river. As she opened the back door, something shifted—a floatie, maybe, or the bags of chips, and my store-bought chocolate cake tumbled over and splattered on her thighs. "For Christ sake," she yelled. Or maybe even, "Fuck sake." All the other little girls gasped. I followed their lead, pretending I wasn't used to such cussing. But I get it now. She just wanted me to have cake. My mom always made sure I had cake.

"So, did you make a wish?" says *Ajarn* Som.

Chewing, cake pinned to my throat, I nod.

ECONOMICS

SIX DAYS AFTER my birthday, Noel notifies me and the others on his mass email list that he has joined Myspace. I scour his page, inspecting photos of Noel, holding an infant tiger beside a bespectacled monk; on a boat, back to the ocean, the blue colors hyper-saturated.

I send a note: "Love your photos! Glad to see you've started a blog. Wish I were as dedicated as you are."

In my first flat and in my first weeks here, I wrote and wrote and wrote about Bangkok and uploaded much of that writing to my blog, *Natalie's Dawn*. And then I moved to a flat slightly bigger than a bathroom stall, got Wi-Fi, found friends and took up drinking again.

He replies: "Wow, are you still in Thailand? Man, time flies."

"Yes, still in Thailand. Busy with a new semester. Seven sections times about forty-eight students. I'm bad at math, but I know it works out to a lot. Too much. Come to Bangkok! That beer you said you'd have with me is long overdue."

He replies: "Yep, that beer is in order. I'm going to Chainat this weekend, but I could possibly rip into Bangkok for a night..."

FRIDAY AFTERNOON: A CALL. I'm marking papers at the Victory Monument campus. Stepping outside the office so the other teachers don't hear, I lean on our third-floor railing overlooking the student courtyard and say, "Hello?"

"Hey," he says.

His voice is a bit raspy. Heavy, yet gentle. The curl of his words, like home itself. It's the first time we've spoken on the phone, so I try to ignore the big-hearted tone that says it before he does.

"Doesn't look like I'm going to be able to make it."

The picture of the night I have imagined—us across from each other at a table, tipsy, laughing under patio lights—it flickers, fades. Maybe we'll make plans another time, maybe not. It's already been months since we first connected, and I'm starting to wonder if we'll ever meet. Maybe he has a girlfriend. Maybe he's just not interested in me.

"Hey, no worries."

Below, a group of students is getting ready for another one of their festivities. Three students, on their stomachs, color a poster. Two girls and a *kathoey* rehearse the dance moves for a Tata Young lip-sync entry. She's a half-Thai pop star, and from the concrete, her music—in English, about dressing too sexy—blares.

"What's going on over there?" Noel asks. "A little Friday afternoon dance party?"

I roll on my ankles and a heel slips out from under my foot. Two students pass me and *wai*. "They're rehearsing... for one of those... things."

He knows what I mean. Every week, it seems, at any school in the country, there is some kind of contest or game day or celebration of a god or a king or a Buddhist event. Stages are erected. Dances are performed. Songs are sung.

"Nice. I got to be the judge at one of those last week. A singing contest. Two hours long and twelve of the twenty girls—twelve of them, not kidding—sang that Céline Dion song from *Titanic*. Good old Céline."

Two days after *Titanic* opened, I saw it with my dad in Medicine Hat. He was in town, visiting. I would have been embarrassed to be at the movies with my dad, but it was dark, the late show. The lineup outside The Monarch went all the way around the block. Winter breath and all the things we could have said swayed above our heads like an old lady's skirt.

Behind Noel's words, I hear a creaky, rocking noise.

"And what are you doing?" I'm trying to keep him on the phone in hopes he'll hear how amazing I am, change his mind and dash to Bangkok. "What's that sound?"

"My hammock."

I hear fingers flicking the wheel of a lighter.

"Really. In the middle of a school day?" I want my voice to say, *I'm fun and witty. Couldn't care less that you're not coming.*

"Yeah. One of the dudes that works here, a Thai teacher, he lives behind the school, so he lets me come back here and just chill when I have a spare." He inhales. "It's pretty rad." And exhales.

The *kathoey* imitating Tata shakes his hips twice one way, twice another, then leans down and shimmies.

"Lucky."

When the conversation ends, I stare at the screen on my phone, as if it has failed me.

HALF AN HOUR passes before we get to the lesson. It's been weeks since Thongchai and I last met. Above the library in a room with space-age-looking white plastic seats and rounded walls, we catch up. His family has been going to Hua Hin a lot because his nephew likes riding the ponies on the beach. He and Wipawan are looking for jobs. I don't teach Thongchai anymore. I have all new classes this semester, including two sections of diction and speech. I love this class. All I have to do is talk. Every afternoon, about fifty nineteen-year-olds study my lips and teeth and tongue to see how the athletics of the mouth achieve "r" sounds and "l" sounds. Last week I concocted what I think will be my best teaching tool, a diagram of a head drawn on a sheet of transparency and a red shard of felt that acts as a tongue, flicking and folding on the projector screen as we move through the double-consonant section of the workbook. *Sp*-o-*rt*. *Pl*-a-*st*-ic. For once, even I understand the workbook. Now the students laugh with me as well as at me. They stay awake, forget the clock, ask to have their picture taken with me after class. These students want my voice and my skin so much that I confuse it for adoration, and bask in it. I think I might stay.

"How about you, *ajarn*? What did you do lately?" He's still in his university uniform, but one button around his neck is undone.

Lately I went to Cambodia with my pregnant best friend. Lately, I found Noel. Lately, I made friends, some really great friends, on Koh Chang. Lately I have a sad, immature relationship with a lamp seller. I sigh. "Oh, a little of this, a little of that."

Thongchai grins. He brushes the hair that's crawling over his ears.

I unfold a square of paper. I've made a list of the words I wanted to ask Thongchai about. Before, Thai was a stranger and I wanted to keep it that way. Now, as I learn one word, "want," and another, "September," and another, "why," I think I've found a friend. When I reach for a motorcycle taxi driver's spare helmet, I look him in the eye and I say, in Thai, "Right at the United Nations, left on Thanon Prachatipatai." I tell him to slow down when you see Wat Tritosathep, and to stop beside the old Thai Hotel, the pool end. "How you sa-peak Thai?" they ask sometimes. I smile. "Ben *ajarn*." I'm a professor. In effect: I live here.

"Thongchai."

"Yes?"

"What is the word for 'milk'?"

I've been wondering about this for a while. Since most people don't have fridges, sometimes you'll see students with tiny plastic milk bottles bought at convenience stores or street stalls. I don't think they even sell actual cartons of milk here. AJ, the American who used to teach here, thought Thailand's lack of milk intake prior to this decade is the reason why we see so many hunchbacked old ladies. I kind of miss milk.

Thongchai looks down at his papers. "*Ajarn*," he says, then stops and takes a breath.

"What?" My fingers are wrapped around my jaw, eyes on his.

"The word is *nom*. But this is the same word we use to mean women's, uhhh…" He sighs, then resorts to sign language. His fingers, spread apart, wave over his chest in a circle.

Ahh, milk is the same word for breasts. Well, that makes sense.

"Oh… OK," I say, and with any other kid my face might have gone red and I might have switched topics, but Thongchai feels more like a friend. I am only three years older than him, and although I find most students about five years behind their Western counterparts in terms of maturity, Thongchai is an exception. He is still innocent, though, his brown eyes filled with wonder and lacking worry. How old was I when I lost that look?

My mind swings on this new knowledge. *Nom* means milk. And boobs. "Oh God. Fudge, fudge, fudge."

"*Ajarn*, what? What's wrong?" Thongchai's brown eyes bulge.

"I just remembered something that happened last week with the word *nom*." Why, why, why did I wait so long to learn Thai?

Over the next two minutes, I recount for Thongchai an episode from last week's diction and speech class. It was about syllable stress and I was using the word "economics" as an example because none of the vowels make their alphabet sound (when the letter "e" sounds more like *eh* than *eee*) and because it has all three kinds of syllables: stressed, unstressed and reduced. The stressed syllable, the one that's said longer and more clearly, is nom. So I said to the class:

"Repeat after me: 'eh-kuh-NOM-icks.'"

Forty-eight voices replied: "eh-kuh-NOM-icks."

They didn't have it. "Again: eh-kuh-NOM-icks."

Louder, they tried once more. "Eh-kuh-NOM-icks."

But they kept saying that syllable like "gnome" rather than "nawm," like their *nom*. "Stop. Repeat after me: 'Nom! Nom! Nom!'"

Laughter.

I gave a glare.

Forty-eight voices echoed, "Nom. Nom. Nom."

"Now try the whole word again."

But most of them were laughing so hard they couldn't talk. I thought they were laughing at me. See, I'm funny. Aren't I great?

I'd been asking a class of twenty-year-olds who have the maturity of twelve-year-olds to listen and repeat: "Boobs! Boobs! Boobs!"

Thongchai is laughing. It's a girly laugh. "*Ajarn*, I think they will remember you for a long time."

MOLLY CHUGS TWO-THIRDS of her Long Island iced tea and tosses the glass on the table. "Not strong enough."

My phone buzzes. Molly and Liliwen look over.

I set down the phone. "Nung."

They nod.

"Does he want to know where you are, again?" says Liliwen.

"Of course." Nung doesn't like it when we're apart. He wants to know where I am, who I'm with. He wants to come here, but I tell him no and begin a vague text about being out with the girls. I don't think about how it would feel if things were the other way around.

"My students were absolutely doing my head in this week," says Molly.

I look up from my phone and smirk.

"Spoiled brats, all of them. They don't know any of the answers and they just stare at my chest the whole time. It's like, yeah, look at my tits, you little twats. Now, can you count to twenty?"

She giggles as she talks so I can tell in class she was probably more amused by her students than upset with them. She'd be the pushover aunt who'd buy your cigarettes. I suspect she started smoking before she was even a teenager. Molly was the sort who hiked up her skirt on the way to Catholic school. At twenty-six and as the youngest of her seventy-year-old parents' three children, Molly was a mistake. Born to a mother who was a nurse and speaks Queen's English despite a common life, and an Irish father who worked as an elderly care aide, Molly tested her parents' waning patience with substances and boys. When she got tired of those and of a boyfriend and of going to the pub every night after her thankless job as an office receptionist because her literature degree was useless, Molly suddenly knew last year she had to get away, far away, and responded to an ad to teach in Thailand. Molly, Liliwen and Yonni all work at an international school for boys who are rich and coddled and not very bright, despite their parents' illusions about them. They get paid three times as much as I do.

We all spend our paychecks and our Friday nights at a bar on Khao San called Hippies. We end up on Khao San every weekend.

We complain about the dirty and ill-informed tourists all the time, but we keep coming back. We can't afford the expat bars.

Here at Hippies, an indoor/outdoor bar with '60s decor—green couches, Warhol-style portraits, Doors' music—the waiters know us by name. We consider it *our* bar, and share it with contempt. We understand it's a public place and there is an owner who is trying to make money; we just wish they weren't so eager about it. Because this is our bar and we are not tourists, we do not, ever and no matter what, hit on the waiters. Though most of us would like to most of the time.

Before Hippies we usually eat at one of two places: Ranee's, which serves the most beautiful pizza in the world, or the Israeli place, which we have never known the name of, and which serves a mouthwatering, heaping plate of shawarma. These are also places we begrudgingly share with tourists. After Hippies, we often go to Dong Dae Moon, a second-floor outdoor bar where you can play pool or sit on picnic tables and listen to house music and pop songs by '90s groups like Oasis. A lot of teachers and the Khao San boys who work around here hang out at Dong Dae Moon. We also frequent Shamrock, a second-floor indoor bar where bands play live music and where a lot of locals hang out. Post-Hippies, we indulge. Flirt and dance and end up on a table. Show off the little bit of Thai we know with a crew of Khao San guys who sell leather, jewelry and t-shirts. They are the bad boys, a gang of fake dreadlocks and enough English to pick up girls ("How long you be in Bangkok?"). They have no concept of commitment or time, and a brotherhood that permits them to live like the Lost Boys. Every day is Saturday. If one has money, they all have money. No bank accounts. Three- or four-letter nicknames like Mitt. And the girls who've been around awhile know why not to get caught up with them.

IN THAI, NUNG'S name means "one," firstborn. His parents are beside his bed, in brass frames and brown paper that make them look old, never mind their wrinkled, tired, teeth-missing faces.

"This is my mother and this is my father," Nung declares. His voice is soft, drowsy, perhaps, from the pain medication.

I bend down to look closer.

"Every day, I must to do this." His hand waves over their shrine—the frames, a bowl of pink incense sticks. "I must to pray to them. You too."

"Nung, I don't—" I wanted this to be a short visit, hadn't wanted to come at all. But Nung was just in that motorbike accident, and I thought I ought to. Seeing him like this, out of it, blood seeping from cheesecloth bandages on his head, makes me feel woozy and guilty all at once.

His wet eyes beg. This means something to him. "Follow me."

So I do. Soon this part of his apartment is smoky with incense and we *wai* his parents' images, then pray.

I open my eyes long before he does. I glance at Nung and his tightened lids, then his mom and dad. How can he pray so hard to people who abandoned him?

Nung was a temple boy, left on the white steps of a Bangkok *wat* one day during rainy season. The monks who took the toddler in gave him an orange burlap robe and taught him the alphabet. They let him walk among them, barefoot, bald and brow-less. When he left the *wat*, he only wanted long hair. When I met him, it was in a ponytail. "It makes me more handsome," he said. Thais still use old-fashioned English adjectives. To the girls, yes, Nung's hair makes him more handsome. To the tourists on Khao San Road, where he sells leather bags and plastic lamps in his "shop" (a red blanket on the ground), he is cool. To the other guys who sell things, like misspelled t-shirts, charcoal portraits and paperback books, he is bad. Think twice, that ponytail tells the world—the backpackers asking for a discount, the police waiting for rent, his minions, who go on noodle and beer runs. That ponytail, it says he didn't go to school, he doesn't have a boss, he has twenty-nine brothers (friends) but no family. His ponytail, frayed from his motorcycle helmet, says: *I am One and I am not the same.*

I shouldn't say Nung has no family. He has a sister who ran off with a *falang*. Now she lives in Sweden and she's not happy. Nung wants to save up to bring her home, but it would take him thirty-six years to earn the airfare.

Nung makes a *wai* to me. "Thank you."

When he does that, it reminds me we have this thing where it's like he's a bellboy and I'm an old lady, and we're using each other. And we're wasting each other's time and I should bloody well know better.

Sitting back down on his bed, the headboard shelf a plate of candle-wax tears, Nung stares at his parents with his cheeks in his hands and sighs.

I want to ask what happened to his mom and dad, but it has been only four days since his motorbike accident. Also, I need to break things off.

This was a boozy tryst that went too far. So far for a moment I forgot my promise to not settle for sevens, even here, even now. Even here, even now, I want a partner who reads novels and newspapers, and wants to discuss the meaning of life. Is that too much to ask?

Also, the affection has become one-sided, and the more I see that and step back, the closer he comes. There's a side of him I don't know, can't know. And that scares me too.

I take a breath, and I say, "Nung, listen..."

BACK IN MY own apartment, I'm marking papers on my bed when Molly calls.

"Hey, Moll."

"Hello, honey," she says. "You all right?"

"Yeah. How are you?"

I stand and walk to my window with knees sore from using them as my desk. Eyes even with the gilded pagoda of the Golden Mount, a bell atop a mountain, I wonder how many men helped get it up there. Rama III gave up on it. The ground was too soft to stand the weight of all those bricks. Rama IV, King Mongkut, carried on with the construction of the edifice, bringing in 1,000 teak logs to fortify the mountain. Today you have to climb 318 winding steps to get to the top. There, where the tapering spire is blinding to those standing inches away on the landing, is a gallery of Buddha's relics, including a genuine shard of bone. In the 1960s, Golden Mount was one of the highest points in the city.

"Yeah, I'm all right. Bit hungover. So?"

"He's OK. His head is all bandaged and his room smells like old blood. But I think he'll be fine."

"And?"

At the Golden Mount's foot, below the staircase, is Wat Saket. Once it was called Wat Sakair because the temple was surrounded by *sakair*, small trees bearing seeds that were used to kill skin-invading worms. Returning from Laos in 1782, Emerald Buddha in hand, General Chakri stopped at the *wat* for a ceremonial bath before moving on to Thonburi. Then the temple was renamed *saket*, washing hair.

"I broke it off."

You leave someone a little bit each day, and then in a breath. Like packing, over time, for a long trip. And then it's dawn and the taxi's headlights trinkle down the block and you're thundering down the stairs, puffing, patting pockets, suitcase wheels clacking. Like you could miss today and the rest of your life entirely, even though you've known about it for ages.

She pauses. "What did he say?"

"Oh, it was awful, Molly." He cried, and I don't know how real those tears were. But he knew too.

"You did have to, didn't you?"

"Yeah, I did." I sigh, fan the neck of my shirt, damp. "God, it's hot in here. I'm just sweating."

My eyes shift back to the Golden Mount and Wat Saket. Below this dazzling yellow bell, such horrors once. For many years, the grounds were a crematorium. In 1897 the explorer Maxwell Sommerville wrote of it: "No matter how carefully we walked, we stood upon the ashes of human remains. Most of the flesh had been consumed, and dogs were there to gnaw their share from scattered bones."

What does it do to the DNA of man to set hips alight, ingest charred skin, trample ashes? What does it do to the DNA of dogs to carry traces of their masters, the sick? What happens when you bait, take, enrage a man already spitting mad for having to live like a dog?

There were gut-eating birds too; vultures, hundreds of them whose claws, along with the scorching cinders, killed the branches of the tall silk-cotton trees. To appease the appetites of their favorite birds, caretakers threw choice limbs at them. During the reign of Rama II, a plague brought 30,000 bodies—many carried out of the city walls through Pratu Pii, Ghost Gate—to the birds' beaks. Then it was the penniless who burned here, their bodies lying, as Sommerville writes, on "pyres built of sun-baked cow dung." The departed who left money had the oils of coconut sprayed over their corpses to "hasten combustion." Bones became a powder that never blew because there was no wind.

I suppose we all step over people at one point or another, but I ought to tread carefully.

BANGLAMPHU

OUTSIDE HIS SHOP, he leans against a pane of ad-splattered concrete.

Standing on the sidewalk, I wait until the light down the road goes red before stepping on the street. I look left to watch for oncoming cars and we catch each other's eyes.

He smiles and nods at me, hands folded behind his back like a hotel porter. The man is old and missing one of his two front teeth, but he still oils his thick, dark hair. Still keeps a plastic comb in his pocket. He stands there or sits on a stool all day, watching traffic, nodding at neighbors, making change for customers. The bed he and his wife sleep on is just behind the freezer, which also serves as a TV stand. I refer to him as the old man, and his face is now the first I see every day.

Smiling back, I adjust the briefcase on my shoulder and remember walking with my mom on the path behind our house in Medicine Hat. I was maybe eight or nine years old. Along a cliff overlooking Riverside, the ribbon of concrete wound around cacti and tumbleweeds and the Teeoda Lodge retirement home. We passed a man wearing a fedora sitting on a bench, his cane resting on planks of wood etched with initials and hearts. My mom smiled and said hello, then turned to me. "Gotta smile, sweetie. Especially for them." Them, the seniors we stack in boxes with green walls, oxygen tanks and TVs. "Might be the only smile they get that day."

In my old neighborhood on Soi Suan Aoi, I had the family. Their chatter and their shrimp soup without shrimp and the puppy I called Mairoo. Now that I don't walk past their tables every day, I don't see them. Now I see the old man.

The light turns red. Motorbike exhaust tingles my legs. In an hour, I will scratch my leg and a brown-green film will curl underneath my nails.

Tiptoeing in heels around tires, I dart to the other side of the road. Just as there's a chance to go, sometimes the national anthem starts. It's played on loudspeakers everywhere at eight o'clock in the morning and six o'clock in the evening, and if you're walking, you must pause. If I'm halfway across the street when it starts, I scuttle on. If I waited, wedged between a truck and two buses and a motorbike, they'd run me over when the light turned green. My bus-stop bench is just outside Wat Tritothsathep and its school, so I wait for the Number 12 watching boys and girls in blue shorts being corralled into the gates by grandparents. The elderly don't live in old folks' homes here. They live with their children and their children's children, whom they mind while the others work. I have to take the Number 12 today—not the coltish Number 56 bus—because on Monday mornings I teach a class at a satellite campus near Victory Monument. I've gone there this way dozens of times, but today, for some reason, I'm seeing the route as if it were the first time.

A chesty woman whose wet hair is tied back in a banana clip stomps down the aisle carrying her change box, a metal cylindrical thing that rattles with coins. Her job is to watch for new faces and collect fares.

She's hovering over me. When the bus jerks to a stop, she grabs the torn corner of my seat. The smell of dust and foam rises. She catches my eye and her raised eyebrows ask, *Where to?*

"Anusawari," I say. Victory Monument. Handing her the change, I notice her legs, hairy-dark all the way down to her rolled white socks.

She hands me a ticket and moves on, snapping the mouth of her change box.

Outside my window, I watch kindergartners whose handkerchiefs are safety-pinned to their chests, women walking to work with umbrellas over their heads to block the sun, zoo staff on their way to its entrance in yellow, floral-print shirts. It's not even eight o'clock and the sun has thrust itself on everything— the hoods of cars and little girls' noses. My hair is warm from the window. Beside me, a woman in a short-sleeved pink blazer is slumped on my shoulder. Thais sleep so easily.

Having just passed my university's main campus, the bus is about to stop at Soi Suan Aoi, my old neighborhood. I look to see if I can spot the dad or the mom or even the puppy, but it's too early.

The bus lurches on.

I turn my eyes to my hands, tanned and veiny, so much older than they were a year ago. Once, when I was on acid with Zora, I thought I had an epiphany about hands—that we wear rings and paint our nails pink so our fingers look pretty, but the palm, this is where the story and the beauty is, the living, in all the blisters and scars and people held and lost. Zora said, "Oh! We should write that down." I think we did.

Soon enough the bus is at Victory Monument, the six-lane traffic circle around which hundreds of vehicles are always inching or charging. At the edge are four quadrants where buses stop and shops sell everything from noodles and t-shirts to pedicures and drip coffee. A freeway ramp rises in the distance and massive concrete towers mark the skyline. Hundreds of feet above the bus is a walking bridge and the snaking underside of the skytrain tracks. In the middle of it all stands the monument, built in 1941 to commemorate a brief war with France and the fleeting victory of colonial land in Cambodia and Laos. The core of the monument is a concrete spire in the shape of five linked bayonets (the suggestion of masculinity) and five dark statues representing the army, navy, air force, police and civilian bureaucracy. It was sculpted by the Italian-turned-Thai national Silpa Bhirasri (Corrado Feroci), the bushy-browed man behind many of Thailand's monuments.

When my bus pulls into its quadrant, I let an old lady and two teenage boys get off ahead of me. In front of the Dunkin' Donuts hut, I contemplate getting something doughy and chocolatey. *Nah*, I'll get raisin toast off the lady set up in the *soi* by McDonald's and a syrupy iced coffee from 7-Eleven. After throwing my briefcase strap across my shoulders, I take the stairs two by two. Eighty steps lead to the footbridge that circles the monument and carries people from one quadrant to another. My heels clack on the edges, my ponytail loosens and my knees nearly knock against my chest. At each landing, I pick up speed. There is no reason for me to be smiling quite so wide.

Up top, on the path, I swerve around slower walkers and catch glimpses of the traffic below. A clang in my blood, wings at my chest. That feeling I sometimes get. The world, winking: We're doing this. You're here. You're here.

I pause at the ledge to feel it all the more, let the chord still. I'm having the time of my life.

MOSTLY IT'S BECAUSE of Banglamphu, the district where I meet my friends.

Banglamphu, named after the seventy-foot-tall lumphu tree which once grew in abundance here, is a district of borders. To the west is the Mae Nam Chao Phraya, Thailand's longest river. To the north is Khlong Banglamphu, a canal dug in 1783 by 5,000 Laotian prisoners. For more than 200 years, restaurants, passengers and hawkers drifted along the canals on *sampans*, three boards. At the height of morning, there was no room for oars. In addition to the *khlongs*, Banglamphu was once hemmed by fourteen forts. Inside the city's walls, Banglamphu dwellers were self-contained: there were fish mongers, flower stalls, *wats* and rice. Until thirty years ago, the city's biggest rice market was on Banglamphu's Thanon Khao San, the road of milled rice, now a world of its own inhabited more by backpackers than Bangkokians. Today Banglamphu is a mélange of what it once was and what it is now. A district where a palace has been turned into a tax office, where a handful of families still carve the rounded bowls monks hold out for alms each morning, where dentists speak perfect English, where a school has been converted to a guesthouse and where khaki-clad government officials eat noodles at lunch. There is a line—perhaps the east-west road of Thanon Phra Sumen, north of Khao San, or the *soi*s that vein around the road—which tourists rarely cross and where the Thais will be surprised to see a white face. On six of the seven weekdays, this centuries-old neighborhood is also home to the Banglamphu market.

Here, a vendor holds a sheet around me, pretending not to look. I'm surrounded by stalls of watches and underwear, school uniforms and cotton maternity dresses—things Thais need, not tourists. Sweat makes the denim stick to my knees. Under the sun, I am trying on a pair of knockoff jeans. I know the vendor can see me, but the more I rush, the longer it takes. It doesn't really matter. I'm on the pavement of the Banglamphu market and shops upon shops are stacked above me all the way up to the sky. A hundred eyes could be watching.

"No. Thirty-four. *Sam-sip-see. Sam-sip-see.*" Liliwen articulates each syllable with care, like she's in class. The vendor might not hear it, but I can tell she's annoyed. She's spent all this time becoming fluent and Thais never understand her. (Is it her accent or their interpretation?) Even if they make out her request, it doesn't do any good when she's shopping. They never have her size.

"Ahh, OK. I check for you," he says, and runs across the street, smiling and waving back at her.

Liliwen takes over the makeshift outdoor dressing room.

"Twat," she mutters.

"What's going on?" I shout over the blue cloth.

"Think I found a pair. He's just checking for the size. How are you?"

"Too tight. Couldn't even do the button up." Even with hips of 28 inches, I am too big for most Thai clothing. "You can let the sheet down."

Liliwen wipes her forehead, a string of sweat darkening the brown curls around her face. She ruffles her ear-length hair with a hand, then sticks it on her hip.

"The thing is, I just want to look good. Really good."

Liliwen's thoughts flake off her tongue like wet toilet paper. If I didn't know what we were shopping for, I wouldn't know what she was talking about because we were just discussing where to go for lunch. What Liliwen wants to look good for is her exhibition on Friday. She studied art in university and she still paints, even though she's in Bangkok, teaching English.

We are at the stage of this, this living abroad, where the place is no longer bigger than us. Specks of our selves—our painting, writing, music-making—emerge, as if issued from under a rock at the bottom of a river. I myself have been drawn back into the story of a German greenhouse owner I wrote about for *The News* after he died. Now I'm crafting something else with it, something longer and less true. Sometimes, as I smoke between paragraphs on the deck and hug my knees, I feel a warmth from somewhere. And the sense I am closer to something. What?

A few days ago, I wrote an article about Liliwen's show for the weekly arts and entertainment insert in the *Bangkok Post*, one of Thailand's two national English dailies. The editor was quick to accept my email query, but let me know they can't pay writers. Of course, I did it anyway. My byline, it's as if it makes me real, known. Someday I'll get back to it, writing for a paper, for others, for change. For a living, back in Canada. Hopefully, working my way up to writing features—longer pieces that afford a bit more story and style. For now, writing on my porch for me is enough.

Liliwen has only been here two years and yet somehow she knows everything, everyone. She knows where to go if you want to hear house music or if you want a Long Island iced tea for less than 100 *baht*. She knows which bars, if you say a certain few words, will serve beer after midnight. She knows her way around Chatachuk, an outdoor market the size of a stadium. And she knows a great bar by the Pin Klao bridge frequented only by locals because it's not listed in Lonely Planet. Yet. It also has a rooftop restaurant and a gallery on the second floor. Of course, she knows the owner and he's agreed to let her use his white walls for a month-long exhibition. The opening night is in a few days and the one thing Liliwen doesn't know is what to wear.

"Think I'll wear my black boob tube and some nice earrings, maybe those jade ones I bought last weekend, you know, with the bracelet, but I don't know about bottoms. I don't want to wear a skirt—that just says *teacher*. However, jeans might not really be dressy enough."

I laugh every time I hear Liliwen say how-*evuh*. Her British accent was made for this word, as was Liliwen, so indecisive. I tell her I agree with her about the jeans, although I'll probably wear a pair myself. We wear jeans even though it's far too hot for it because we want to prove we're not tourists.

Liliwen is peering into a jeweler's window, tongue pinched between her lips. Necklaces, earrings and rings are about the only things Liliwen will spend money on. Even though she makes loads of money and grew up in an affluent family that spent summers in France and winters in Norway, Liliwen is a miser, even carries a calculator to split dinner bills. Also, she's saving so that when her teaching contract expires, she can paint and live on a remote Thai island in the South for a few months. Liliwen started learning Thai because she had a boyfriend on said island, who, like many island boys, had many girlfriends. We've never met him, but we think he liked her, loved her, even. Even as much as the others. It's likely he also had motives that were mercenary. How could he not? How do so many not, when they'd barely find enough coins for a bowl of noodles in a day? And yet we cry out, we Westerners, when we show up with overstuffed suitcases and freshly pressed bills and buy the soup, and they eat it.

The vendor returns panting and grinning. "OK. Hello? Miss. Miss," says the vendor.

Liliwen turns around, index finger fiddling with the silver stud in her nose.

"We no have thirty-four. Thirty, yes."

"I need thirty-four," Liliwen says, drawing a circle around her waist. She pulls her black t-shirt down to cover the part of her body she hates most.

He shrugs and points at her belly. "You like bee-a, *mahk mahk*."

"Yes, I like beer very much," she says, seething. Her voice rises. "So does *she*."

Liliwen points at me, at my waist, smaller than hers. For a moment, Liliwen sorts out what she wants to say. She knows he's only joking, about the beer and her waist. It's the Thai way, to laugh in nervous situations and at someone's shortcomings, especially chubbiness. Liliwen's students think nothing of calling her fat.

"You know what? Never mind," she says, and stamps through the crowd down the street, her blue scarf bobbing among brown necks.

Liliwen could have said a thousand things.

FRIENDSHIPS UNFOLD ON shopping expeditions, but they seal over wine.

It has been eleven months since I last had wine. When Cécile sends an email to say she sent a little something with her sister's friend, arriving in Bangkok tomorrow, I almost cry. I know it's wine. French wine. As teachers at a public university, Cécile and I couldn't afford wine even if we could find it. It comes to Thailand imported from all over the world at Western prices—almost a week's salary. Taking a taxi, or even bus-sky-train-bus to the slick expat neighborhoods to find one of the three wine vendors in the whole city would be an hour's work in wages, and we'd be too broke to truly enjoy the taste. Cécile and I often talked about the things we missed. Depending on the day, men might be first, or wine.

"Hello?"

"Ah. Allo. This is Natalie, yes?"

"*Oui.* Is this Cécile's friend?"

"Yes."

"Oh, good. Where are you?"

"I am right now in a guesthouse not so far from Khao San. It's on Si Ayuthaya Road with very much wood. Do you know?"

"*Oui.*" I don't know why I continue this facade of being able to speak French. "Can I come now? Please?"

"Yes. Yes, sure."

I run through back lanes as best I can in flip flops and even though it's dusk. Two little boys on the sidewalk almost drop their pork balls on a stick as I round the pavement near their knees.

Prayers are being sung in the *wat*. A lady whose porch is strung with birdcages sweeps her step. A front-room store owner naps in his chair. *Soi* dogs lick fallen eggs in a gutter.

I'm almost out of breath and my back is coated in sweat. I grin, grin with my mouth wide open. Air mists the insides of my cheeks.

I spot Cécile's friend on a street corner. I'm tipped off by her dreadlocks and piercings and flowy burnt-orange fabric. She's an old-school backpacker. Not one of these bikini blondes drinking from a Starbucks cup after a pedicure. The teachers and I know a few of her type, who came to Thailand from France in the early '90s, when Khao San was a dirt road home to the rice market and the shacks of a few families who let the odd traveler sleep in a back room. The veteran travelers and the teachers run in different circles, but we respect each other.

Seeing my damp forehead and teary eyes, she holds out the bottle, like I'm a silly child who left a stuffed bear behind. As we hug, her dreadlocks scratch my neck. I say thank you and I leave.

It has crossed my mind that I could jog back home and down the whole bottle in one gulp. I could also just have a little bit every night for a week, an hour before bed. I run my fingers along the little bumps at the bottom of the bottle. Or, I could share. Liliwen is at Pranakorn Bar with Molly, starting to set up for her show. If I do that, I'll only get a glass and a half. I stand on a bridge above Khlong Banglamphu, equidistant to home and to Pranakorn, debating.

Soon I have the attention of a motorbike taxi driver who insists I want to go to Khao San. I shake my head. Too excited to get flustered, I explain where the bar/gallery is, just off Thanon Ratchadamnoen and down a *soi*.

He hands me the helmet. "OK. OK."

Fastening the clip, I climb on. Nothing compares to being on the back of a motorbike in Bangkok. Cowboys on concrete, they are. Weaving around cars and buses and *tuk-tuks*. Stopping, rarely, for lights. Or anything. If they do, they halt with a screech, take off again with their front tires jackknifing in the air. Long hair fanning out of an elastic band. Orange vests shimmering. The engine, heating my calves, my thighs vibrating, our pant seams rubbing. Ripples of warm wind blowing across my cheeks, my eyes watering. People in cars, staring at me, at the red hair under my helmet, the ivory legs against the kickstand. I lean when he leans and hope my heels won't fall off. In all these months, if nothing else, I have mastered the art of riding motorbikes in Bangkok.

A minute later, I tell him to stop. Hopping off, I pull the bottle out of my bag to find my wallet and hand the driver 30 *baht*.

Inside, Molly and Liliwen are on the floor, cutting string. Usually they get up to kiss me on the cheek and say hello, but I motion for them to stay where they are. Liliwen looks tired, stressed. Molly looks amused; her right eyebrow arches. I stand awkwardly at the gallery door, the smell of fresh paint filling my nose. I can't say, "Guess what? I have wine." It just wouldn't do this miracle justice. I draw it out of my purse and reveal it. Like Vanna. The longer I hold the bottle, the less I want to let it go.

Molly gasps. "Oh my God."

"Where did you get that?" asks Liliwen. "Is that for...?"

I nod.

Liliwen stands, skips downstairs to ask the owner for a corkscrew and three glasses.

"I can't believe this," says Molly. "Actually, I can't believe you're sharing,"

⋅ I laugh. But I have true friends to share the wild air with me.

What do we want, us girls? After this?

Why does there have to be an after?

Why can't we forever be this—these freckled teachers who can't say our students' names but see ourselves in their dewy foreheads, their confused, sanguine eyes. These freckled, leggy teachers who drink mugs of beer like men and ride motorbikes sidesaddle through the fug of the capital. Who try at this language, this summery extravagant land, where things are only what you want them to be. Not what they are.

Someday, maybe someday sooner than later, we will want an after. We will want jobs where we will earn as much as men, want to be as respected as our nurse-engineer-social worker mothers, but be less tired, more young. Always young. We will want an old character house walled by our grandfathers' paintings and Ikea shelves and Oprah-recommended books. We will want a man to share life with, to create a child in our image, the grainy black-and-white ultrasound strip of its tiny feet. And if it's a girl, we will want her to grow up smart and charismatic and talented, and, perhaps most of all, brave enough for an adventure.

Someday.

Right now, we are abroad, being twenty-five, twenty-seven, twenty-eight.

And there is wine.

Liliwen pounds back up the stairs. "Can't remember the word for wine," she says, breathless, reaching for the bottle.

I hand it to her.

"Never had occasion to say it."

Liliwen comes back balancing the wine, three plastic cups and a roll of tape in her paint-stained palms. I have visions of it all crashing to the floor, the wine's burgundy dye soaking Liliwen's paintings—patterns of blood-red gills and petals—instead of our tongues. But it doesn't. She makes it to the middle of the room and passes us each a glass, then me the bottle. I tell her to pour; I'm afraid I'll spill. I watch the liquid, a merlot from the South of France, cascade into our cups as if it were my first time with wine (a much less sophisticated atmosphere: me, Zora, a fourteen-year-old boy's garage and a bottle of his parents' Hutterite wine, which I later hurled on my mother's white nightgown). We are all laughing, like schoolgirls into mischief.

"Cheers, ladies," I say. "To Liliwen's show, which will be a huge success. And to us, of course, our first glass of wine together."

"Cheers."

"Yes, cheers," says Liliwen, nearly blushing.

I hold the glass below my nose and inhale the wine. Its spice alone makes me feel light and lulled. This would be enough. But I taste it too, let the first sip creek around taste buds before sliding down my throat, falling into my belly. My belly, flush and loose with the night, with life.

For a moment, we say nothing. We let the wine warm us again and again. We sip and we smile.

AS THE TAXI closes, my phone rings.

"It's Nung," says Molly, a few cabs behind me. "He's following you."

Through the dust of the taillights and the streetlights and the moonlight, I see his hair, wild. Nostrils flared. No helmet. Sweaty brow.

"Oh God."

Too-strong Long Islands and a round of pool with some Aussies and another teacher, a Brazilian Casanova who told us how last night, for free, he bedded a Thai woman with C-section scars across her stomach. From the rooftop patio, I saw Nung's pink and orange lamps, balls of light as stiff as yellow dandelions, not blowing—for there is no wind in Bangkok. A little lesbian Thai, who wears army pants and latches on to tourists such as tonight's Louise, tapped me on the shoulder with her pool cue.

She smiled. "Bank saw you, you know." Teeth too big for her face, for her buzz cut. Bank, Nung's head minion.

Eyes on the tile, eyes in the soup, eyes in the loo.

Last Friday, on a beach blanket where a boy was selling bottled Singha after hours on the lane of Soi Rambuttri—the same lane where Nung sells lamps—I led a group of tourists through a rendition of "Wonderwall." Before the beer boys shushed us and said, "Please, singing no. Police." I curled into the lap of a chubby half-Thai tattoo artist with lip piercings. And held his hand through Phra Sumen Fort, through laundry lines and rooster cages, to his room above the river.

Molly: "Is he still there?"

We drive past the last of the late-night noodle-eaters and the rats of Rambuttri north, past the Banglamphu bus loop, over the *khlong* and into my parkade. I toss a 50 *baht* note to the driver and run. The security guard drops his feet from his desk as I pass, breathless, room card in hand and the lights of Nung's motorbike looming.

"*Mai ow!*" I scream. Not want.

Nung grabs my shirt.

"You are sa-lut! Everyone knows."

Twisting free, I slam my card against the scanner and yank open the door. Nung catches the handle. The security guard— with a figure not unlike a grasshopper—jostles Nung from behind and loses his grip.

I kick the glass door of the lobby to close it. Too heavy. I punch the elevator button. Floor three.

Outside, Nung elbows the security guard, who tumbles into the stone planter of a lady palm. "My pride!"

Floor two.

He pauses, wipes the hair off his face. "You cannot do this to me."

Floor one. The steel panels open, but the door does not.

Nung searches for something to throw at the glass door and catches my eye. "I will be hurting you!"

I lunge for the stairs, flip flops clacking. Up and up, round and round under white-white lights, panting, crying. The door rattles below. Nung and the guard's voices holler, then still.

I reach my room, stand behind it for a minute and listen. Eventually, I slip off my sandals and lie on the bed, dirty feet and purse still across my shoulder. Is it minutes, or hours afterwards, when I hear knocking on my door? And then Nung.

"Natalie. I am here. I am sorry. Let me in. Please. I must to tell you something."

IN BETWEEN HAMMOCK naps, Noel, the teacher from Medicine Hat, emails for the first time since he canceled on meeting up and says he's going to work at an English Camp in Khon Kaen, up north, this weekend. They need one more person, if I want to come. I consider it: I don't feel safe here since that night with Nung, and now I know he has some way of getting in the building. Playing dead, or at least asleep, might not work next time. And yet I don't want to go. I want a break from teaching this weekend. Even more, I want the day we meet to be ours alone.

No, Noel, this is not how we meet.

"Tempting," I reply. "But I feel like I do enough of a monkey act from Monday to Friday. Have fun!"

It is August 17, two weeks from the anniversary of my arrival in Thailand.

RUNE

THE SINGER'S LONG blue nails clench the microphone. The baggy black t-shirt hides her flesh. Her face, curtained by waist-length hair, sways with each word of Michael Jackson's "Billy Jean." She doesn't even need the mic.

The vibration of her voice and the tarry black floor beneath our feet, they say this night could go one of two ways.

Molly and Liliwen and I dance. There isn't supposed to be a dance floor, but we've made one. Others have joined, edged back their tables and let their middles twist, heads lilt. We're all trying for the same thing, together, like fish in a net.

"She's bloody good," says Liliwen. Liliwen, whose face could light up a lake when she dances. She closes her eyes and smiles as she rocks from foot to foot in a circle. She always wants to dance. To be Liliwen is to dance.

"Is she ever," I say, arms above my head, nose ticking near my armpit. I love to dance too. I took jazz and ballet lessons as a girl. Even though, at home and at school, I was always stubbing my toe, dripping milk on my chin and going around in bumpy ponytails, somehow my body shed all that doing *pas de bourrées* on the glossy, hardwood floors of the Cultural Centre. And yet because I still put too much stock in the thoughts of others, I usually need to be a bit tipsy to dance in public. Tonight, though, everyone is happy and the music is good.

It's Saturday, and it's Jessi's birthday. We're at Shamrock, the second-story bar on Khao San Road where we come just once in a while, when we want to dance in front of a band and alongside the general traveling public. We don't know how old Jessi is. He doesn't know how old he is. His birth date was probably guesstimated late in life. Some of these Khao San guys from the South don't know what year they were born. Calendars were not household objects. Still aren't. Though he is somewhat peculiar in that he has a long-term *falang* girlfriend—Kat, an Australian teacher friend of ours—Jessi is one of more than a dozen just like him. They wear dreadlocks and boots and bell-bottoms. They idolize Bob Marley and his song "No Woman, No Cry." They earn enough money selling leather accessories and silver jewelry to buy the rice and beer that gets them through the day. They sleep around, have slept with far more women than the average number of bones in an adult body (206). They are artists—intuitive, brilliant with their fingers—but they lack either ambition or information about the ways of the world, and many will never really profit from their talents. Instead, they will remain on Khao San Road until their hair grays. Between now and then, they live for the day.

I tap the bottom of my empty glass and point to the table. Liliwen nods as I walk off the dance floor. Molly leans against the edge of the stage, exhaling onto the ground and looking at Oil, her new love interest. Behind the column where our table is, all of the guys are sitting and smoking and drinking and talking and laughing. Kat is the only girl there. She's between Jessi and his twin brother, a replica with a shaved head and softer skin, who came up to Bangkok to celebrate. Lips cinched, brows creased, eyes darting, Kat is trying to sort out what they're all saying. Even though she has been here two years and lives with them—Jessi and a handful of others—she doesn't know much Thai. But she's trying. Only Rune, Jessi's friend, looks up when I reach for the tall Singha beer bottle and begin to pour.

His hands flutter over my glass and his face cringes.

"What?" I ask, beer bottle in hand.

"This," Rune says, imitating my pour, palm upside down, "no good." He scratches the hair above his forehead, mining the dictionary in his head for the words. Of all the guys in their group, he is the most shy and he knows the least English. But his eyes—big, brown, always shifting—say he understands everything just the same. That he is quiet, an outsider in this way; that he isn't using English to get into some blonde's guesthouse, is what I find most attractive about him. That and he's taller than me. In Thai, Rune means "happy."

"Oh." My voice lightens. I smile. I've heard about this superstition: if you pour a bottle backward, palm open, you invite a ghost into your glass. I try again.

Rune spreads himself out on his seat and smiles. For a moment, he forgets about his teeth, crooked and pointy, and opens his mouth. His eyes are holding me here, before him. Feeling the pull, I step forward.

I reach for his hand. It's dry. With my other hand, I point to the dance floor.

He shakes his head. "No dance."

Here I go again. Trespassing, fishing, fists slick with worms. Why can't we just stay back awhile, when we see the line?

Liliwen sees us talking and heads over. She says something in Thai to Rune.

Rune's eyebrows arch like branches. He flicks his dreadlocks off his face, something Rune does as often as he blinks, and studies my face. His own face is long, pulled down by his hair.

He has high cheekbones, a pointy nose. Perhaps there are foreigners in his family tree.

A boy in a Shamrock t-shirt takes the empty glasses off our table and adds them to a tower of cups resting on his shoulder.

I tap Liliwen's bare, freckly elbow. "What did you say?"

"That you fancy him," Liliwen says, and wanders back onto the dance floor, straw in mouth.

Rune points at me, then back at himself, his white tank top bearing the UK flag. His pupils grow darker. He has a hold on my eyes and he's reading my mind. At least it feels that way. And what I'm thinking is, I like the ring of that, "fancy."

How easy it is, to abandon reason when there's a possibility that another human would like to see you naked.

The lights go on and the band stops. Suddenly able to see, my other senses kick in. The walls emit a moldy, smoky scent. The room is humid with the sweat of dancing bodies. Voices that were dulled by the band, now fueled with need, wanting to know where friends are, where they'll go next. It's too early to go home.

Jessi and Kat and Rune decide to have a party at their house, in a village a half hour's drive away from Khao San. Rune searches for me in the crowd. When he spots me, he grabs my hand, not even asking if I want to come, then clenches my waist. I tell myself he doesn't know, he isn't with girls often. Standing on a stair, we wait for the crowd to move. We're all knocking around like reeds in the wind. He scans my eyes for my intentions. Rune is pensive and I don't know why. I smell his whiskey breath and wonder what kind of kisser he'll be.

AS THE SUN rises, rice husks form shadows in the paddies. Someone has a guitar and we're all sitting outside sharing the tall beers we bought at 7-Eleven. Kat and I are the only ones speaking English. We're in a Thai neighborhood and everyone else, save for flies and the cats, is asleep.

"It's so nice out here," I say, closing my eyes and inhaling the leafy air.

"Yeah," says Kat. She looks at me and then the moon, ever yellow. "Took a bit of getting used to. I mean, I'm the only one around here."

The only *falang*.

"And Jessi's the only one who knows English and he can barely speak it. So I thought, 'OK, I'll learn Thai.' Well, it's fucking hard, man. But I'm learning, I'm really trying, and then when Jessi talks, I can't understand him." Kat smooths back her bangs. Her fingers are studded in silver rings Jessi has made, and they complement her hippie-tomboy look. "Sounds like there's rocks in his mouth, but some of the other guys have said they have trouble hearing him."

"Really?"

"Yeah. The ones from the South, it's like they have their own language or something."

Because Jessi couldn't say Kathy, she started going by Kat just so he could call out to her.

We're sitting on stools, leaning against a fence. Kat's petting a dog. She doesn't know whose dog it is. The dogs out here look more like the ones back home rather than the wound-infested, hairless animals that stalk *soi*s in Bangkok.

"Don't know how long it'll last, though." She exhales and eyes the guys, passing the bottle, faces swaying to the music.

Kat is someone who could be two people, the person you hope she is, and someone else, a girl who drinks too much and forgets who she is. Like me.

A youth spent outdoors in Tasmania has left her skin pink and cracked. Her short hair, stiff and yellow like wheat, is always falling out of a ponytail. Kat used to have dreadlocks, but when she got hired to teach English at a kindergarten, even though she doesn't have a degree, they told her to cut her hair. She met Jessi on Khao San a few years ago during a trek across Asia with a girlfriend. They were supposed to go on to Laos together, but she held back, called Jessi on his cell phone, and soon after she was living with him and all of his "brothers" (friends), in this house. She'd like for them to have a place of their own someday. Last week she helped him set up a bank account, his first one. Jessi is the youngest of seven or eight, she's not sure, and he sends money home to them.

"In some ways, their family system is so admirable, you know. It's like, what's mine is yours. But, then, they can't do much on their own. I honestly don't know if Jessi would ever leave them. But this is OK for now, you know," she says, pointing her cigarette at all the people sitting around us. "They're pretty cool people."

I nod. This is a world I haven't seen, the Thai bohemian outside of Khao San. I wonder, *Could I fit in here? Could I be almost Thai like this?*

When the guy who was singing "Stairway to Heaven" stops, I tell Kat I need to get a cigarette out of the pack I left inside. I found my purse where I'd left it, just behind a door beside the bathroom. I open the pack, count four Marlboros and slide the top back down. The cigarettes are in one hand and a beer is in another, so I use my toes to open the door.

On the other side of it, Rune is frozen but for his blinking eyes.

I smile and tell him in Thai that I'm going to the washroom.

"Two minute," he says, and kisses me.

I let him, the beer and the cigarettes in my hands.

His teeth ram my lips. His chin digs and twists against mine. His fingers claw my ribs.

I step back. I say I have to go to the bathroom again and try to bend around him. But he pushes me against the wall.

"Rune. *Mai ow.*" Not want.

He jerks my shirt sideways. His fingers are warm, scratchy, pinching. He smells like sweat and straw.

"Rune. *Mai ow!*"

He shoves my shoulders, trying to fall me. His weight, towering now, and his eyes, alight, I won't be able to stop them.

His nails slit my arms all the harder, each time I scream no. *NO no no.*

But I have to.

"No!" I try to swerve my head around his, give my voice a path to travel. "No!"

I wait until both his hands are on me, one under my shirt, one fiddling with my belt. I twist myself around him, topple, land with my knee on his chest. I reach for my beer bottle. I picture it smashing between his eyes, blood and glass sprinkling his skin. For a moment I know I can, and I wish I would.

Jessi and Kat heave open the door. I fall over, to the ground. Jessi knocks Rune against the wall. Kat steals the beer bottle from my hands.

A breath, a scream, tears. I run, to the gate at the edge of the driveway. Kat's behind me, holding out a cigarette. I take it.

"I heard someone shouting, but it was Thai, so I thought it was one of the neighbors. You don't mess with the neighbors," she says, her eyes scrambling for mine. "I'm so sorry."

The stars. You can see stars out here. Even the stars are sorry.

"How did that happen?"

"I said no." Snot sags from my nose. My shirt is torn and my skin is stung and red, sheared of knowing people are good.

The rice paddy, toes sinking in its chill, letting the mud choke my throat, my nose, my eyes.

Kat puts me back together. Lifts the sleeve of my shirt. Tucks away my bra strap. Wipes my cheeks, still hot and wet and black with makeup. Creaks open the courtyard gate. One of the older brothers will drive me home.

I hear hooves and look up to see a water buffalo ambling across the road. *Khwai*, water buffalo, Thailand's worst insult, for there is no animal more stupid and stubborn.

I REACH MY sheets, tear off my clothes and chuck them on the floor, under my bed. I am still naked and staring at the ceiling when Molly texts and asks if I want to go for breakfast. Turning my head toward the phone was the first time I've moved in hours. I haven't slept yet. My thoughts are caught like burrs on what happened. I don't reply.

Awake, a stranger, sorry, unknotting, bad-lucked, found out, *lost lost lost*. My fault.

Two hours later Molly phones and after a while, I answer.

"What are you doing?"

I unravel from sitting cross-legged on my computer chair. "Flights."

"What?"

"Looking up flights." It's going to cost at least $1,000, and I don't even have a quarter of that in my bank account. I'm going to have to ask my mom for the money, and she'll want to know why I need to leave.

"Why?"

"I'm going home."

"You're what?"

"I'm going *home*." I'll take enough clothes to keep warm on the plane. Everything else, I'll just leave.

"What happened?"

I tell Molly two words at a time. *Tried, rape*—my tongue can't quite make them. Finally, I confess so matter-of-factly I don't think she believes me. I'm dull to it. He didn't *rape* me, but he *tried. He tried. Rape.* I'm back in that room with Rune clawing my ribs. Pinning my bones against the floor. Strangling my nos. *NO no no...*

I guess I should feel lucky, that I got away. I guess I got myself there, didn't I?

Why do we offer fault?

I tell Molly I had a daydream that I was standing on top of D&D Inn, like a hawk on a hay stack, waiting for him. I swooped down to his stall and clenched his face in my claws, hauled him over to the River Chao Phraya. Let go. Didn't look back.

Molly sighs. "Oh dear."

I'VE MADE THIS all up. Sometimes, that's what I think. That maybe this is not some magical find-myself quest. There were no signs, no special messages from strangers. Or books. No winds of fate turning my feet this way or that. I'm just a twenty-five-year-old who daydreams too much during the day, and drinks too much at night. Almost a year I've been in Thailand, and nothing divine has happened.

It's been four days, and I'm still scouring travel sites. I haven't told my mom yet. I don't want her to know what I've been up to. Back home, I wouldn't have hung out with glorified street urchins disguised as artists who treat rice better than women. *Why am I doing it here? Why am I here at all?*

The jeans and the green top I was wearing that night lie crumpled under my bed. I see them hanging out from under my sheet sometimes.

THE FAINT SOUNDS of a rooster from the roof next door fade and return. The bird never knows what time it is, or is it a myth that roosters only crow at dawn? Trying to sleep, I wrestle with sheets and thoughts. My mind sails along memories: Feeling one with the world under the moon on Hat Rai Leh. Learning how to *wai* by copying *Ajarn* Nand in the hotel lobby. Waiting for the steam to slow on a bowl of *tom yum gung* at the family's restaurant. Song, hand clasped to my arm, showing me how to cross the street.

Faces flicker and mouths hum, like an old projector. I remember kneeling on the balcony at Saxophone with Cécile, twisting my neck to see the band. Crying as Zora's tanned face bounded toward me with a Thai broom behind her head. Revealing my mouth's inner workings so students could pronounce "explore." Catching myself in the mirror with Nung behind me. About to bat Rune's ear with a beer bottle.

My body rolls. Lands on my stomach, in that innate position which becalms babies. There are four kinds of memories: The kind that still sting that you keep at the front of the closet, because they're your excuse for all that is wrong with you. The old and new ones that bring joy, hung throughout, chronologically. The everyday-unusual ones that you may never make sense of or don't need making sense of but that stick out somehow. And then there are the ones you bury at the back.

MAGIC
ROOSTERS

I SPRINT IN FRONT of buses, wend around silver vendors and t-shirt hawkers and the women who wash tourists' clothes. Under a corrugated metal roof, the alley is dark, dripping. Rusted pipe drains vent the stench of sewage. This lane, Trok Mayom, the lane I so desperately wanted to find my first night, is like Khao San Road's intestine exposed. Newcomers usually have their noses plugged, but I can bear it. I've been coming this way ever since that night at Jessi's. And now, now I'm behind a pole between the alley and the courtyard of the Sawasdee Guesthouse, the same place I stayed eleven months ago before visiting the university for the first time. My heart is beating louder than the record of any memory. And I see him.

Three minutes late and he isn't looking at his watch. Never wears watches, never has, I suspect. Instead, he stands with an elbow on the lobby desk, fingers pinching his almost goatee. He's dressed in baggy jeans, Birkenstock-like sandals and a green cotton tunic with branches of stitching around the neck. His hair is covered by a brown striped beanie. I yanked shirts off hangers for nearly an hour and fiddled with my hair for almost as long to create a messy ponytail that would give the impression of being windblown, carefree. He is watching for me facing Khao San Road, but I've come from the back. When he raises an index finger and begins to chew the nail, I take a step. And then another. Until I am just a few feet away.

My voice prances, as if we were in the hall in high school. "Noel."

He turns around, pitches his eyes at mine. "Natalie."

I walk his way. We hug. He's damp and I'm not sure if it's because he just showered or he's sweaty. His hug is whole, and it tugs breath out of my chest. Even this is so much.

He steps back. "Nice to meet you. Finally."

"You too."

One hundred and seventy-one days have passed since he wrote, "You've probably never heard of it. It's called Medicine Hat."

"What do you want to do? Are you thirsty? Hungry?"

"Both," he says, drumming a water bottle against his thigh.

"Follow me." I am taking him to Ranee's, the Italian place on Trok Mayom. If he doesn't fall in love with me for me, he'll fall in love with me for having taken him to this pizza.

Inside, we sit near the oven and the plank of wood where dough is rolled. Noel's eyes poke around the restaurant, outdoors and dimly lit. Plants adorn the sun-faded wooden fence. Somehow Ranee's is so far away from the chaos of Khao San.

"You'd never know this place was here," he says, taking off the beanie and folding it on the chair beside his. Noel's hair is brown, not light brown or dark brown, just brown.

Studying his face, my eyes move from the lines around his eyes to his strong jaw and his lips, dark, full. I want to kiss him.

"I know. Isn't it great? That's the owner," I say, pointing to a man with olive skin and dark freckles. "But his Thai wife is actually the cook, not him."

He lights a cigarette and leans back on the white plastic chair. "Cool."

I light a cigarette too and pretend to study the menu, but I already know what I'm going to have: penne carbonara or the funghi pizza.

The waiter, tall for a Thai and with almost no neck, asks what we want to drink.

"Beer?" I ask Noel.

"Sure."

"*Beeah Sing, kot—*" I say.

"*Beeah Sing, kot—*" Noel says.

We laugh. I raise my hand to him.

The waiter turns to Noel.

He begins again. "*Beeah Sing, kot yai, nung, sai nam keng krub.*"

"That was funny," I say, lingering on his eyes too long. They're dark and small, but they've seen things, been things.

"Yeah. I was wondering how much Thai you would know, living in Bangkok."

"Well," I say. I tell him about Soi Suan Aoi and the family, about trying to learn Thai along with Cécile, the lessons from Thongchai and the time I accidentally had forty-some students shouting, "Boobs! Boobs! Boobs!"

"I've had some serious doozies too," he says. During Noel's first week teaching, there was a troublemaker who laughed and got the whole class laughing every time Noel said "he." *He* is the Thai equivalent of vagina.

And this is how the night goes. He tells a story; I tell a story. All the while, I am both in and outside myself. My mouth moves, I brush my ponytail off my shoulder, I exhale cigarette smoke and laugh so often I find myself massaging my cheeks to break the strain.

Because of the incessant talk and the long glances, you can tell it's our first date, or what I call our first date. For Noel, I think, this is a weekend to drink beer with someone who speaks English and stock up on books before heading back to his village.

Our conversation flits between here and home. I don't tell him that my real dad lives in a Saskatchewan hamlet I can never remember the name of. I do tell him I grew up with three brothers, one biological. I don't tell him that the stepbrothers' dad and my mom just got divorced. I don't tell him that a few months ago my mom was here, in Thailand, with Wayne and a few other couples from Medicine Hat, including my brother's ex-girlfriend's father. He was a former police officer who slept with the mother of that babysitter (yes, that sitter) on a washing machine at a party while on duty and calling on a noise complaint; he tore up the ticket, of course, and went on to become a city councillor—a role he eventually left after an alleged affair in which the lover's husband told the whole town in an email. During one leg of their tour group's stay, my mom paid for Cécile and me to stay at their hotel in Hua Hin. We could have been at a resort anywhere in the world, and the visit was mostly boring: we drank beer with them on the beach in the afternoon, and ate bacon and cheese with them at the buffet in the morning. I wanted to like Wayne. I went to high school and was friends with his two daughters, who are both intelligent and lovely. And my mom seemed happy, so I was tempted. But I ached with the plain gnawing of something not right.

Noel, on the other hand, tells me he grew up in "the valley," in a dome-shaped house his dad built alongside nine others at the west end of the South Saskatchewan River. There was just one bunny-eared black-and-white TV in the dirt-floor basement, in the center of the four boys' rooms, and since the boys were loud and the volume had long gone off, Noel learned to lip-read watching Kevin and Winnie on *The Wonder Years*. He developed a keen ability to block out everything else around him: hat tricks in mini hockey games, the DDTs of wrestling matches, little boys with an affection for flatulence.

Because they lived outside city limits, he went to school in Seven Persons with the farm kids, from whom he learned how to rope and bellow Garth Brooks songs. His mom loves music. Not country, though. Fleetwood Mac, Dire Straits, the soundtrack to *Cats*. She was always playing music, and loud too. Now Noel is like that, always after a song and setting the volume to ten.

We talk about how lucky we were to be kids in Medicine Hat, the dozens of ways we might have met. Turns out one of my friends is stepcousins with his best friend, his aunt was a teacher of mine, his cousin had a crush on my little brother, he worked as a waiter with some of my friends at Earls.

We talk about having the feeling we had to leave. How he left, at once, for Vancouver and never returned, not to live. How I left—to Regina, to Kananaskis, to Calgary—but kept moving back.

Now we're on the subject of Thailand, how we got here. Noel arrived in April 2005, six months before I did.

His eyes are glued to his thumb, currently flicking the butt of an L&M brand cigarette.

"Eric was here." Eric, his best friend, not Eric, his older brother. Eric H. works for a Bangkok company that recruits English teachers for Thai schools. "And he wrote and said he could get me a job and I fought it for a while. Like a few months at least. And then I said, 'Yeah, dude, I need to get out of here. Now.'"

Three years earlier, on November 25, 2002, Noel's brother Jon died of a cancer that crippled and spread from his shoulder. Jon was twenty-two, a small young man with hair the color of corn and eyes a lonely blue. He was the Appleton family's only rebel, staying out late and running with a bad crowd, though he starred in school plays and was the favorite of toddler cousins.

I met him once. A party, maybe. I don't remember where. I can just see him standing there, in his denim Lee jacket. His eyes, so blue. His cheeks, rosy. And I knew that he died. Medicine Hat's so small. I think it was Zora that told me.

After waiting a week for each of his three brothers to get to Medicine Hat and to his bedroom (their mom had called around and said it was time), the Appleton boys watched one last hockey game together on November 22. Vancouver beat Detroit four to one. The Canucks would have had a shutout, but in the last eleven minutes, Brett Hull, Jon's favorite player, scored on a power play. Noel remembers sitting on the floor, all of them so close you couldn't tell whose sock was whose, the white of the ice reflecting on their faces. Trying to watch, trying not to. Hours later, Jon was in a coma.

"After that, things got pretty bad. It was like sleepwalking for a few years. And I knew this was something Jon would have loved to do."

I want to hug Noel so much I have to dig my wrists into the table.

Long after its metal surface has been cleared of our plates, I glance at the door. Head cocked, a finger over my ear, I say, "My apartment has a deck."

"Guess we better go there, then."

With glazed eyes and deliberate steps, we make our way out of Khao San, stopping just once at a 7-Eleven for a few beers and a bag of ice.

OUR ASHTRAY IS a pop can. Our view is a vacant building's brick wall. Noel sits on my desk chair. I am beside him, on an upside-down blue laundry basket. I insisted. Behind the sliding glass door is a plastic bag filled with marshmallow-sized ice cubes and two tall bottles of beer. Outside, the sky is black and starless. It's tempting not to talk.

There is so much to say it's hard to know where to start, and yet, it doesn't matter.

"What do you miss, about home?"

"Oh." He strokes his sideburns with his knuckles. Grins. "Sour cream. Sunday dinners."

I miss wine. Sometimes my mom and my brother. But now that's all. "Do you have a big family?"

"Yeah." His mom is the oldest of six. She and her sisters take turns hosting Sunday dinners.

"Me too." My mom is smack in the middle of seven siblings born of Irish and English-Italian parents who moved a lot but lived the longest in Thompson. My grandmother's uncle Chil ran rum from Saskatchewan to Chicago for Al Capone. My grandfather's grandfather, I want to tell him about that.

"Wanna hear a story?"

Noel nods. "Sure."

"I think it was 1898, maybe 1897. My grandpa's grandpa— his name was James Allen, but they called him Jim—he took a team of horses up to a wood camp. On Riding Mountain. In Manitoba. All the farmers went there, for wood."

His wife, Ada, nine months pregnant with their first child, waited for him at her parents' farmhouse, where they were staying until spring, when they would finish building their own homestead, just a few miles away. A blizzard set in. The other men at the camp told him not to go, to wait out the storm, at least until morning. But James said, "I have to get home to my wife." James, a man of six feet and two inches who served as the Lavinia district Sunday school superintendent. So he left. One of his horses turned up first, then the sleigh of wood. Finally, a day later, the men found James just a few feet away from a homestead shack, frozen to death, on his knees, praying.

This image, this lineage, it asks me to be thankful for this life, to do something with it that would make James and Ada and their Allens proud.

"There was an article written about him in *The Western Producer*, in the sixties, I think." Aunt Cindy showed it to me the night of the grilled cheese sandwich, not long before I left Calgary. "Sometimes people need stories more than food to stay alive"—a Barry Lopez quote my aunt Donna shared with me when I was working in Lethbridge after leaving *The News*, and the idea of other leavings started shooting up like white-tufted dandelions. Now I wonder, what if we don't just *need* stories, what if we *are* stories? Braids and braids of them, like veins. Or muscle. The stories something greater than us tells the grasses, of wishes for us, in whispers we ingest on walks. The stories our grandparents tell, of sailing and starving and saving, to get here, for us, that come to our tongues on dumpling skins and rocking chairs. The stories we tell ourselves about why we can't, to protect the heart. *It's too*... When, in truth, every day that we keep closed that chamber, that arc, the heart starves.

But now I've spoken too long. I much prefer to listen.

"What do your parents do?" I ask.

Noel's mom is a teacher. His dad and a friend own a bakery. His grandpa Vic was a school principal and coached minor league hockey. In the late '60s, with nails saved from before the war, Vic built a cabin on a hill in Elkwater. This is the park where a lot of Hatters spend their weekends, and where the lake is so cold, even in August, that it steals your breath when you jump in. We talk about May long weekends in Elkwater, the drinking-under-age-and-in-public tickets I got there, and his family cabin as a never-ending party for him and his brothers.

"No matter how many people there were, and there were tons, always—from all different groups, because we all had different friends—everyone just got along. I don't know, there was just something about that place."

Noel is already like a campfire.

We keep so much from some, and then, with others, strip to our skin and bones at the start. Do we know already that they'll love us entirely, that whoever loved, loved in truth?

We let the weight of our stories and what is sit for a while.

And then, the kiss. Our lips reach, enwrap, pause. In this perfect silence, we are still. Something like love swells from my mouth to my heart, as if I've swallowed it. A force borders our faces. *Can he feel it?* Still kissing, eyes closed, I watch us in my mind. My red hair waves over my bare shoulders; his is as dark as the night. Our lips press and part and we open our eyes. We breathe.

By the time Noel leaves, the sun has painted the clouds pink. A rooster from the other building swaggers along a cement windowsill. A fifteenth-century Thai poem, *Phra Law*, tells of twin princesses in an enemy city who fall in love with the prince, Phra Law, from hearsay, and use a magic rooster, *kai fah*, to lure the prince into the wilds, toward them. What I would have given—weeks, months ago—to have had a magic rooster bring Noel to me. There was no rooster. Magic, yes.

At the door, rocking the handle in my palm, I watch him shuffling down the hall. "Goodnight," I say. My mouth opens, I take a breath, and then the words just... sit.

"You mean good morning."

I WAKE UP smiling. With my eyes still closed, I think of Noel's face when he was talking about his brothers. The way he lit a cigarette with conviction. The way he peered at me, rambling in a language and of a land he used to know. I picture us back on my deck, staring out at the Bangkok sky, barely blinking, chests rising.

Hours later, we are on our way to buy novels from a bookseller I favor on Soi Rambuttri, just off Khao San Road.

Noel stops at a CD vendor's table. He dreams of seeing the inside of an album cover and a song title of his and the words "Written by Noel Appleton."

"Workin' on it," he says, flipping through the dominoes of discs. When he lived in "Van," he played with a few guys. They would attempt to coerce their instruments into making the sounds that were in Noel's head; Noel sang the words. Even though he'd been deemed a genius at age three, he never went to university. He despised the guys with commerce degrees and Camaros paid for by their parents, and the professors who introduced students to groupthink. He despised the hockey-playing oafs who took turns with girls on the bench seats of their trucks, from behind. And he despised the doorbell boxes and subdivisions both camps moved into. Noel has always known what he didn't want. But he didn't know what he did want. So, he bartended. And on those long walks home at the edge of Cambie Bridge, lyrics coasted like cars past his ears, so that by the time he reached his bed, a song was waiting patiently for his pen. When he got to Thailand, he had to teach himself how to play guitar, and tried, on the face of a cheap blond-hued guitar he bought at Tesco. During his last trip back to Canada, he bought Black Betty, a Yamaha electric-acoustic. These days, on the guitar he can manage a few Johnny Cash songs and a bit of Pearl Jam, but that's it. His favorite artists to sing, just to sing, are Bob Dylan and Neil Young.

"My music teacher told me not to blow air in my recorder for the Christmas concert," I say. I don't know if this is true, or if I've just said it for so long I believe it. I do remember the wilt of her face every time I blew into the plastic instrument once she discovered it was me making *that sound*. A later music teacher let me play in the handbell choir because all my friends were in it, but she gave me the biggest ones, G and F, which were only used for single, long rings. I used to resent music. Growing up,

I only ever bought a handful of CDs. One was the Tragically Hip, which every Canadian teenager of my era bought. The other was Sarah McLachlan, which every Canadian teenage girl of my era bought. "Music was too much like math for me, I think."

Or maybe I just couldn't hear myself because I was listening to everyone else, aware they could hear my music too.

We pass Wat Chana Songkhram at the end of Khao San, and the guy who sells purses and toy trucks and all manner of things made out of Coca-Cola cans, and we turn onto Soi Rambuttri.

"It's hard, man. I'll probably take lessons, when I go back," he says. Back, to Canada. Someday he wants to live in a big old house like the ones in his parents' neighborhood, the hill. I'm sure, if I stood at the top of the cliff behind the house where I grew up, I would have been able to see the lights on in Noel's kitchen across the river. His own house, he says, will look like a library.

I might pinch myself. When Stuart and I were looking at houses to buy, we walked through a yellow, two-story home on the hill that had a den just off the kitchen with wall-to-wall bookshelves. I saw myself holed up in that room, cocooned in blankets on a wingback chair with a coffee and a book. Stuart didn't like the house, not at all. Stuart wanted the black-and-white bi-level with the double garage, the one that was the former home of a childhood classmate who'd moved away in eighth grade and, just a few months later, died in a head-on collision with a cube van. Sometimes I'd whispered, *I'm sorry, Grant*, when I twisted the key in the front door. Looking back, I was always uneasy at that house.

My book guy nods and waves. Seeing me giddy, with Noel, he nods, smiling, and steps back, arms behind him.

Noel coughs. "I have many leather-bound books and my apartment smells of rich mahogany." It's an impeccable impersonation of Will Ferrell's character Ron Burgundy, from *The*

Anchorman. This is something about Noel. He does movie voices all the time and he doesn't talk about serious things for too long without acting silly. Partly he is a born goof with a parrot's talents. Partly, after Jon, he can't take life too seriously.

I laugh. "Oh, I love that movie."

"Sweet."

"People in TV are like that, you know. I mean, they're not quite like Ron Burgundy, but they do like looking at themselves in the mirror." I tell Noel about being a TV station intern in Calgary, and how I couldn't wait to get back into a newspaper newsroom, where reporters wore wrinkled shirts and sometimes didn't shower.

Noel, biting a nail, reads the blue-and-coral back cover of *Shantaram*, which all the backpackers are reading right now. When he was fourteen, his family took a trip to Mexico, and while the other boys threw footballs in the sand and dodged jellyfish in the ocean, Noel was sitting under an umbrella wearing a black turtleneck, reading a book.

His phone rings. He reaches into his bag, says, "Hello?"

I can tell by the drawn-out words, the still air between responses, that he's talking to a Thai. He steps out of the bookshop and into the lane. I turn a carousel of novels and pretend not to listen.

SECOND
STREET

M Y MAKESHIFT UMBRELLA is a yellow plastic bag. Noel's is blue, from the old man's shop. The rain is wild, but it's too dark to see drops except in the light of an oncoming car. Water slips between our fingers and as we run across the street, our hands fall away. I reach instead for Noel's arm, dripping and bare.

A few minutes ago, we ran out of beer. Wanting to be nowhere else but on my porch, alone, I suggested walking to the only shop open this late, a 7-Eleven.

"Man, it's really coming down," says Noel. His glasses are streaked and drops of water have teared around the hair on his jaw.

All week, I thought about Noel. On Wednesday, he called to see if he could come back to Bangkok on Friday. I didn't know how to word my answer: "Are you going to... will... do you want to... stay here?" He almost cut me off. "I don't care. I just want to see you again." And because reality started to run alongside the stream of a story I'd hoped would unfold, my heart swelled and I had to pause before whispering, "OK."

Tonight, he is staying over. It was dark by the time he knocked on my door. I opened it, let him take two steps before my bare right foot pinned his to the floor. Our bodies, both hot with wanting, pressed. My lips dragged along his neck, his jaw, his lips. We kissed, for a long time.

Later that night, I introduced Noel to Molly, Liliwen and Yonni at the Ride Bar, an establishment more like a hut on Trok Mayom. It reeks of rotting fruit and wok oil, and you half expect to see rats, but tourists never go there, so we like it. Very much. Molly and Liliwen were charmed by Noel, who topped up our glasses with Thai rum and told them about how his neighbors in Nakhon Nayok have thought he was a bit off since the day he meandered through town on his bicycle wearing an umbrella hat. Each of its nylon panes bore a Canadian flag. I couldn't stop smiling. Molly peered at me; she knew there was something to know. I felt light, almost high, and it wasn't from the drinks. "Sorry," I said, when Noel was off in the washroom. "I can't stop smiling." Molly swung a cigarette from her mouth to her ear. She squinted and said, "It's like a fairy tale."

Except instead of crowns we wear bags. After leaving Khao San for my place, and then my place for 7-Eleven—populated only by us, a bucktoothed clerk girl and two wieners rolling on a metal rack—we leave the convenience store with three tall beers and walk back to my apartment unable to hold hands because he's clutching the bottles with arm and pressing the blue plastic bag to his head with the other.

"Almost there," I say, as we near the gate of the hotel next door to my apartment. It used to be the Thai Hotel, but now it's called something else I can never remember because it's French. When the hotel opened in 1962, its fifty-five rooms brought the total hotel rooms in Bangkok to one hundred. I think of going there to eat or to see if I can swim in the empty pool, but I never do. I tell Noel about how I waited forever to go into the old man's shop.

"I don't know what I was afraid of. Really."

Before we went out to meet the girls, Noel and I ducked into the old man's shop. Charmed by Noel, the way he spoke Thai and tried to joke with him, the old man dug for the coldest bottles at the bottom of the freezer and patted Noel on the shoulder. We waved as we left and he returned the waves with the flap of his palm and that beautiful, toothless smile. In the elevator up to my room, I said, "He never does that to me."

"Can't," said Noel.

"I guess," I said. "Isn't he cute?"

"Yeah," said Noel. "He's a pretty cute old guy."

My sandals are like soggy leaves. I'm wet, but I'm warm. The whole street, the night, like it's ours alone.

In the apartment parkade we have to walk through to get to the main door, we pull the bags off our heads and shake off the water.

The security guard's eyes follow us and glare. "*Mow.*"

Yes, we're drunk. We are drunk and falling in love and it's raining. Just try to wipe the smiles off our faces.

On the fourth floor, I have to hold a piece of my t-shirt around the handle to open the door.

"Nice one," says Noel.

Nothing gives me greater pride than being resourceful, even in such small ways. I think I would make a good MacGyver. I was rather proud of myself when I recently had menstruation cramps and, in the absence of a hot water bottle, set the hot base of my laptop on my abdomen.

Inside, we rub towels over our legs and feet and faces and arms. He sets up the bar, pours two glasses and waits for me out on the porch. Seeing my reflection beside his back, I pause. He is books and song and laughter. Bravery. Wonder. Gentleness.

And family. His is as sturdy and right as a pew. Mine is a tattered spider's web clutching crickets and flies. Maybe there are philanderers and drinkers and kooks in his line too, but you'd never know. Not so with me.

I step out onto the porch and assemble myself on the underside of a laundry basket, now my seat.

Noel flips through his CDs and slides into the laptop a recording of him singing and his friends on guitar one night in Vancouver. The two guitars beat softly, like drums, and then the chords emerge. Noel's voice enters and I can't tell what he's saying but his voice—his voice, my God. Slow, throaty, the truth. His soul, staggering off his tongue, tingling my body's edges.

He wrote "Gemini" about a friend whose twin brother died in a car crash at twenty-two, the same age Noel's brother Jon had been.

"We got ripped off—no one is supposed to die at twenty-two years old, no one, you know—but at least we knew it was coming, right? With her, though..."

Noel coughs, his fist a punching bag for words his lips never issue. He pauses. Turns to the laptop, switches the track and plays "Jonesy's Bench," a song he wrote not long after Jon died.

"They put up a bench in the park on Second Street, the park by where my parents live. It says, *In Memory of Jon Appleton, Let His Sense of Fun and something else Be Remembered*. Or something like that."

Second Street. Could I go back now, or ever? Or with Noel? I picture the windows down and my bare feet on the dash while Noel drives past the brick WELCOME TO MEDICINE HAT—THE GAS CITY sign. Sunburnt. Backpacks in the trunk. I give him directions to my mom's new apartment by the river. Noel nods while bellowing a Johnny Cash tune. Yesterday a Medicine Hat friend who is cousins with Noel's best friend Eric sent an email asking how things were going with Noel and me. I told her I think if he asked me to marry him nicely enough, I'd say yes. But I don't know if it's the same for Noel. Thai girls—thin, soft-skinned, that hair—they toss themselves in his path. And he doesn't know that a cheating heart brought me here, that someday, my mind intends to pack off too.

When the song starts, Noel is somewhere else.

On the recording, he whispers, "One, two, three, four." The guitar enters and the tin of it, the tallness of the chords, they tell you it's a sad song. His first words, they nearly totter. It's not an improv recording. He knows the lyrics too well.

Love and sorry trample to the walls of skin around my chest and my eyes, reaching for him. And yet I have no words.

He sings of Jon knowing for a year, of Noel not being around, of how Jon waited for all his brothers to get back, of how being able to do that brought a fleeting smile to Jon's then-sallow face.

When the song ends, Noel bends his head, rubs the back of his neck and says, "I don't even remember writing it."

The words came to him as he was crawling into bed after a late shift at the bar. He'd struggled to stay awake through the last lines, woke to a world where people got upset about "stupid shit" like broken-down cars, and eventually carried a wad of tips into the office of a travel agent.

ON MONDAY MORNING, my every other thought is of Noel. Of his eyes, closed. Of his mouth, open. Above me.

We woke even in the middle of the night for more. Noel and I were sweating before it even began because Bangkok's heat doesn't cease in the night. Our bodies, dripping, kept sliding. In the end, we had to use our tongues. Hours later, long after dawn, I crawled back onto the mattress, where he lay, still sleeping. He woke, but once he was inside, his eyes closed again.

When Noel opened them, in awe and awayness, I thought, *I want to do this with you, only, ever.* That face, it filled me more than he did.

Days later, when he's gone and the sheets have been washed, I think of that face and reach that same startling peak.

There's a prickle at my neck, a warmth that sweeps my stomach. It feels like there's someone with me, but I'm outside, alone, smoking in front of the gate. Exhaling in the direction of traffic, I remember a conversation between my seven-year-old self and my grandpa Allen.

He was so tall I had to stretch my neck to see his eyes, dark dots behind burgundy-rimmed glasses.

"Grandpa, what are some other 'N' names?"

"'N' names?" he asked, eyes on his feet, shuffling along a path around Henderson Lake in Lethbridge. He was a plumber, but, in letters written to my grandmother during the war, amidst talk of getting an ice box for drinks, he wrote about wanting to write for newspapers for a living.

"You know, names that start with the letter 'n'?" I squinted in the sun. "Boy names."

"Well," he sighed. My grandpa never asked why I wanted to know something. He just answered. He'd raised seven children, two of whom were born in his forties, and I've seen photos of him dressed as the devil in red tights as he took the youngest trick-or-treating. Of course, that was years after he "saw the white light" and gave up the drink. Anyway, the man had patience by the time I came around. Plus, it hurt his heart, I think, that a child should have to go without much of a father. "Ned. Ned is a name that starts with 'n.'"

"Nope. That sounds like a grandpa name, Grandpa." I slipped on a rain-soaked leaf. Grandpa gripped my hand, half-covered in the sleeves of a wool sweater that was too big for me, and pulled me up. It was autumn, a Saturday, and the crown of my head was warm from the sun. I spent a lot of Saturdays with my grandpa. Rocking on the bumpy swing in his backyard, picking raspberries from his garden, walking. Always, though, I was asking him questions. My grandpa, he knew everything.

He nudged his glasses up his nose. "Nathan. Nathaniel," he said. "Those start with 'n.'"

I stopped and gave his suggestions the verbal test. "Natalie and Nathan." I paused. "Natalie and Nathaniel."

He took his hands out of his pockets and tapped my back. Earlier that morning, we'd done yoga together. I'd spied a number of books with the word "psychic" in the title on his shelves.

I took a few steps and caught up to him. "Good ones, Grandpa," I said. "What else?"

The Gate 3 guard's whistle bleats as a car pulls in.

Did he say "Noel"? My chest fills with missing my grandpa and gratitude for this memory. I light another cigarette, exhale hard. I wonder if he's watching me, watching all of this.

SIX-THIRTY A.M. PULLING back the shower curtain, I reach for a towel and hear the trill of my phone. *Why would someone call so early?* My fingers slip around the edge I need to flip.

"Hello?" I sit on my bed, wrapped in the towel, hair dripping on the sheets.

"Natalie."

It's Song.

"Something happened last night." She sounds tired, struggles to explain. "Politics."

Last night, while I read with a flashlight in bed, tanks rolled into Bangkok and parked a block away from my balcony. The barrels of the tanks' rifles were wrapped with yellow ribbons. Yellow, the color of the king's Monday birthday. Seeing soldiers pass on the streets and not knowing why, Thais took pictures

with their phones. Already there were whispers: "It's a coup."
The elite and middle classes have been protesting and calling for Prime Minister Thaksin Shinawatra to step down for
months. His family sold the controlling shares of their telecom-
munications empire Shin Corp., a national asset, to a Singapore
firm for $1.9 billion, allegedly without paying taxes. Members
and supporters of Thaksin's *Tai Rak Tai* (Thai Love Thai) party
have allegedly been receiving kickbacks on construction of the
new Suwarnabhumi Airport. Thaksin, they say, has done nothing to resolve the conflict in the mostly Muslim South, where
separatist violence has led to the deaths of 1,300 people over
the past two years, including the three killed and sixty injured
in six simultaneous motorcycle bombings in the southern town
of Hat Yai three days ago. Oh, and Thaksin's *Tai Rak Tai* won
an unprecedented second term in 2005 by a landslide of sixty-
two per cent after rural villages received $5,000 or more each
in exchange for their support. For this last reason, outside
Bangkok, rural voters, who make up seventy per cent of Thailand's sixty-four million people, are fiercely loyal to Thaksin. To
counter antigovernment protests earlier this year, some rode
tractors to the capital.

"Song, is everything OK?"

"Yes. Yes, don't worry."

Not long after the troops filed into my neighborhood, a
man approached a soldier atop a tank and handed him a bag of
steaming food, perhaps noodles or rice and curry. Relaxed but
hungry, he ate sitting on the green hood of the vehicle. Neighbors passed around a collection plate to get food for the other
soldiers. In the red-light district, emptied not long after happy
hour ended at ten o'clock, bar girls turned up the volume on
the little TVs hanging from ceilings. Prime Minister Thaksin
Shinawatra, in New York for the UN General Assembly, said
he has fired the army chief, Sonthi Boonyaratglin and declared

a state of emergency in Bangkok. Minutes later, his statement was taken off the air. All TV stations, including international ones, were blocked.

All of this, so close to my doorstep. And yet so far away.

"Oh. Good."

"But, anyway, there is no work today. Like a holiday. I think you are not supposed to go outside."

What? I stretch my neck to see outside the porch window. Everything is in its place, the broom on my deck, the building next door, the sun. "What?"

At eleven o'clock last night, a body calling itself the Administrative Reform Council issued a statement saying the army and the national police have seized control of Bangkok. Without firing a shot, troops took over Thaksin's office at Government House, the Shinawatra building and the iTV station.

Food vendors rushed to my neighborhood—to Government House and the United Nations building—in hopes of making money from feeding the troops. A woman who cooks smoked chicken on a stick told a journalist, "Tomorrow everything will be back to normal. Everything is OK because we have a king."

Song yawns. "Just be careful, *na.*"

"OK," I say, walking to my desk to turn on my laptop. I hang up and dry the sides of the phone. Trying to type while holding up my towel, I let go of the terry cloth just long enough to get the *Bangkok Post* address up. The website is frozen on the main page headline: "COUP D'ETAT."

Racing to expat forums, I see strings about everything from the falling *baht* to a six o'clock curfew. No one is supposed to be outside. *What am I going to do?* I look at the plastic bag below my desk where I sometimes keep crackers and juice. *Nothing.* I have to go out.

On the sidewalk I expect to see those two little boys, eating rice soup and shoving a stray dog away from their bowls; those old men by the café, smoking and smiling; the fruit lady clanking bells and cutting pineapple. But they're not there. The road I cross to catch my bus in front of the *wat* is empty. By now there would be four lanes of traffic, stalled and colored with the blue-gray smoke of the fifty-year-old green buses. Still, I look both ways and cross, making my way to the intersection and looking at the street—the buildings, the sidewalk and the signs—as if I've never been on it before. It's still and it's quiet and the air is clear, but that's not what's wrong. It's the whistles. Without whistles it's like Bangkok has lost its breath.

Feet away from the 7-Eleven sign and the Royal Thai Army Headquarters, I spy rifle-bearing soldiers lunged over a second-story rail. Eyes follow me, but I'm not afraid. They're bored or they're surprised to see a female *falang*. I consider waving.

A woman peers out from behind the bars of her noodle shop, bowls of uncut white and green vegetables behind her, watching the soldiers as if they were birds in a tree.

Back home, I smoke and read about the coup online. I eat canned tuna and crackers. Noel texts and reminds me to stay in. He says not to worry too much, though; his coworkers told him this is the country's nineteenth coup. It's business as usual. I write a piece for *The Medicine Hat News* about how exciting it is to have history happening just outside my window. Having emailed my TV internship boss to say if they needed anything to let me know, I get a call from a producer in Toronto. She asks if I'll do a phone interview for their morning show, which involves me waking up at four a.m. I agree. For just a few seconds, in my mind I tape my face to the body of a female CBC foreign correspondent, her backdrops of gunfire and protests. Her belly, flat, cold. Her skin, flaky dry from the recycled air of planes and warn-torn capitals. Crow's feet from squinting in desert suns, from standing alone a lot. And I see all she gave up rather than all she gained to do what she does. And I see my adventure, my awayness as temporary. Because not now but soon I want my own family more.

The last point-form note I make about the coup before shutting down my laptop is that the king declares his support for Sonthi. Just as I am pulling back my sheets again, Song calls. We're going back to work tomorrow.

The producer forgets the fifteen-minute heads-up call.

"So, can you give us a picture of what yesterday was like, Natalie?" This is the voice of the morning-show host. We're live.

My mouth, beyond dry. It's dark. *I can't*, can't find my water. "Well, it wasn't... it wasn't that different." *Fuck*. Of course it was different. More different than if there had been crowds and shouting and shots.

She asks another question. My voice gets broken up by incessant swallowing and seizing. I can't talk. The host cuts the interviewer short.

Later that morning, I get an email from Scott: "Hey Natalie, heard you this morning. You were great."

At first, it surprises me, how little those words reverberate. How wanting that kind of approval, that kind of spotlight, led me here. And now I don't care what the Scotts of the world think, and I don't want that life anyway.

Of course, he was just being polite. I was terrible.

Was it the hour, the husky pitch of the anchor's voice, the pressure of being live, the clamping of my throat? Perhaps all of it, it reminds me I'm not meant for TV correspondence— foreign or domestic. I just want to write. Someday maybe I'll get back to writing for the kinds of thin grayish pages that will actually be read by others (and then promptly used to catch bird droppings). I crave the alchemy of story. The machine of the industry, not as much. But I see now, I don't *need* to write for a big paper in a big city, simply because I don't need to tell it to people from my past. I just need to write.

ZORA GOES INTO labor.

Seventy-two hours later, she sends me an email. She says it's hard to type and breastfeed Ella at the same time. Zora started calling the baby Ella a long time ago. Zora's not sure if she looks like an Ella now that she sees her, but it's what they're calling her. She said she looks like her father, Drew, who is half Trinidadian, and Zora wouldn't know it was her own child if she hadn't felt the doctor's fingers pluck Ella from the bloody nest of her loins.

There is a picture attached of Ella at that moment, fresh from birth. Her brown hair slicked with mucus. Her nose, too big for her face. Dark eyes, wide open, facing the camera, as if she were posing for the photo, as if she knew things we hadn't or couldn't teach her. Beautiful, alive, of her mother and father.

Tears dam under my eyelids, a blink away from falling. I'm not there, beside my best friend, where I should be. I will only know about Ella through Zora's poorly spelled emails about being a milkmaid.

Writing Zora back, I say, "In my mind, I've sent you a hundred hugs. Ella is beautiful, and I can't wait to meet her. I'm so sorry I'm not there."

Noel stirs in the sheets. He hears me sniffle and asks what's wrong.

"I have a new niece."

This is what's hard about being so far from home. You miss the milestones and you fear that your friends and family won't forgive you, or worse, that one day they'll forget about you.

LOST BOYS

THREE FLASHES GO off at once. I'm standing next to Tida, Song and *Pii* Sinn, sandwiched on a bench. Song's eyes are focused on Nok's camera; so are mine. *Pii* Sinn is gazing at *Pii* Fah's lens, and Tida is smiling for Soon. Next to Tida, I look anorexic and sad. The veins of my arm are like blue yarn and my face is coated in the film of my conscience. A giant blue Pepsi poster looms in the background, behind my head. It could almost be mistaken for the sky.

We are waiting to get on a boat that will take us from the Don Wai Floating Market down the River Nakhon Chaisi and feed us along the way. This is my farewell party from this *rajabhat*. I've taken a job at the university next door. Both universities were once a part of Dusit Palace, King Rama V's royal compound. Inspired by trips to Europe, the king flattened a fruit orchard for the tall trees, wide boulevards and colonial-style mansions of his new royal city, and called the district *Dusit*, heavenly gardens. The king's private garden—and, eventually, one university—was named after the consort Sunandha Kumarirat, one of thirty-six women whom Rama V either married or kept as a minor wife. In the dusty, teak-floored rooms where women of the royal court once spent their days dressing and waiting, we chalk English letters and sums and teach young adults how to spend their days dressing and waiting, on foreigners. Starting in the 1930s, the thirty-two residences of Suan Sunandha slowly became classrooms and dormitories for two colleges, one for domestic studies and one for teachers. In 2005, just before I arrived, the king elevated these *rajabhat* institutes to universities.

Last month *Ajarn* Tan asked, "Do you want to stay, in Bangkok, in our department?" Ten months ago, I thought no, no, I absolutely wouldn't want to stay after my one-year contract is up. And then, day by day, Thailand grew on me, and I in Thailand. And then I thought, *I don't ever want to leave*. Ever. The only part of life in Bangkok that I could do without is work, though it has, in turn, taught *me* a great deal about how and why we want to know what we want to know, how humans convince and comprehend, and how I was not put on this earth to be a teacher. Not so deep down, we know where we should not be.

I show up every day and I try to plan lessons that will help my students learn something, and I hope that if and when they remember me, years later, they'll think, *she saw us, she listened to us*. But I don't count on it. Despite my shortcomings, a few weeks ago I was asked to teach at another *rajabhat* university. The department head there said my schedule would be cut in half, I could come and go as I please and he wanted me to start and run a radio program to help students learn colloquial English. My mind drew up an image of the old Natalie, who interviewed strangers and who was known. I accepted.

This is my last day with these women, as coworkers anyway. I put off telling them I was leaving as long as I could, but they could tell long before then, I think, because whenever they said "next semester," I took a breath and kept it in and only nodded,

"Umm hmm." They would never think of going to work for the university next door. When I confessed, I went on about the radio show, and being able to use my journalism background. And then they held back their breath and smiled, lips closed. *Ajarn* Tan was the only one who spoke: "That is good. Good for you, Natalie." But I could sense the steam in her cheeks.

Now she's telling an animated story and the other teachers are laughing. I grin, as I usually do during moments like this, both to say *I understand the story and it's funny*, and to say *I don't understand, but don't mind me*. Sometimes I wish I were one of them. Tida steals the conversation and the women's eyes chase her ring-less hands, skipping with the story.

Pii Fah's and Mee's eyes widen at Tida's words. Song listens expressionless—she's already heard the story. It's so odd to see them out of their suits. Today they are all dressed in sandals, jeans and the green-and-blue English Camp shirts of years past.

We left the university in cars and headed for the other side of the river. I was with *Ajarn* Nand and the air-conditioning was so cold that on the way here I looked not out the window but at the field of goose bumps on my arm. Turns out we are in Nakhon Pathom Province, at a riverside market renowned for its duck and sweets.

A dark wooden boat with open windows drifts toward the dock. *Ajarn* Tan marches over to the captain. The others follow.

It hurts to look these women in the eye. They took me to the bank and the passport office and to both of my apartments. They taught me how to eat noodles with a spoon, how to discreetly dissect a pineapple to share, how to show less skin and somehow be more attractive. They reminded me to never worry, *mai ben lai*. They called me *Norng*, little sister. If I understand at all what it is to be a good Thai, it is because of these women.

One by one, we crawl into the cabin. It's a two-by-ten-foot room with blue plastic chairs and a skinny white table in the center. Just enough space for all of us to sit at the table, but it feels bigger because of the windows, opened to a calm river and a horizon of mangroves.

I set my bag on a chair below an orange life ring. Tida sits next to me, and so does *Ajarn* Nand. Even now, most of the teachers would rather not. They like me, but they'd like me better if I spoke Thai.

Song bends over the table, around *Pii* Fah and Mee, and squints behind her camera. "Natalie, smile."

In the midst of a discussion with *Ajarn* Nand about the verb "to be," we look up. My arms are pinned to my sides so no one will see my sweat stains. *Ajarn* Nand, in a collared blue shirt rolled up to his elbows, gazes at the glass of ice before him, waiting to be filled with beer. His face is shiny and the curls at the top of his receding hairline are wet. His lips are turned down.

Pii Fah catches my eye. "Natalie, see that? The white sign."

Hands on the wooden windowsill, I study the river houses. Some are shacks on stilts with canoes tied to a ladder. Some are three-story buildings of white wood or curved terra-cotta balconies with rock terraces. Beyond their docks and flower beds, past painted yellow shutters, residents' roofs bear hand-painted signs faded by rain and sun.

"Yes. I see it," I say, then glance down at the water. My fingers could graze the currents without bending down. Behind and ahead of us, the river is still and flat and shiny in the middle from the sun's reflection, like a skating rink.

Ajarn Sinn's fingers trace the sign's words. "It says, 'This house has nothing left to steal because it has been'..." She asks around the table for the English version of the verb. "Yes, 'robbed.' This house has nothing left to steal because it has been robbed many times."

"Really?" I check their faces to see if this is true.

"*Chai*," says *Pii* Som. "But then everyone along the river did this. They all put up signs all the time so the robbers would not want to break into their house."

"Did it work?"

They all laugh.

Pii Som answers. "It is more like a joke now, but maybe at one time."

Our heads weave around the server, setting dishes on the table.

"That's funny."

"Yes, so now, the signs mean nothing," *Pii* Som says, puffing air up her face so her bangs blow off her forehead. She ties her ponytail into a knot. In her thick lenses, I can see the other side of the river.

Conversation falls. I watch the white of the table disappearing as more and more food arrives. The steel, tiered bowl of *tom yung gung* is placed in front of Tida. Fish cake squares and shrimp corpses swim in the oily red soup. Two pots of rice are planted at each end of the table. The *som tum* salad is set in front of me. I inhale the aroma of garlic, lime and chilies. My finger rubs the bowl, tempted to dip a long bean in the juice.

"We wanted to get your favorite, Natalie," says *Ajarn* Sinn, sunglasses atop her short, curly hair. With her red lips and fitted plaid shirt, she reminds me of models from the '50s. "But they could not do it. So sorry."

My favorite Thai dish is *yum tua pu*, winged-bean salad. It's made from plier-shaped beans found in central Thailand. The sauce is a mix of peanuts, palm sugar, chili paste, and the milk and meat of coconuts. Slices of hard-boiled eggs are served on the side. At the mere thought of *yum tua pu*, my tongue waters and burns with its spice. They know this, and that makes my heart burn too.

"Oh," I say, swallowing. "That's so thoughtful."

"Another time," she says, and winks.

By now the rest of the food has arrived, grilled chicken with a sweet chili sauce, fried noodles and smoked sea bass served on a bed of banana leaves and dressed in yellow flakes of gingerroot.

Eating begins and lasts for hours. This is the way Thais eat, slowly and in the background of conversation. Plates are cleared only when diners part. Because of me there are two strands of conversation, the first between the Thai women at one end, the second in English between *Ajarn* Nand, me and occasionally Tida at the other end. *Ajarn* Nand, who usually talks on and on, as if he'd been saving sentences all week for us, is quiet. Without the croak of his voice, our end of the table is silent. I don't notice it now, but later, after he dies of cancer, I will wonder if the next life was on his mind.

"Natalie," Tida shouts.

The deep-fried fish cake from the *tom yum gung* lies on my tongue, soup oozing from its flakes. I cover my mouth and turn to her.

Tida coughs and noses my empty plate. "You really like Thai food now. But," she says, eyeing my bowl of spicy shrimp soup without the shrimp, "you still don't like seafood."

I blush, hooking my hair behind my ears.

At the other end of the table, *Ajarn* Tan thrusts her chair back and stands.

"Listen please, everyone," she says, folding her sunglasses into her shirt pocket. Her eyes are fixed on mine.

Shoots of guilt wade in the food I've just eaten.

"Now, as you know," *Ajarn* Tan says, stiff voice slicing the lazy afternoon air, "we are here today to say goodbye to Natalie."

My eyes block out the rest of the boat and fasten to her small dark eyes, her wiry hair pulled into a ponytail and her yellow shirt, flecked with white roosters and their red combs.

Ajarn Tan goes on to say it's been a pleasure to have me, that I'm special in their hearts and they will not forget me. They know I will have good luck and a happy future. And I am their sister, always.

The other teachers clap.

Tida pretends to cry and sets her palm on my shoulder. "Oh, Natalie, please do not leave us."

I flick her shoulder. "Tida."

"And," says *Ajarn* Tan, "we would like to present you with something to say thank you, *na*."

She angles over the table and hands me a small box with a card stuck to the top. Before reaching out for it, I *wai* her. The card was made on the computer by Song and on the outside it says, "Good luck." Inside, the teacher's signatures offer well wishes in blue and purple ink.

Before I unwrap the box, I exhale. "You..." My stomach creaks like an old wooden floor. "You have all been so wonderful to me. And I'm so grateful, for everything." Breath jerks out of my mouth. My eyes pulse and tear and ask for their forgiveness.

I unwrap my present. It's a set of matching earrings, a bracelet and a belt. Plastic pink and yellow balls and shells are linked with silver beads. Tida's thumb brushes my wrist as she fastens the bracelet, then turns the belt the right side around on my waist. Once everything is on, I lift my head and sniffle. Song takes a picture.

"*Suai*," says *Ajarn* Fah. Beautiful.

"Natalie, you cannot go," Tida says, eyes darting to take others in. "We will never find another teacher who will leave the shrimps for us."

OUR KNEES TOUCH. Mine are bare, but Molly's wearing fisherman pants, so light you can dry them with your breath. We're sitting cross-legged on the sand, leaning back on our wrists. We move only to bring cigarettes to our lips.

Feeling pensive, I ask Molly questions I myself want to answer. "How will we ever leave here?"

Here is Thailand. Home is home. For me, that's Medicine Hat. For Molly, that's London. As English teachers in our twenties, we are like Lost Boys, stalling adulthood in a wild we want to claim. If we wanted to stay in Thailand, we'd have to stay in this state, like *soi* dogs, out, not in. A half life. Liliwen, who is leaving in a few months, always says, "No matter what, you will never *be* Thai." Not to them. Our white skin will mark us as outsiders and stop our feet from rooting. And yet home, the plain normalness of it, isn't the place for us either.

Molly slurps through her straw and shakes her head. We are about to finish a Thai rum and Red Bull, watered down by melting ice in a plastic cup.

Thirty minutes ago, the four of us—Molly, Noel, Yonni and I—stepped off a speedboat driven by a long-haired guy called Jimmy. Liliwen had spoken to a taxi driver in their village and explained Molly and Yonni wanted to go to Koh Samet, and on the way out of Bangkok they needed to pick up Noel and me at Khao San. Liliwen teaches on Saturdays, so she's coming tomorrow. In the Friday-afternoon traffic, it took the taxi almost two hours to get to us, standing in our sandals at the edge of Ratchadamnoen Road with two Burger King bags. While we waited, Noel told me a story about his mom pulling up to a sister's house in a station wagon in January, and leaving the car running outside, in the snow, while Noel, nine months old, slept buntied in a blanket on the seat. His mom said goodbye into a puff of winter breath, then turned to the street and screamed. The car was gone. Stolen. Then returned, forty minutes later, not long after the teenage thief heard Noel's first cry.

When he arrived, the driver, a chubby older man with a missing front tooth, didn't mind the food in the car, even smiled and turned up the volume on his radio, set to a station that played the country music Thais call *luuk thung*, children of the fields. And then he asked where we wanted to go. I looked at Noel, then Molly. Molly looked at me, then Yonni. Yonni, in the front seat, trying to block a tomato from falling out of his bun, looked at the three of us in the back. We weren't sure if we should say Koh Samet, a tiny island along the Gulf of Thailand, since that's our final destination, or Ban Phe, where the closest pier is, or Rayong, the province Ban Phe is in, 137 miles from Bangkok. Noel rubbed his hands, leaned toward the driver's ear, and said, "Koh Samet." And he said, "OK. OK. *Dai.*" Can. As if this was news to him. But he smiled and sang and danced a little in his seat so we liked him. We even offered him French fries, but he shook his head no. Later, Yonni reckoned he probably had to be reminded to eat each day. Just as he had to be reminded where we wanted to go approximately every twenty minutes. Quickly losing faith, we tried to watch for the signs of cities along the way—Chonburi, Si Racha, Pattaya and Sattahip— but not all of them were in English and it didn't matter if we could read; our driver couldn't. So he stopped, about four times before Rayong, to ask gas boys and other drivers if he was going the right way. Afterward he'd climb in the car grinning and give us a thumbs-up. During one of the traffic jams, we'd showed him how to do the thumbs-up and he made an "*Oooay*" noise when he saw my thumb, a perfect "L." It was during one of these moments I thought, he's never been this way before, he's never seen the ocean. I've met Bangkok taxi drivers, many of whom hail from the North, who say their dream is to see the ocean and I'd think, well, just start walking and you'll be there in a day or two. But it's not like that for everyone.

We realized later that we didn't want to go to the main Ban Phe pier, where the ferries to Koh Samet are, because it would be too late to take one. Liliwen had told us to go to a deserted pier around the corner where a guy she knew knew a guy who had a speedboat, and for 1,200 *baht* ($34), he'd make the twenty-minute drive over the ocean to Koh Samet in the dark. Somehow, we made it. Sitting on a red metal gate at the end of a pier lit by one fluorescent light, Jimmy was waiting for us, keys in one hand, a cigarette in the other. We had to roll up our jeans to walk onto the beach below our guesthouse, where a mustached DJ/barman standing under a neon green light threw Yonni the keys. Molly and I walked barefoot all the way from the boat up to our bungalow. We changed out of our city clothes so quickly neither of us had bothered to turn on the light.

Now, at the beach, we can't take our eyes off the ocean. "Can you even think of where you would be if you were at home?" I feel high. "Can you?"

"I know. God, I'd probably be in a pub, after work, getting pissed."

I'd be hungover on the couch, a cigarette butt dangling from yellow-brown rings on my fingers.

Waves tumble toward us and skim the sand near our toes. There is no line between the ocean and the sky. It's all dark, endless. A breeze flutters up my top and draws the cotton against my back. I study the moon, as far away as Medicine Hat. Right now, my mom is getting ready for work, curling her hair in the bathroom, an elbow raised as she winds and unwinds the rod. My brother is stepping outside in unlaced runners to start his truck and light his first cigarette of the day, smoke clouding in the winter air.

Noel totters in the sand. "Ladies."

He and Yonni both have four plastic cups between their fingers. Molly and I raise our hands, faintly, to help.

"Right." Yonni's eyes scan the table, far below his knees and filled with the cups of those who were here before us. He hovers. "OK."

Noel takes the cups from him and places all the drinks in two neat rows in the middle.

"So, Moll, where were we?" Noel asks. He rubs down the dark chest hair crawling out of his white t-shirt, given out for free at Spectrum, a summer festival in Medicine Hat. Noel prefers to wear free t-shirts, and he has a tendency to nickname people at the start.

My fingers circle the drinks. I look for the one with the least ice. "We were just guessing what we might be doing at this instant if we were back home. *Home* home."

Molly draws a drag of her cigarette and turns to Yonni.

Yonni lights his own and inhales. "I don't know, man. I've been gone for so long. Three years. I've now gone from China to Japan, back to China, and now to Thailand. It's addictive, man." Addictive—new neighborhoods, odd sounds, different food, being no one and the new foreigner—like tobacco. He ashes his cigarette with two quick taps and looks at Noel.

"Hell if I know." He strokes his jaw. "No, I do know. Downtown Vancouver. Pouring a pink martini for some blonde whose boyfriend drives a Lamborghini."

Molly is quick to turn Noel's shame into a smile. "Couldn't have been all bad."

"No, it was good money, that's for sure." He looks down at his fingers and spins the wooden beads on his wrist. Home is on Noel's mind now more than ever. The Thai government is cracking down on teachers with forged degrees. Noel, some kind of genius and the perfect teacher, doesn't exactly have a degree but he doesn't want to embarrass his school by being thrown out of the country so he's leaving at the end of the term, next spring. Last week Noel told me about his decision. "It's time," he said.

"I was a barmaid for a while and I quite liked it," says Molly, fondling the earrings that fall just below her bob. She's fallen for teaching. Thailand, she knows she'll leave someday sooner than later. But now she knows she wants to teach, the little ones, with lisps and tales and scrapes and potty-talk. "Money was shit, though."

I hated serving. Hated the way people treated me. Men think "waitress" means prostitute. Women think "waitress" means I want to steal your bald husband who treats me like a prostitute. I see flashes of French-manicured fingers waving me off and thick, hairy hands patting my ass. If I left Thailand, I'd probably have to go back to that. No more *Ajarn* Natalie, no more *wai*s.

"Well, all the best people are poor," says Yonni. He beats the table as if it's an African drum. He is always dancing from the waist up. Always quoting Frost, talking in poetry. Wants, I suspect, to someday write something brilliant himself. Something happened to his father when he was a boy, and I think he wants that too, fatherhood. These things we want, more than we know. Closer than we know.

"The most interesting people I have ever met did not have a suit in their closet," he says.

Yonni's t-shirt features a tree, which says to a man: "Hug me." The man replies: "No." Yonni, half-Malaysian and raised in England, often wears a shirt that says, "Someone stole my visa." He belongs nowhere even more than the rest of us.

"They didn't," he says.

Molly nods. "Exactly."

"But being awesome doesn't pay the bills, does it? If it did, I would be *ri-ch*." Noel sings the word "rich." Movie voices and caroling, they often spike his speech.

He says this as I'm taking a sip and I laugh and snort the drink out my nose. Molly tries not to laugh. I wipe my chin with my shirt.

"Why aren't we running the world?" Noel shouts at the sky, thrusting his arm into the air.

Molly thumbs the spaghetti straps of her black tank top. "Yeah!"

Two shirtless bar boys in jeans and bare feet strut past us carrying sticks soaked in gasoline. Everyone who was on the dance floor at Silver Sand Bar is making their way to the beach, fumbling in their 50-*baht* shoulder bags for silver digital cameras. Flame-throwing is nightly island entertainment, but we've all seen it before.

Noel and Yonni joke about having abs like the bar boys. Molly turns to me. "We never asked you."

"What?"

"What you would be doing, if you were at home."

Somehow, in my mind, the words "home" and "Noel" have dovetailed. He makes me remember the Medicine Hat of my childhood, tobogganing over coulees, building forts in the dirt hills with my brothers. But that's not my Medicine Hat anymore. I can hardly picture myself there now, with my already stitched-over family separated again, with the rift between me and my friends who think I think I'm too good for them, with the chance I could run into Stuart at every turn. I broke up with Medicine Hat too, and I worry it might always be awkward around her.

What now?

What do I want not if but when I go back to Canada? A desk. Some writing I'm proud of. The city, I don't know. Now that I've lived in one of the world's biggest cities, I know it doesn't mean you've made it. It only means you are less known and have more restaurants to choose from. Vancouver, maybe? Maybe smaller, like Whistler. Where people will be a little more carefree, a little more caught up in just being. Anyway, somewhere neither too far from nor too close to Medicine Hat. Noel, if he'll have me. A few green- and brown-eyed faces that resemble ours and bear the names of our grandparents. Stories I'd never tell my own grandchildren.

Facing the waves in bare feet, the first flame-thrower's body forms an angel. The fire colors half circles between his legs and his arms. He looks like an eagle, saluting the sky.

WAVES ROLL OVER my stomach. Leaning back onto my elbows, I slide as water tugs weightless toes. Sand pools between the seams of my bathing suit.

I never would have known this. The ocean's skirts and light. My heart, my feet, at peace.

The sun is somewhere behind the beach, past the trees, but it's waltzing on my skin, warming it more with every step. The straw cowboy hat I bought Noel for his birthday shades my nose, more freckled already than it was yesterday. The leather chin strap dangles on my bare back.

Then I hear Noel's voice. "You, uh, come around here often?"

The ocean is so loud and the sand so quiet I didn't hear him approaching. My neck twists so I can see his face. "Hi."

"Oh, man," he says, surveying the horizon. With depth, the water's color shifts from white to turquoise to blue.

How would we fare somewhere slightly less romantic? Like the tiny yellow-green kitchen of one of those townhouses for low-income families—a toddler and a baby filing our legs and drifts of bills on the counter and a charcoal March morning out the window? What then? What if this love, this story, weren't enough? What if I still become my family's most unlikable characters: the philanderer, the drinker, the middle-aged mother who loses her mind? What if—as much as I want a noisy, messy, happy little house someday—I'm not cut out for it?

Rising in stages, I smooth the sand out of my bikini bottom. I reach for Noel's hand and place the hat back on his head. We stride through the water until it reaches our knees. His arm finds my shoulder. He's warm. When his fingers stroke the skin above a dotted birthmark on my back, I feel the craggy, chewed edges of his nails.

The echo of my bones, each one knows this story, knows him.

Noel draws my waist to his, kisses my forehead. "I love you."

And it's tempting to believe in all of this.

LANTERNS ON
THE RIVER

FINGERS, SPINNING A sarong around my waist. Fingers, draping a sash over my shoulder. Fingers, decorating my arms and ears with costume gold. And so many pins.

The moon has stamped itself in the clouds by the time I'm ushered into the costume room. I feel like Cinderella's mannequin when the mice and the bluebirds are lofting thread and bows to finish her ball gown. The teachers sing words I don't know but understand. Their soft, busy arms blanket me.

I am in Nakhon Nayok, where Noel lives. More specifically, at the school where he teaches. It's the night of the twelfth moon and everyone from the school is dressing up for Loy Krathong. Tonight, the entire kingdom will give thanks to the river and ask it to carry their troubles out to sea on a float of flowers and banana leaves. It has been one year since Song helped me relinquish a *krathong* to the rocky waters of the Chao Phraya in Bangkok. Here in Nakhon Nayok, the whole town gathers by the school and the river to sing and dance and light the night with the candles of their *krathongs*.

After a stop at the town salon, where my hair was pinned into a French twist stiff as a lampshade, and my bangs molded into an ocean wave, *Ajarn* Win, one of Noel's coworkers, braced my shoulders and said, "Ahh. *Suai mahk*, Natalie."

Her touch kindled shivers from my wrist to my chin.

"Almost forgot," she said.

Ajarn Win scurried over to a plastic bag by her seat and lifted up an orchid with purple petals and a belly of white. She dug through the hairdresser's tray, then folded my left earlobe as she slid a bobby pin across my neck and over the stem. A petal tickled my ear. Above us, the moon was inching up the sky as if being pulled by string. It was orange, pregnant with light and hazy with waves of heat.

"*Deegwa*," she said, hands clasped at her chest. Better. Then *Ajarn* Win showed me the way to the costume room.

As the teachers flutter around my waist in front of the wardrobe I catch glimpses of myself in the mirror. Barefoot on a wooden floor, I am wrapped from neck to ankle in white and gold fabrics that shimmer when I move. Later, I will find out this is a traditional Thai wedding dress used in plays. On me, the hem is too short and even on its last latch, the golden bejeweled belt clamps my lungs, but my hair and makeup look less silly now. All of this, it makes me heady.

The teachers see it. I don't know if it's because happiness is radiating from every goose bump on my body, or if Thais are better at hearing what hasn't been said. After all this—the highways and oceans, the buses and motorbikes, that led me here, to Noel and to myself—I have to believe the universe loves extravagant stories too.

Corkscrewing my body to see the dress from all sides, I study myself as if in pictures, years from now. And I'd remain giddy, but a knot is bobbing up my middle. I need to tell Noel.

IN THE FIRST of many photos that night, you might not notice we're almost holding hands.

His thumb rubs my wrist and lingers there.

"*Noel.*" I scold him but his touch jangles, wanting too.

It isn't proper for couples to show affection in public, and here in this small town, everyone is watching us. We prefer to be respectful, but we haven't seen each other in five days. Which is a long time when you're in love.

How will I start this story? *Noel, I have something to tell you...*

Noel smiles at *Ajarn* Win. Frizzy stubs of dark chest hair poke out of his yellow King shirt even though he trims the area to avoid chest sweat showing up on his shirts. The navy pants he's wearing were bought at Tesco in Chainat. During a month-long trip back to Canada last year, he gained so much weight they didn't fit when he returned to Thailand. Noel continued wearing them, though, zippered but unbuttoned. In class, he would turn to the board and raise the falling zipper, then face his students with a chalk-dusted crotch. The pants fit now. Noel wanted to be wearing a costume too, but he decided too late and everything had already been signed out. I have only been wearing my dress for twenty minutes, and already it's wrecked: my belt, studded in the middle with a faux red gem, is left of center and the sash across one shoulder is unraveling.

First, I'll tell the inciting incident: *You know how the night before Christmas Eve, everyone used to go to Gringo's? I was there two Decembers ago, and I ran into Scott, Scott Wicks—tall, runner, Student Association president, moved to Ottawa? Anyway, he said, "Natalie, what are you doing here? I thought you'd be somewhere." Like Toronto or New York or something. I told him, "You don't have to be in a big city to make a big difference, you know?" I said, "Hey, I'm happy here."*

"Ready?" asks *Ajarn* Win. She had us standing the other way around before, but she couldn't see my gold armband so we had to switch places. Behind us, the hair-like branches of a banyan tree break up the sky, now black. Incense wafts out of the temple windows and we hear the footsteps of those going inside to make merit.

But I wasn't. Happy. The next morning I woke up and I thought I was going to throw up. I knew I had to go. But it was Christmas, and I owned a house with Stuart.

Noel leans into me a little more. Our fingers sift into one another's palms. Touching him, even a little, quiets me. We think we're getting away with something, but if you look close enough at the photo, you can see our wrists touching.

The rising action: *I left. All these weird, bad things kept happening in Calgary. I thought this guy was going to shoot me, but he had a pigeon, not a gun. It's funny now, but I wondered. About going back.*

"One, two, three." *Ajarn* Win steps back, eyeing our faces instead of the camera screen. "Maybe one more."

The protagonist's internal struggle: *But there was something inside me that was so sure everything was going to be OK. And Medicine Hat, I could always go back. I could always go back.*

Before long, our cheeks are sore. Students who still have baby teeth want a picture with Noel. The other Thai teachers want pictures with us, standing between our armpits. Strangers smile.

I wrote Gil. He told me I should travel. I got a job. Found a flight. Suddenly, here I was, in Thailand. I kept trying to figure out why I was here.

A woman on the path by the river, out of ear range of the school stage, shouts at me. "You look beautiful!"

Turning to find her voice, I see her, an older woman in a baggy t-shirt over capris. Our eyes meet.

"Like Thai woman," she says. Her arched eyebrows are question marks: Do I understand?

Shock stings my face then fades. I return her gaze and nod. I understand. I do. Tonight, if I'm special, it's not because I'm white; it's because I'm trying to be Thai.

Noel looks confused. "That was weird."

"No, I get it," I say, watching her disappear into the crowd of people on the road.

And then you sent that email, "You've probably never heard of it. It's called Medicine Hat." I must have read that line a hundred times. My mind swims past quitting *The News*, leaping up the snow-dusted stairs with Scott, seeing Stuart's reflection in the driveway, ketchup on my ankle, my plea to Gil, meeting Pippa, even Rune. I cried and I prayed and I wished and I listened. Still, I had to wait.

Between the school gates and the pier, the whole town is here. On a stage skirted with yellow fabric, a dozen girls perform a traditional Thai dance. They're wearing costumes like mine in peach and pink, and dance not with their feet or their hips but their hands, fingers curling and twisting to a recorded singer's voice and the lonely croak of a wooden drum.

My eyes break from the dancer's knuckles. "What do you want to do?"

Noel looks both ways, the reflection of white lights strung by the river dotting his glasses.

We walk toward the moon, strung above the dark forest on the other side of the river. Our feet reach the water's edge by following a trail of candle smoke and giddy children. They've waited all year for tonight. Joy bounces through their knees, up to their elbows and into their noses. But it's quiet. Save for matches being struck and mothers whispering instructions into little ears, there is only the sound of banana leaves bathing.

The whole time, I wanted to tell you, "Noel, it's me. Don't you get it?"

Sometimes we need the story almost as much as the ending, don't we?

The love story, that's just one strand. The other is the story of a young woman who was suffocating. Her heart spoke. The wind showed her the way. She left. She stumbled. Stood. Found her feet. Turned mistakes into tickets. Tiptoed. Changed, into a woman not wiser, not stronger, but trustier. She knew that if she trusted her gut, she would be OK. The universe would make sure.

Both stories, how I've needed them. Needed every minute of showing myself. And finding him.

Noel is taking pictures above the pier. His lens frames a school of *krathong*s, clumped but upright like the contents of canned vegetable soup. This river is a gentle thing compared to the rocky girth of Bangkok's Mae Nam Chao Phraya. I remember my Loy Krathong experience last year with Song, my float toppling in the waves and her saying, "Maybe you will have better luck next year, *na*."

A tear emerges but does not part from my eye. It dangles, like a toe over a boat.

The conflict and twist: *I nearly gave up. In August, I was almost… Something happened. I almost left. But something told me not to.*

Noel ducks around a little girl on all fours, crawling on a cement wall above the water. She wants to see where her *krathong* is now, if the candle is still burning. Thais believe it's a good omen if the *krathong* stands and sails downriver, candles still alight. The girl's hands are at the edge of the picture, now a snaking line of yellow and pink flowers. Every six *krathong*s or so are still lit and drifting.

"Wouldn't it be cool to do this in Medicine Hat?" Noel's camera still covers his face. "On the river?"

"Would it ever." I picture it: us, back in Canada, launching a *krathong* between the cottonwood trees, into the South Saskatchewan. Us. Does he see us there, together? My mind has only erected the scene of our drive from the airport and a welcome-back party where Noel would shake my brother's hand and I would hug his dog and everyone would ask what it was like, and what now. Would we stay and go to Tigers games and Ralph's country bar? My chest twists. Can I go back for good? Can he?

We don't have to know the answers.

With my back to the river, under the still leaves of a palm tree, I lean on the wall's ledge. And what about, will my mind drift, or my fingers slip? What if?

The climax: *Finally, you came to Bangkok.*

"Ready?" he says.

I nod. Noel's been putting off picking out our own *krathong*.

A Chinese boy with an overbite stands behind a table of *krathong*s, hands held behind his back. There are hundreds of them, and more waiting on a patch of a grass below the trees. Schoolgirls and their mothers spent the day making them. These *krathong*s look healthier than the one I bought in Bangkok last year. These banana-leaf bases are ripe and green, and the orchids have opened. Other flowers—white and yellow ones, mostly carnations—have been planted around incense and a thin, yellow candle.

"What's that?" I say, pointing to the little white slip of paper between the incense sticks.

The Chinese boy thinks I'm choosing one, and leans in, lifting it for me.

"I don't know. Guess we could open it," says Noel.

"No." I block his hand. "It might be bad luck. It's probably written in Thai anyway."

"True."

"Do you care which one we get?" I ask. The teachers told us we should float a single *krathong* together, though some couples float their own and believe that if, downriver, the *krathong*s stay together, so will they.

Noel shrugs. "They all kind of look the same to me."

They're not. My hand hovers around a handful of *krathong*s at the center of the table. In my head I think this choice really means something, that there is only one right one.

"Here," I say. The *krathong* is simple. Purple orchids pinned to the banana-leaf base circle a center of yellow carnations, two red candles and an incense stick.

Noel nods. The Chinese boy stuffs the money into his shirt pocket.

Heading back to the river, I carry the *krathong* like a cake. My elbow brushes Noel's, and then it is our eyes that meet. Like the whole world knows.

We have to walk down a set of wooden steps to get close enough to let go of our *krathong* so it can join the others on their brief but beautiful voyage. People are lined up on the bank. Waiting, Noel watches to see how others do it, to see their *krathong* ebb and sway into this waterborne-garden, to see their faces when, after all, it floats. Their joy is his. This is just one of the qualities I love most about Noel.

The night is still hot. My upper lip is moist with sweat.

Noel makes way for those ahead of us to leave the bank. "Our turn."

I pass him the *krathong*.

His eyebrows furrow, and his hands are still.

I continue holding it out for him. Even though it's as light as a bouquet, it feels heavy in my hands. "You do it."

Before I let go, I say, "But we have to make a wish."

Our fingers hold the banana-leaf base together. I feel its little ridges, smell the perfume of the orchids.

My eyes and mouth close. I ask the universe to please keep us together.

Noel makes a wish too.

With the *krathong* flowers between our faces, our eyes meet and pause. We know what this means.

The denouement: *Noel, I think I came here to find you.*

I feel like the caterpillar that crossed the road. Here I am.

Noel's hand stains the small of my back with warmth.

See, see, see, says my heart. Here we are.

"Noel."

He looks up, hopeful and sweet. Innocent of all this.

"I have something to tell you."

Our *krathong* lands and sways forward, then back the way it came. With a little wind, the *krathong* will sail in a chain of floats through the night. Sometime before dawn, I imagine, it will break free and drift toward the sea.

EPILOGUE
2017

I N THE HOURS when they are near sleep but can't because they're ill or afraid of monsters or we're somewhere strange or they just don't want the day to end, I tell them The Story of Bennett, or The Story of Eddie, depending on which son lies awake, teary-cheeked, stalling my creaky rise from his little twin bed.

The first line is always the same: "A long, long time ago, in a faraway land called Thailand, Mommy was—"

"Mama, how far is it? The faraway land?"

Not long ago he began copying the way one of his French friends at day care says Mama, and I love it too much to correct him. His breath is sweet, like bubblegum toothpaste. Or sour, because he's been throwing up. He is three, or five. Very concerned with distances, especially as they relate to the mere handful of places we have been brave enough to take him and his brother.

"Two oceans and a hundred thousand miles." These numbers, I've typed and read them so many times.

"Farther than Grandma Dar's?"

Grandma Dar, Noel's mom, who lives in Medicine Hat. I always think it's funny how children call a grandparents' home after the grandmother, not the grandfather. We women, we steer ships for longer than we know. For our own, for our children's own.

"Farther than Grandma Dar's."

"Farther than Saskatchewan?"

"Farther than Saskatchewan."

Their grandfather, my dad, still lives there, and we marvel at the thorny sound its letters make when his packages arrive. *Sas-kat-chew-an*: swift-flowing river, in Cree. We also have a saying in our house, when a balloon is lost to the skies or a plastic sword to cracks, "Long gone Saskatchewan." Gone, never to return. Like the buffalo. Like farmers' daughters.

We live two provinces away, in Vernon, BC, a mountain town not unlike Medicine Hat in size. Four months after moving back to Canada with Noel, I was eating spicy shrimp soup without the shrimp at a new Thai restaurant in Medicine Hat with Zora and baby Ella when my phone rang. It was the editor of a Vernon daily, where I'd applied for a reporter position.

Zora dropped her fork. "Jesus, Natalie," she said, "Here you go again."

I had never been to Vernon, but Noel had driven through the Okanagan on his way home from Vancouver, and said it was at the tip of a breathtaking valley of lakes and orchards. That hippies and painters and outsiders and outdoor enthusiasts lived there. And that was enough for me. I knew from my time in Thailand that I was calm near water. I also liked the idea of living in this other idyllic land where people paddled and hiked in Mother Nature's arms, took care of her and created art about her. But mostly I wanted to be warm.

Noel and I had returned to Medicine Hat at the end of March, its dirty snowdrifts, crooked winds and short days seeming to

get longer. In the beginning, we sat around in our Thai fisherman pants, which weren't warm enough and suddenly looked
like rodeo clown's clothes next to those butt-hugging yoga pants.
We also ogled at the sea of white faces every which way and
pouted a little at being nobodies again. At my childhood house
on 7th Street, where we were housesitting for my ex-stepdad,
we spoke bits of Thai to each other. We ate with spoons. But we
also watched hockey, drank wine, made love under the covers
and occasionally ventured outside, onto the ice.

When I met his parents and cousins and aunts and had to
answer their questions about my family, when I took hot baths
and the water licked my neck and swallowed my knees and I
had to answer my own questions about my family—not together
at all and not even split, now, but each member alone, hurt,
hurting—I drowned in all the things I had been able to ignore
on the other side of the world. The architecture of this family
tree, my sliding place in it. And all the more it set me off again,
away from breaks I couldn't fix and determined to grow a family
of my own that would stand.

When he finally heard all my fears about the family I wanted
and the family I had, and met a good number of the people I
was related to by blood or marriage, it hardly dissuaded Noel.
One night we were on the steps outside, smoking, and I said
something like, "It's not too messy... for you?"

"God no. You know I'm a Dee, right?" Dee, his maternal
grandparents' last name. And he told the story of an alcoholic
uncle at a family reunion, bitter that Noel's older brother and
cousin had returned to the campfire empty-handed. "Bet you
didn't even bring me a beer," he slurred, mustache webbed
with spit. "Well then, you can just get the hell outta here. We
don't want ya, and we don't need ya." It was a story that made
you laugh, rather than one that was tough to swallow, like most
of mine, but now I knew what I'd needed to hear to move on,

with him and on my own: I am not them. We just lived in a house together once.

In Vernon, I found us a Vancouver couple's summer home overlooking Okanagan Lake, with a pit for fires and two chairs on the sand. One morning, we were sitting barefoot on the beach when a blanket of sparrows flew from the knuckles of a giant willow tree. The sun was already casting nets of light on the lake. I couldn't stop my tongue.

"I think we should get married here."

My son, yawning now. Of course, I don't tell him about how he nearly was never made. Or about how, after we told our families and went home for Christmas, I ran into Stuart.

I'd had a feeling I would run into him. It was exactly three years after the eve of Christmas Eve that set me in the bathroom stall of a bar with Scott's words ringing in my ear. I opened that green metal door knowing I wasn't happy in Medicine Hat or with my boyfriend, and left both within weeks. Now, in this other bar, the Silver Buckle, there were a dozen heads between us. Because the ceiling was low and we were all in sweaters, everyone's cheeks were pink. Mine too.

After shuffling through the crowd toward him, I opened my arms and said, "Hi."

"Hey," he said, and let me in.

My face pressed the yarns of a green sweater I had bought for him. Somehow the sweater was familiar, but not him.

"Heard you got engaged."

His eyes, if nothing else, still blue. Still kind. A reddish beard about his smile.

We forgot about all that other stuff. The money. The renovating mishaps. The maybe somedays.

"Yeah."

"He's from Medicine Hat? That's what I heard."

"Yeah. He is."

I stretched my neck to see if I could spot Noel. I caught a patch of his beanie, next to his cousin and a guy named Moose. It was still hard to believe I'd found him on Khao San Road, wearing that beanie, no idea who I was, all the time we were in Thailand, all the time we were in Medicine Hat. All the ways we could have met before, all the people who could have introduced us. Now, I wondered, were we divined? Lucky? Or just determined?

"Crazy."

Stuart stole a look at my fingers, the ring. White gold and the band, dotted with diamonds, forks before the rectangular stone, green tourmaline. It has an antique look about it, and I'd spotted it myself in the window of a jewelry store while I waited to go in and interview an MLA for some kind of year-in-review story. Stuart's mom had emailed me once and said, "Would it have made a difference if Stuart had bought a ring?" I don't know if *she* wondered or if she was wondering for him. I told her no, it wouldn't have made a difference. From the outside, it looked like we had it pretty good. Or good enough. I told her I just had a feeling I had to go.

And I did. I needed to see the world, make my way, meet Noel.

It's too simple, almost. With Stuart, I had doubts. With Noel, I didn't.

Soon, Stuart and I ran out of things to talk about.

"Well, I should probably..."

"Yeah," he said, tipping his beer bottle at me. "Take care."

My eyes locked with his, blue as ever. Forgiving, sure.

"You too."

My son's eyes, heavy now and yet needing to stick out the story's end. His hair, it smells of baby shampoo or pee or lake. He loves hearing about the wedding, about how it was the hottest June 28 Vernon had ever had, that aunts and uncles and cousins and friends and grandparents drove for days to be there.

"Even Oakley?" he asks.

Oakley, their "uncle." He was Jon's dog, now Noel's parents' dog.

Was Oakley there? I don't remember. Molly and Liliwen were there. Noel and I were maybe the only ones from Vernon, so perhaps not in the best interest of the environment to have ninety-odd people driving vehicles for days to join us. But my son, he smiles when I say that everyone we knew and loved was on the landing of one of his favorite lakefront parks. That we ate ice cream cake at the end and some stripped off their collars and socks and even their pants, and went swimming in the dark.

At some point in the night when we were all still dressed and seated, and the wine was making us sentimental, too sentimental for Noel's taste, he plucked the microphone from its stand.

In that voice of Ron Burgundy from *The Anchorman*, he said, "Well, good evening, everyone."

The guests laughed.

Noel paused for effect, made that character's smirk of vanity and idiocy. "Hey, if you, uh, ever want to meet a nice girl from Medicine Hat, just move to the other side of the world and wait awhile."

For a while after the wedding, everything was mostly as wonderful as it had been in Thailand. We were so poor, but we didn't care at all. And then the paper I worked at became a sinking ship, so I jumped to another paper, and a few months later, as the recession lurched toward us, I was laid off.

One of my last tasks at the paper was to write a blurb about a Canadian woman writer who now lived in London, UK, and was giving a reading in Vernon. She was also the director of a creative writing master's program that focused on long-form narrative non-fiction—true stories that use the literary devices of fiction. Yet again, I had that feeling, that something was happening for me, and I could yank it by the tail and hold on, or let it scurry off into the woods. At the end of her talk, I was introduced to her and I said, "Your program, that's exactly what I want to do."

Noel and I decided to turn lemons into London, go on one more adventure before we gave in to a mortgage and parenthood. So, with little more than a massive line of credit, a duvet gifted to us at our wedding and some wool sweaters, we moved to the UK and I began that master's degree.

My final project would be to write a book. This book.

For a long time, the story was a lie. A love story would have been too cheesy for me, so at first it was just about me and my adventure in Thailand. And then I admitted it was very much a love story, so I wrote about that. I didn't want the whole of the world to know I was a confused floozy for a while, so I left out the part about what really happened on the eve of Christmas Eve and a lot of other nights. But you could tell something was being left out, and I thought, I may not have done anything particularly lionhearted, this story may not be exceptional, but perhaps that's why someone might need it. I thought about all the books that helped inch me along, how much it would have meant back then to hear the true story of a young woman who had the same kind of everyday unease about a life just enough, and left it. Story, as Barry Lopez wrote, sometimes people need it more than food. What I had was a story, and the chance to tell it with intimacy and honesty.

So, I wrote the whole story. The truth.

My son's eyelashes, so long, ever so heavy now, almost set. He'll hold out, with all his little boy will, to hear the almost ending, about him.

"After we came back from London, we wanted a baby to love, so my belly began to grow and grow and grow, but when it was time, the baby did not want to come out."

"I didn't want to come out of your belly?" He inspects my belly, his "house." "That belly?"

That belly, the curdled folds of skin, the faded *linea negra* that suggested a son was growing inside me.

Seven days overdue and eleven hours of back labor later, the baby emerged, screaming and red and cone-headed. So relieved were we that it was only several minutes later we thought to check its gender.

"Daddy cried, 'We've got a little guy!' And we brought you home and you screamed and you cried and you screamed and you cried. For months. But we loved you so much we thought we ought to do it again so you could be a brother."

Two weeks after our eldest's second birthday, ten days overdue and on the heels of a steaming plate of chocolate crêpes made by my friend Olivier at the farmers' market, our second son was born in our dining room in a planned yet sudden home birth. After the midwife caught him, he made not a peep, just poked his eyes around. Though he also went on to cry for nearly four months straight.

My boy, asleep, finally.

Somewhere in between giving birth to two sons and starting a copywriting business, I would come back to this book. I had a feeling, from the way strangers' eyes swam when I told them this story, that it had a place in the world and could do good things.

It's morning now, just a tail of light out the bay window in the living room. My son steps out into the hall, spies me on the sofa in my housecoat, typing, and waits. He's wondering if I'll be cross that he's gotten up so early.

"Mama, why are you pressing buttons on your compute-ee-er?"

That's what they think writing and my work are, pressing buttons on a computer, which he always pronounces with an extra syllable. I never correct him, on either count. I suppose he's right, about the buttons.

This is my early-morning writing time and my instinct is to scowl, shoo him off, but they're so sweet when they've just woken up, pink-cheeked and soft limbs after a cuddle. And he'll only be three or four or five for just a little while.

"My little boy. Come here."

He tucks into me, his cheeks to my chest, his kneecaps on my lap. I will wait to type my parting thoughts. To tell you—to tell him, when he's much, much older—when you hear that voice, please listen. Go.

What if it's something greater than us, nudging and fastening synchronicities to make it easier? And yet, if it is the universe that stakes signs, it's us that recognizes and interprets them. Noses out the way.

The way, I found it. My voice as a writer, my great love, my sons.

Our tens, we ought to go after them.

ACKNOWLEDGEMENTS

I THANK JIM McFetridge. He's the family friend and former college registrar who, upon hearing my plight of feeling lost, said, "Seems like a good time to travel." And then connected me with friends and a job in Thailand.

Next, I must thank my mother, who, without a second thought, bought my plane ticket to Bangkok. Thank you, Mom.

And then, more than anyone, Noel. Not for inspiring the ending of this story, but for his part in carrying it forward since then, and, even more, giving me the precious time to write this book. So many mornings, after he'd been working late, he woke with our sons and the birds so I could duck out for an early-morning writing session. How fortunate I am to have a partner so wholeheartedly supportive of this thing I must do.

Before kids and while Noel was sleeping, I wrote a first very embarrassing draft of this manuscript in a tiny studio flat in Nansen Village, an affordable residence for married and parenting students in London, UK. The light, the leafy block, the low rent, it all helped a great deal.

A remarkable group of women and one man gave kind and insightful feedback as I read aloud chapters from that first embarrassing draft during my studies at City, University of London. A special thanks to the clever and lovely Anne H. Putnam for her careful early reading, and for her humor.

A remarkable group of women continues to inspire me to write well, and write at all. I owe so much gratitude to my sisters-in-writing, The Spokes: Hannah Calder, Michelle Doege, Kristin Froneman, Karen Meyer and Laisha Rosnau. A very special thanks to Kerry Gilbert, who, after I received one rejection letter or another, talked me out of throwing myself or my laptop into the lake, and told me of somedays.

I wrote one of the latest drafts in a room on the second floor of the Caetani Cultural Centre, a converted heritage home dedicated to the making of art. Thank you to Sveva and all the beautiful energy you left behind, and to the people who carry forth your vision today, namely Susan Brandoli.

It was in my little studio at the Caetani House that I first spoke with Page Two principal Trena White, and made a plan to make this book happen. I am indebted to you and your team, especially Gabrielle Narsted for keeping things ticking; Helen Reeves for pushing me and this book into deeper waters; Erin Parker for her keen eye and enthusiasm; Jenny Govier for her superb proofing; and Peter Cocking and team for their gorgeous design work. Thank you to Thai-British artist Kat Jones for allowing me to use one of her stunning paintings on the cover of this book.

Several early teachers encouraged my writing: Bob McDougall, John Baty and Gillian Steward. Thank you.

So many friends and family members have shaped me and my writing in ways I will always be grateful for. Thank you. Thank you, Aunt Cindy and Aunt Donna. Thank you, Sabrina Moore, Erin Norrish, Ursula Maser, Sian Pittman and Lucy Tierney. Thank you to the late Cecil Allen, and his great-grandfather James Allen, who came so far. I hope I can make you proud.

SOURCES

PAGE xvii
Mark Evan Prado, http://www.thailandguru.com/buses.html.

PAGE 31
Paulo Coelho, *The Alchemist*.

PAGE 65
Joy Harjo, "She Had Some Horses."

PAGE 83
Chris Baker and Pasuk Phongpaichitm, *A History of Thailand*, second
   edition.

PAGE 97
Facets of Thai Cultural Life, Foreign News Division, Government Public
   Relations Department.

Erik Seidenfaden, *A Guide to Bangkok with Notes on Siam*.

Abha Bhamorabutr, *The History of Bangkok: Summary of Political and Cultural Events From the Age of Establishment to the Present*.

PAGE 98
Edmund Roberts and W.S.W. Ruschenberger MD, *Two Yankee Diplomats
   in 1830s Siam*.

PAGE 99
Sombat Planoi, *Thai Kitchen*, Office of the National Culture Commission.

PAGE 105
Steve Van Beek, Insight Pocket Guides: Bangkok.

PAGE 107
P.A. Jackson, Dear Uncle Go: Male Homosexuality in Thailand, qtd. in Richard Totman, *The Third Sex: Kathoey: Thailand's Ladyboys*.

Richard Totman, *The Third Sex*.

PAGE 115–116
Sombat Planoi, *Thai Kitchen*.

PAGE 203
Erik Seidenfaden, *A Guide to Bangkok with Notes on Siam*.

Maxwell Sommerville, Siam on the Meinam from the Gulf to Ayuthia..., qtd. in *Descriptions of Old Siam*.

PAGE 208
Stever Van Beek, *Bangkok Then and Now*.

PAGE 242
http://www.hoteldemoc.com/.

PAGE 247–249
Chris Baker and Pasuk Phongpaichit, *A History of Thailand*.

Hannah Beech, "A Violent New Year's Eve in Bangkok," TIME.com, http://content.time.com/time/world/article/0,8599,1573283,00.html.

Jocelyn Gecker, "Thais and Tourists Clear Bangkok Streets after Military Coup," Associated Press.

Grant Peck, "Thai Military Launches Coup against Prime Minister," Associated Press.

Shino Yuasa, "Yellow Scarves—and Calm—on Bangkok's Streets," Agence France Presse.

PAGE 253–254
Michael Smithies, *Old Bangkok*.

BOOKS

Baker, Chris, and Pasuk Phongpaichit. *A History of Thailand.* 2nd edition. Cambridge: Cambridge University Press, 2009.

Bhamorabutr, Abha. *The History of Bangkok: Summary of Political and Cultural Events From the Age of Establishment to the Present.* For Distribution Commemorating the Bangkok Bicentennial Celebrations, 1982.

Bickersteth, Jane, and Joshua Eliot. *Bangkok and the Beaches Handbook.* Bath: Footprint Handbooks, 2000.

Coelho, Paulo. *The Alchemist.* San Francisco: Harper San Francisco, 1993.

Cooper, Robert, and Nanthapa Cooper, *Culture Shock Thailand...and How to Survive It.* Singapore: Times Book International, 1982.

De Beze, Claude. *1688 Revolution in Siam: The Memoir of Father de Beze.* Translated into English with introduction, commentary appendices and notes by E.W. Stuartinson. Hong Kong: Hong Kong University Press, 1968.

Descriptions of Old Siam. Compiled and introduced by Michael Smithies. New York: Oxford University Press, 1995.

Facets of Thai Cultural Life. Foreign News Division, Government Public Relations Department. Bangkok: Office of the Prime Minister, 1984.

Gillett, Freeman Joseph. *The Famous Medicine Hat in Poetical History.* British Museum Colonial Copyright, 1923.

Mehrer, Peter. *Run That by Me Again.* Medicine Hat: Medicine Hat News, 2000.

Neale, Frederick Arthur. *Narrative of a Residence in Siam at the Capital of the Kingdom of Siam with a Description of the Manners, Customs and Laws of the Modern Siamese (1850).* London: Office of the National Illustrated Library, 1852.

Planoi, Sombat. *Thai Kitchen.* Translated by Suttinee Yavaprapas. Bangkok: Office of the National Culture Commission, 2000.

Roberts, Edmund, and W.S.W. Ruschenberger MD. *Two Yankee Diplomats in 1830s Siam.* Introduced and edited by Michael Smithies. Bangkok: Orchid Press, 2002.

Seidenfaden, Erik. *A Guide to Bangkok with Notes on Siam.* Oxford: Oxford University Press, 1984.

Smithies, Michael. *Old Bangkok.* 2nd edition. New York: Oxford University Press, 2003.

Thailand in the '90s. National Identity Office of the Prime Minister, 1991.

Totman, Richard. *The Third Sex: Kathoey: Thailand's Ladyboys*. London: Souvenir Press, 2003.

Van Beek, Steve. *Bangkok Then and Now*. 2nd edition. Nonthaburi, Thailand: AB Publications, 2001.

Van der Cruysse, Dirk. *Siam & the West, 1500–1700*. [city published?]: Silkworm Books, 2002.

Waugh, Alec. *Bangkok, The Story of a City*. 3rd edition. London: Eland Publishing Limited, 2007.

Wyatt, David K. *Thailand, a Short History*. 2nd edition. New Haven and London: Yale University Press, 2003.

NEWSPAPERS

Beech, Hannah. "A Violent New Year's Eve in Bangkok." TIME.com. January 1, 2007. Accessed June 2015. http://content.time.com/time/world/article/0,8599,1573283,00.html.

Gecker, Jocelyn. "Thais and Tourists Clear Bangkok Streets after Military Coup." Associated Press. September 19, 2006. Accessed [date?]. [source web address?].

Peck, Grant. "Thai Military Launches Coup against Prime Minister." Associated Press. September 19, 2006. Accessed [date?]. [source web address?].

Yuasa, Shino. "Yellow Scarves—and Calm—on Bangkok's Streets." Agence France Presse, English. September 19, 2006. Accessed [date?]. [source web address?].

WEBSITES

Prado, Mark Evan. http://www.thailandguru.com/buses.html. Accessed April 10, 2011.

HEATH FLETCHER

NATALIE APPLETON is an award-winning writer whose stories have appeared in publications around the world, including *The New York Times*. Natalie won Prairie Fire's 2016 Banff Centre Bliss Carman Poetry Award, and her prose has been longlisted for the CBC Creative Non-fiction Contest. Natalie is a graduate of the University of Regina School of Journalism and the MA in Creative Writing (Narrative Non-fiction) program at City, University London, UK. In her former life as a journalist, she worked at newspapers across the Prairies. Natalie lives in the Okanagan, BC, with her husband and two sons.

Be the first to find out about Natalie Appleton's readings and news, and access *I Have Something to Tell You* bonus material, such as photos, videos, and more at:

www.NatalieAppleton.ca

f @natalieappletonwriter

t @n_appleton

If you enjoyed *I Have Something to Tell You*, please share your review on sites like:

- Amazon Canada & US
- Barnes & Noble
- Chapters/Indigo